Joyous Torah Treasures

משמחי לב

A Collection of Rabbinic Insights
and Practical Advice for Daily Living

Volume 1

SAM FRIEDMAN, M.D.

DEVORA
PUBLISHING
NEW YORK ◆ JERUSALEM ◆ LONDON

Joyous Torah Treasures
Published by Devora Publishing Company
Copyright © 2008 by Sam Friedman, M.D.

COVER DESIGN: Benjie Herskowitz
TYPESETTING: Koren Publishing Services
EDITORIAL AND PRODUCTION MANAGER: Daniella Barak
EDITOR: Chani Hadad

All rights reserved. No part of this book may be used or reproduced or transmitted in any form or by any means, electronic or mechanical, including photocopying, recording, or by any information storage and retrieval system, without written permission from the publisher.

Hard Cover ISBN: Set: 978-1-934440-51-3
                Vol. 1: 978-1-934440-20-9
                Vol. 2: 978-1-934440-21-6

E-mail: publisher@devorapublishing.com
Web Site: www.devorapublishing.com

Printed in the United States of America

To my grandparents,
of blessed memory

To my mother, of blessed memory, for her genuine
faith, optimism, and devotion to our family

To my father, may he be blessed with a long
and healthy life, for being a great teacher and a
constant source of inspiration and support

To my wife's parents and grandparents,
of blessed memory

To my *rebbe*, Rabbi Shmuel Scheinberg,
may the memory of the righteous be blessed

They will always be known for their devotion to
transmitting to future generations the joys of
living according to the Torah's teachings.

And to my wife, Nora, for her love; for her unfailing
assistance in helping me confront life's challenges; and
for the kindness she displays to everyone she meets.

And to our daughters, Miriam, Chana, and Nava,
who inspired me to write this book.

RABBI CHAIM P. SCHEINBERG	הרב חיים פינחס שיינברג
Rosh Yeshiva "TORAH ORE"	ראש ישיבת "תורה אור"
and Morah Hora'ah of Kiryat Mattersdorf	ומורה הוראה דקרית מטרסדורף

מכתב ברכה

It was my pleasure to receive a selection of דברי תורה from Dr. Friedman's forthcoming ספר on the פרשה. The receipt of this draft is especially meaningful because of the very special relationship the author had as a student with my dear brother, Harav Shmuel Scheinberg zt"l. One of the hallmarks of my brother's relationships with his closest students was enthusiasm for family-oriented Torah discussions that serve as a foundation for growth in בין אדם לחבירו, which is clearly one of the strengths in Dr. Friedman's ספר.

Another theme my brother emphasized through his teachings, and by example, is the large amount of שמחה (happiness) and meaning learning Torah brings to our daily lives. Dr. Friedman has told me that he is thinking of naming the sefer משמחי לב. How appropriate then that Dr. Friedman's ספר, which includes many of his Rebbe's insights to the פרשה, emphasizes this concept.

הנני מברך ר׳ יהושע that he should be זוכה to continue his wonderful work מתוך מנוחת הנפש והרחבת הדעת and may he be able to inspire all those who read this ספר with שמחת הלב

רחוב פנים מאירות 2, ירושלים, ת.ד. 6979, טל׳ 537-1513 (02), ישראל
2 Panim Meirot St., Jerusalem, P.O.B 6979, Tel. (02) 537-1513, Israel

דוד קאהן   ביהמ"ד גבול יעבץ
                           ברוקלין, נוא יארק

בס"ד

I have perused the work of Dr. Samuel Friedman ‎יי on the sidras of the week and enjoyed his essays.

I found an anthology replete with many commentaries — both classic and current. The author's taste is such that I am certain that every reader will find beautiful thoughts which teach and inspire.

The very fact that a busy cardiologist puts away time to learn Torah and publish novelae is uplifting. More power to him.

ג' קה"ח ‎3/3
ג' אייר תשס"ה

Rabbi Hershel Schachter
24 Bennett Avenue
New York, New York 10033
(212) 795-0630

בס"ד ג' כסלו

קא אשר הב'ה יכול וקאו
ש'בת פרשת ויצא אלחנן

Kislev, 5768

Over the past several years I have studied many of the essays contained within this Sefer. I have found them to be thoughtful presentations on various topics, mainly of Hashkofa and Middos. I also found the essays to be informative on the historical level, identifying each of the Torah commentaries. I personally found the essays of great value. Kol Ha'Kovod to Dr. Friedman for this Torah accomplishment.

With great admiration,

Hershel Schachter

FOUNDED BY
RABBI SHLOMO FREIFELD זצ"ל

SH'OR YOSHUV
INSTITUTE

מכתב ברכה
September 30. 2005
26 Elul, 5765

Our dear and esteemed friend, ידיד בן ידיד ר' יהושע העשיל נר"ו בן ידידנו הדגול ר' משה נ"י Dr. Sammy Friedman is publishing a collection of דברי תורה on the פרשה. I have read through many of them and found them to be exciting, meaningful and a דבר השוה לכל נפש, where layman and scholar, man and woman, adult and child alike can find inspiring thoughts for the פרשת השבוע.

In this week's סדרה we will read ומל ה' אלקיך את לבבך ואת לבב זרעך גו', "Hashem will circumcise your heart and the heart of your offspring." The question is obvious: if הקב"ה guarantees that in the future all of כלל ישראל will return to Him, why does the פסוק single out our children? The שפת אמת stresses that the reality of רוחניות will be so real and deeply vivifying to a person that his feelings will immediately affect his children. They will perceive their father's excitement and שמחה של לימוד התורה (true joy of studying Torah); they will see that the hours for learning Torah are their father's most coveted hours of the day. In the spirit of this שפת אמת, Dr. Sam began his writing. His wish was to ignite his own children's love of Torah. לא ללמד על עצמו יצא אלא ללמד על הכלל כולו יצא.

We have shared a warm relationship with the Friedman family for generations. Dr. Sam's illustrious grandfather, Reb Ezriel ע"ה and his splendid father, Reb Moshe, נ"י, president of our Yeshiva, together with his אשת חיל ע"ה, were very dear to my father in law, Rabbi Shlomo Freifeld זצ"ל. They were partners with Rabbi Freifeld and helped fuel his vision of Sh'or Yoshuv. Dr. Sam grew up in this unique environment, and one can clearly see the result of such a special relationship. May his ספר help others to be as passionate as he is about Torah learning and result in another link in דעה ומלאה הארץ דעה.

Rabbi Naftali Jaeger

בס"ד

ישיבה יוניברסיטי **בישראל** ע״ר
Yeshiva University in Israel
RIETS Kollel - Aaron Rakeffet
Caroline and Joseph S. Gruss Institute
40 Rechov Dudevani, Bayit Vegan, Jerusalem
ISRAEL Tel: 972-2-530-3000 Fax: 531-3001

ב אייר - 30.4.07
בס״ד:

To all my students and Friends:

Happy are the Torah people that we now have medical doctors who are also sensitive and learned savants of the Torah. This continues the Traditions of our חכמים when so many medical doctors were also קהלי ישראל.

In this vein I am happy to recommend the Torah writings of Dr. Samuel H. Friedman to you. It represents a world of Torah knowledge, insight and sensitivity!

With the blessings of the Holy City!

Aaron Rakeffet

Contents

Acknowledgments xiii
Author's Note xv
Introduction 1

SEFER BEREISHIS

פרשת בראשית
Parshas Bereishis 7
  What Was So Bad About the Snake's Punishment?
  Everything Is Hinted at in the Torah

פרשת נח
Parshas Noach. 17
  Try Hard! Don't Be Afraid of Failure
  The First Comma

פרשת לך לך
Parshas Lech Lecha 27
  The Heights of the Universe
  I Will Make Your Name Great

פרשת וירא
Parshas Vayera 37
The Formula for a Successful Marriage
An Essential Lesson

פרשת חיי שרה
Parshas Chayei Sarah 45
A Marriage Manual for All Times
God's Language

פרשת תולדת
Parshas Toldos 53
Whoever Honors the Torah
Let's Try to Solve the Great Mystery

פרשת ויצא
Parshas Vayeitzei 63
Ancient and Invaluable Advice for Every Husband and Father
Everything Is Hinted at in the Torah – Two Magnificent Abbreviations

פרשת וישלח
Parshas Vayishlach 73
The Image on God's Throne
Masters of Silence

פרשת וישב
Parshas Vayeshev 83
The Torah of the Yeshiva of Shem and Ever
Yosef and Chanukah

פרשת מקץ
Parshas Mikeitz 93
Couldn't Yosef Have Been a Little Nicer?
The Amazing Vision of the Vilna Gaon

פרשת ויגש
Parshas Vayigash..................................103
Kind Words – A Tribute to Rabbi Shlomo Freifeld
Yehuda, Jews, and Judaism

פרשת ויחי
Parshas Vayechi 113
The Brilliance of the Ba'al HaTurim
A Principle by Which You Will Understand the Book of Bereishis

SEFER SHEMOS

פרשת שמות
Parshas Shemos..................................127
The Earliest and Most Respected Biblical Commentary
Kindness Equals Torah

פרשת וארא
Parshas Vaeira...................................137
Freedom
Brotherly Love

פרשת בא
Parshas Bo 143
Reflections
Time and Renewal

פרשת בשלח
Parshas Beshalach................................153
Happiness and Torah
Rabbi Deutch's Precious Jewel

פרשת יתרו
Parshas Yisro..................................159
What Did Yisro Hear?
Left and Right

פרשת משפטים
Parshas Mishpatim..............................167
Everything Is Hinted at in the Torah
Starting a Sentence with the Word And

פרשת תרומה
Parshas Terumah................................175
Inside Out
Jewish Joy

פרשת תצוה
Parshas Tetzaveh...............................185
God's Keys
Is Moshe's Name Really Missing?
Let the Spotlight Shine on Your Brother

פרשת כי תשא
Parshas Ki Sisa.................................195
A Life Saving Measure
Don't Confuse the Big Letters

פרשיות ויקהל־פקודי
Parshios Vayakhel and Pekudei 201
The Torah of Life – How Fortunate Are We!
Just Try!

Acknowledgments

Like a completed jigsaw puzzle, many pieces had to fit together correctly for this book to become a reality. A partial list includes: good teachers, good health, a desire to do the research and writing, an ability to find time for this project despite a busy work schedule, and a supportive family. First and foremost, I thank the Holy One, Blessed is He, who is the master architect that fit all the pieces together.

Without the privilege of my praying in Congregation Beth Abraham, this book probably would not have been written. Rabbi Yaakov Neuburger, the spiritual leader of the congregation, teaches ethical insights into the weekly Torah readings that form the basis for several of this book's essays. Also, at Congregation Beth Abraham I came across a collection of essays selected from the Internet on the weekly Torah portion that is distributed by a member of the Shul, Rabbi Chaim Ozer Shulman. These essays are usually of the highest caliber, and are skillfully merged together into an Internet Parshah Sheet that I read each week. I often have the desire to share some of the beautiful insights that I read in these sheets with others, and they are frequently quoted in this book. I am very grateful to Rabbi Shulman.

This book is primarily an anthology, and every essay is based on someone else's insight into the weekly Torah portion. I express my profound gratitude to all of the Torah scholars who are quoted in this book and to their publishers.

If I have made even a small contribution to Torah literature, I am sure that it is in the merit of my parents, grandparents, and ancestors. Words can't express my appreciation for all that my parents and grandparents have done for me.

I am very fortunate to have two talented friends, Terry Mischel and Meish Goldish, who carefully proofread and edited the entire manuscript, before I submitted it for publication. I am so grateful to them for their friendship and for improving the quality of this book.

I am indebted to Rabbi Binyamin Kamenetzky and to Rabbi David Weinbach for providing me with a fine education. Thanks also to Rabbi Michael Taubes for his advice and for always making the resources of his library available to me; to Rabbi Elozor Preil for all that he has taught me; to my brothers, David and Howie, and to my sister, Elaine; to Reuven Escott and David Felig, M.D., for their friendship and support; to Lawrence Eisen, Gary Munk, Ph.D., Michael Rapoport, and David Schild for their interest and encouragement; and to Rabbi Mordechai Cohen for always being available to assist me.

I am very grateful to Ms. Melissa Raymon, who is a respected educator and the original typist of most of the essays in this book. Ms. Raymon also added some valuable Torah insights that enhanced some of the essays that she typed.

Thank you to my publisher, Rabbi Yaakov Peterseil; my editor, Ms. Chani Hadad; and to the entire staff at Devora Publications.

Leaving the best for last, I am most grateful to my partner and wife, Nora, for allowing me the privilege of sharing our lives together. Thanks for helping to raise our family and for keeping our home, work, and Torah study on track. May the Holy One, Blessed is He, allow us to share *nachas* from our children and good health for many more years.

Author's Note

For the reader's convenience, biographical information for most sources is usually written in the text immediately after the source is quoted. Some rabbis are quoted so often that it would have been repetitious to include their biographical information at each appearance in the text.

Biographical notes about these rabbis can be found at the end of Volume II.

Introduction

Observing the commandments and studying Torah lead to a life of happiness, as King David says, פִּקּוּדֵי יְהוָה יְשָׁרִים מְשַׂמְּחֵי לֵב, *The commandments of God are just, gladdening the heart* (*Tehillim* 19:9). We are reminded of this daily in the *Shacharis* (morning) prayer service, when we say, shortly before the silent *Amidah* (*Shemoneh Esrei*), אַשְׁרֵי אִישׁ שֶׁיִּשְׁמַע לְמִצְוֹתֶיךָ וְתוֹרָתְךָ וּדְבָרְךָ יָשִׂים עַל לִבּוֹ, "Fortunate is the person who obeys Your commandments and takes to his heart Your teaching and Your word."

The Rambam teaches, in *Laws of Meilah* (*Sacrilege*) 8:8, that it is proper to attempt to understand the ultimate purpose of the Torah's laws, but he emphasizes that the laws must be observed even if this goal is not achieved. Similarly, Rav Moshe Feinstein explains, in his commentary on *Bamidbar* 19:2, that all the commandments, even those "whose reasons are given by the Torah itself," should be considered as חֻקִּים (decrees without reasons). Even though the Torah's laws should be observed just because God commanded us to do so, and not for any other reason, it is refreshing to know עֵץ חַיִּים הִיא לַמַּחֲזִיקִים בָּהּ וְתֹמְכֶיהָ מְאֻשָּׁר, *It is a tree of life to those who grasp it, and its supporters are fortunate* (*Mishlei* 3:18).

My mother, of blessed memory, my father, and my *rebbe*, Rabbi Shmuel Scheinberg, may the memory of the righteous be blessed, emphasized the happiness and satisfaction that emanate from living one's life according to the Torah's precepts. Torah study is a joyous pursuit, as King David writes in *Tehillim* 119:162, שָׂשׂ אָנֹכִי עַל אִמְרָתֶךָ כְּמוֹצֵא שָׁלָל רָב, *I rejoice over Your word, like one who finds abundant spoils*. Some of the joy to be found in Torah study derives from the fact that every time one studies Torah, one can find something new and interesting. As the *Gemara* in *Berachos* 63b teaches, "On each and every day, the Torah is as beloved to those who study it as on the day it was given from Mount Sinai." Rabbi Abraham J. Twerski, M.D., elaborates on the thrill of learning Torah and compares the joy of studying Torah to an infant who has just learned how to walk:

> The child is fascinated by his new method of moving about, which allows him to investigate his surroundings. The child squeals with glee as he goes from place to place and from room to room, and is excited by all the new things he discovers…There is always room for creative ideas in Torah [study] and one may discover new treasures that were unknown to the ancients…Great Torah scholars have always been innovative, constantly making new discoveries, and in observing them one can see the excitement in their study of Torah. This may not be the exclusive privilege of the dedicated scholar. Every person can experience thrills in exploring the infinite garden of Torah…

The Ba'al HaTurim writes in his introduction to his commentary on the Torah that he sought to present interpretations לְהַמְשִׁיךְ הַלֵּב, "to attract [the reader's] heart." I have tried to do the same – to present some of our Sages' keen interpretations that will attract the reader's heart, thereby bringing happiness to the reader. I have also tried to present some of our Sages' practical advice for daily living, which is מַחְכִּימַת פֶּתִי, [*capable of*] *making a simple person wise* (*Tehillim* 19:8), thereby promoting a life of joy and fulfillment.

When I first started to record insights on the weekly Torah portion, I had no intention of writing this book. My sole purpose was to collect for my young daughters the best interpretations that I could find. My hope was that as they were growing up, they would become interested and read them. Perhaps, because the *Gemara* in *Kidushin* 40a teaches, מַחֲשָׁבָה טוֹבָה מְצָרְפָהּ לְמַעֲשֶׂה, "A good thought is regarded [by God] as a good deed," the collection of Torah insights for my daughters became this book. May God grant my daughters credit for having been the impetus for the Torah study contained within this book, and grant them an appreciation for the Torah's teachings, with the desire and the ability to transfer their appreciation to their children and grandchildren.

Writing this book has been a pleasure for me because of the Torah that I've learned in the process. My prayer is that readers of this book will achieve greater happiness through an appreciation of some of our Sages' keen interpretations and practical advice for daily living that are presented herein. With happiness that is enhanced by our Sages' teachings, a person may be privileged to attain greatness and experience the שְׁכִינָה (God's presence). As the Rambam teaches at the conclusion of the *Laws of Lulav*, "There is no greatness or honor other than being happy before God, as it says, 'הַמֶּלֶךְ דָּוִד מְפַזֵּז וּמְכַרְכֵּר לִפְנֵי יְהוָֹה' *King David was leaping and dancing before God*' (*Samuel ll* 6:16)," and as the *Gemara Shabbos* 30b states, "The Divine Presence doesn't rest [upon a person] who is sad…but rather through the happiness that is associated with [fulfilling] a command of the Torah."

Sefer Bereishis

פרשת בראשית

Parshas Bereishis

> **WHAT WAS SO BAD ABOUT THE SNAKE'S PUNISHMENT?**

The Torah tells us that the snake was punished for its role in enticing Eve to eat of the fruit of the tree. One of the snake's punishments was וְעָפָר תֹּאכַל כָּל יְמֵי חַיֶּיךָ, *and dust you shall eat all the days of your life* (*Bereishis* 3:14). The *Gemara* in *Yuma* 75a comments that God's punishment of the snake contains a measure of kindness, because "when it ascends to the roof, its food is with it, and when it descends below, its food is with it," since the snake eats dust which is found everywhere.

There is a magnificent collection of Torah insights entitled *Likutei Yehoshua* (*Collections of Yehoshua*) published around 1958 by Rabbi Yehoshua Scheinfeld. Rabbi Scheinfeld quotes the comments of Rabbi Yitzchak Kalish of Vorka (1779–1848), a prominent Chasidic Rebbe who was known for his love of the Jewish people, regarding the snake's punishment. Rabbi Yitzchak Kalish of Vorka wonders, what is so bad about having to eat dust? As the *Gemara* quoted above teaches, since dust is all over, the snake's food will be plentiful. The snake will not have to work for a meal and will never go hungry. What is so bad about the snake's punishment?

The Rebbe from Vorka explains that having food everywhere is in essence the great curse of the snake. Since the snake's food is available in abundance, the snake will have limited interaction with God. It will not have to look to God for its food, because it is available everywhere. On the other hand, human beings work hard to raise their crops and rely on God for rain and the proper amount of sunshine. This situation is entirely the opposite of the snake, which finds sustenance everywhere. By telling the snake "and dust you shall eat all the days of your life," God was cutting off the snake from His presence. The fact that human beings rely on God for their sustenance is actually a great blessing. It creates a closer connection between human beings and God.

This is similar to the relationship that God has with the Land of Israel. It is written in the Torah, כִּי הָאָרֶץ אֲשֶׁר אַתָּה בָא שָׁמָּה לְרִשְׁתָּהּ לֹא כְאֶרֶץ מִצְרַיִם הִוא... וְהָאָרֶץ אֲשֶׁר אַתֶּם עֹבְרִים שָׁמָּה לְרִשְׁתָּהּ... לִמְטַר הַשָּׁמַיִם תִּשְׁתֶּה מָּיִם, *For the Land to which you come, to possess it, it is not like the land of Egypt...But the Land to which you cross over to possess it...from the rain of heavens shall you drink water* (*Devarim* 11:10–11). The Torah is explaining the reason that God gave Egypt the Nile River, a constant source of water, yet created the Land of Israel without a large river. Similar to the snake, Egypt's interaction with God is limited because Egypt has a more constant source of water than Israel. God created the Land of Israel entirely dependent on rain, to increase the interaction between the people of Israel and God. Those who live in Israel need to follow God's commandments to be worthy of receiving rain. This creates a special bond between the people of Israel and God. The Torah is emphasizing that Israel is very different from Egypt, which has an abundant natural source of water.

Perhaps this is also one of the reasons that many of Israel's neighbors are rich in oil. It seems that God purposely created Israel with fewer natural resources, so as to increase the dependency of Israel on God. Part of the snake's curse is that it became less dependent on God, which reduced its divine interaction.

Rabbi Benjamin Yudin, a contemporary scholar, teacher, and

communal leader discusses this concept regarding the בּוֹרֵא נְפָשׁוֹת (*Borei Nefashos*) blessing that one is obligated to recite after eating certain foods and drinking liquids, other than wine. In this blessing, we thank God for creating living things וְחֶסְרוֹנָן, *and their deficiencies*. We thank God for creating human beings with deficiencies, so that we need to rely on God for sustenance. Rabbi Yudin explains that this is the reason that human beings weren't created like camels, with a need to drink water only once per week. Human beings need to eat and drink several times daily, so that we rely more directly and more frequently on God. This creates a closer bond between humanity and God. And it is for this reason that we thank God in the blessing בּוֹרֵא נְפָשׁוֹת for creating us with deficiencies.

I believe it was the first Lubavitcher Rebbe, Rabbi Shneur Zalman of Liadi (1745–1813) who points out that it is for this reason that out of all the creations only man walks upright. This is again because human beings rely more directly on God. Human beings are reminded by their upright posture to look toward Heaven, as King David writes in *Tehillim* (*Psalms*) 16:8, שִׁוִּיתִי יְהֹוָה לְנֶגְדִּי תָמִיד, *I have set God before me always*. This concept is so important that Rabbi Moshe Isserles (c.1520–1572) begins his *Notes* on the *Shulchan Aruch* by writing that this is a כְּלָל גָּדוֹל בַּתּוֹרָה (major principle of the Torah). Similarly, Rabbi Shlomo Ganzfried (1804–1880) begins the *Kitzur Shulchan Aruch* (*Abridged Code of Jewish Law*) by emphasizing the importance of שִׁוִּיתִי יְהֹוָה לְנֶגְדִּי תָמִיד. By looking toward Heaven, we are reminded to increase our interaction with God by studying the Torah and observing its commandments.

I read that this may be part of the reason that the prayer שְׁמוֹנֶה עֶשְׂרֵה (*Shemoneh Esrei*) should be recited while standing. This is emphasized by the fact that the שְׁמוֹנֶה עֶשְׂרֵה is often referred to as the עֲמִידָה (*Amidah*), which means "standing." Even though people usually sit during important conversations, the שְׁמוֹנֶה עֶשְׂרֵה should be recited while standing. Perhaps one of the reasons for this is that out of all the creations, God blessed only human beings with an upright posture. As the first Lubavitcher Rebbe suggests, this is to emphasize the importance of looking toward God, and of living our lives according to the Torah's guidance. This leads to a satisfying and happy life. As King David writes in the nineteenth chapter of *Tehillim* (*Psalms*), פִּקּוּדֵי יְהֹוָה יְשָׁרִים מְשַׂמְּחֵי לֵב, *The commandments of God are just, gladdening the heart.*

> EVERYTHING IS HINTED AT IN THE TORAH

Our Sages have have taught לֵיכָּא מִידֵי דְלֹא רְמִיזֵי בְּאוֹרָיְתָא, "There is nothing that is not hinted at in the Torah." The source for this teaching is not entirely clear, as this exact phrase does not appear in the *Gemara* or *Midrash*. A similar but more limited idea appears in *Gemara Ta'anis* 9a, where the *Gemara* teaches that everything written in the נְבִיאִים (*Prophets*) and כְּתוּבִים (*Writings*) is hinted at in the Torah. Perhaps this principle is also based on the last *Mishnah* in the fifth chapter of *Pirkei Avos* (*Ethics of the Fathers*) that teaches, בֶּן בַּג בַּג אוֹמֵר הֲפָךְ בָּהּ וַהֲפָךְ בָּהּ דְּכֹלָּא בָהּ, "Ben Bag Bag says, 'Search in it and continue to search in it, for everything is in it.'" The Ramban (1194–1270), a great biblical and Talmudic commentator, Kabbalist, and physician, teaches that besides the five books of the *Torah*, God also taught Moshe many laws and much Kabbalistic wisdom, such as "the manner of the creation of heaven and earth." According to the Ramban, all of this is hinted at in the Torah, as the Ramban writes in the introduction to his *Commentary on the Torah*, "Everything that was transmitted to Moshe our teacher…was written in the Torah explicitly or by implication…" To support this statement, the Ramban cites the *Gemara* in *Menachos* 29b which teaches that Rabbi Akiva (who lived about 50–135 C.E. and was one of principal authors of the *Mishnah*) derived many laws which were taught to Moshe on Mount Sinai from the crownlets that are attached to certain letters of the Torah.

Rabbi Eliyahu ben Shlomo Zalman (1720–1797) is commonly referred to as the Vilna Gaon, or as the גְּרָ"א (initials of גָּאוֹן רַבִּי אֵלִיָּהוּ – Gaon Rabbi Eliyahu) and was one of the greatest Torah scholars of the last few centuries. According to the *Encyclopedia*

Judaica, the Vilna Gaon was a "semi-legendary figure of saint and intellectual giant, [who] towered over Lithuanian Jewry and influenced its cultural life in the 19th and into the 20th centuries." The Vilna Gaon had amazing insight and often revealed wonderful explanations that were previously not apparent. The Vilna Gaon often taught that לֵיכָּא מִידִי דְלֹא רְמִיזֵי בְּאוֹרָיְתָא, "There is nothing that is not hinted at in the Torah."

In *Torah LaDaas*, Rabbi Matis Blum, a contemporary scholar, quotes the Vilna Gaon as saying that all 613 of the Torah's commandments are hinted at in the first word of the Torah, which is בְּרֵאשִׁית (*Bereishis*). The Vilna Gaon was asked how the law of the redemption of the firstborn son (פִּדְיוֹן הַבֵּן – *Pidyon HaBen*) is hinted at in the word בְּרֵאשִׁית. The law of פִּדְיוֹן הַבֵּן (*Pidyon HaBen*) is based on *Bamibar* 18:15, *Shemos* 13:12, and *Shemos* 34:20. The law is that a father who is not from the tribe of Levi must redeem his firstborn son from a *Kohen* (a member of the priestly family of Jews descended from Aharon), after his son is more than thirty days old. The Vilna Gaon promptly answered that even this law is hinted at in the word בְּרֵאשִׁית, whose letters can stand for בֵּן רִאשׁוֹן אַחַר שְׁלוֹשִׁים יוֹם תִּפְדֶּה (you should redeem the firstborn son after thirty days). It is fascinating how easily and quickly the Vilna Gaon found a magnificent hint to the law of פִּדְיוֹן הַבֵּן in the word בְּרֵאשִׁית.

Rabbi Herschel Schachter, a great contemporary Talmudic scholar, writes:

> In the late 1930s, Rabbi Shmuel Maltzahn published a manuscript written by Rabbi Chaim of Volozhin (a well-known student of the Gaon) where he related the following story: The Gaon was fond of stating that if we look carefully into the Chumash, we will discover allusions to anything and everything that happened both to the Jewish nation as well as to individuals, even in the centuries following the time of Moshe Rabbeinu. On one occasion Reb Chaim asked of the Vilna Gaon, 'Where is there an allusion to the Rebbe?'

The Gaon immediately opened the Chumash to Parshas Ki Seitzei and reviewed it a bit until he noticed that the phrase אֶבֶן שְׁלֵמָה was an allusion to his name. (*Internet Parshah Sheet on Ki Seitzei*, 5763)

In the Torah portion entitled *Ki Seitzei*, the Torah commands us to own only honest weights and measures. The Torah teaches, אֶבֶן שְׁלֵמָה וָצֶדֶק יִהְיֶה לָּךְ, *A perfect and honest weight shall you have* (*Devarim* 25:15). The Vilna Gaon found in the words אֶבֶן שְׁלֵמָה an allusion to his name. אֶבֶן stands for אֵלִיָּהוּ בֶּן (Eliyahu, son of). שְׁלֵמָה are the same letters as his father's name, which is שְׁלֹמֹה (Shlomo). In this manner the Vilna Gaon saw in the words אֶבֶן שְׁלֵמָה an allusion to his name, אֵלִיָּהוּ בֶּן שְׁלֹמֹה (Eliyahu, son of Shlomo).

Rabbi Matis Blum relates in his commentary on *Devarim* 25:15 that the Vilna Gaon was asked where the name of the Rambam (רַמְבַּ"ם) is hinted at in the Torah. The Rambam is an acronym for Rabbi Moshe ben Maimon, who was born in Spain in 1135 and died in Egypt in 1204. The Rambam was a great Talmudist, codifier of Jewish law, philosopher, physician, and author of numerous monumental works including *Mishneh Torah* and *The Guide for the Perplexed*.

The Vilna Gaon answered that the Rambam's name is hinted at in the first letters of the sentence in *Shemos* 11:9, רְבוֹת מוֹפְתַי בְּאֶרֶץ מִצְרָיִם, *My wonders may be multiplied in the land of Egypt*, since the Rambam (רַמְבַּ"ם) was a wondrous scholar who spent most of the latter half of his life in Egypt. These are some examples of the Vilna Gaon's amazing vision, and his ability to point out insights that are hinted at beneath the plain meaning of the words of the Torah.

Rabbi Scheinfeld writes that each year, as we begin reading the Torah anew, we are reminded of the obligation to review the weekly Torah portion because it is also hinted at in the word בְּרֵאשִׁית. The *Gemara* in *Berachos* 8a-b teaches, "A person should always complete the Torah portion [of the week]…reading the

Hebrew text twice and the *Targum* once…for whoever completes the Torah portion [of the week]…merits that his days and years are prolonged." The *Targum* is the Aramaic translation of the Torah by Onkelos, a righteous convert who lived approximately in the first-second century C.E. Rabbi Yosef Caro (1488–1575) writes in his monumental Code of Jewish Law, the *Shulchan Aruch*, that one may read the commentary of Rashi on the weekly Torah portion instead of the *Targum*, but it is preferable to read both (*Orach Chayim* 285:2).

Rabbi Scheinfeld quotes an unnamed Rabbi who suggested that these laws regarding the review of the weekly Torah portion are hinted at exactly in the letters of the word בְּרֵאשִׁית.

ב, which has the numerical equivalent of two, stands for the obligation to read the Hebrew text twice. The letters רשי spell Rashi. The leftover letters are א and ת, which stand for the obligation to read אֶחָד תַּרְגּוּם (the *Targum* once).

Our Sages have taught that these laws regarding the review of the weekly Torah portion are also hinted at in the beginning of the first sentence of the second Book of the Torah, the *Book of Shemos*, וְאֵלֶּה שְׁמוֹת בְּנֵי יִשְׂרָאֵל, *And these are the names of the Children of Israel*. Rabbi Matis Blum quotes Rabbi Mordechai ben Avrahom Jaffe (c.1535–1612, known as the "*Levush*" after the name of his major literary work) that the letters of וְאֵלֶּה שְׁמוֹת בְּנֵי יִשְׂרָאֵל stand for (וְחַיָּב אָדָם לִקְרוֹת הַפָּרָשָׁה שְׁנַיִם מִקְרָא וְאֶחָד תַּרְגּוּם "And a man is obligated to read the weekly Torah portion twice and the *Targum* once") and that this applies to all Children of Israel.

Rabbi Yaakov ben Asher (c.1269–c.1343, great codifier of Jewish law and Torah commentator who is known as the Ba'al HaTurim) suggests a more detailed acrostic. The Ba'al HaTurim writes that the words וְאָדָם אֲשֶׁר לוֹמֵד הַסֵּדֶר וְאֵלֶּה שְׁמוֹת בְּנֵי יִשְׂרָאֵל stand for שְׁנַיִם מִקְרָא וְאֶחָד תַּרְגּוּם בְּקוֹל נָעִים יָשִׁיר יִחְיֶה שָׁנִים רַבּוֹת אֲרֻכִּים לְעוֹלָם, "And a man who studies the Torah portion twice and the *Targum* once, with a melodious voice, will truly live many, long years." The Ba'al HaTurim's acrostic hints to the *Gemara* in *Berachos* quoted above, that also promises "that his days and years are prolonged" as a reward for reading the weekly Torah portion twice, and the *Targum* once.

The *Midrash Bereishis Rabbah* 1:4 teaches that "The Holy One, Blessed be He, foresaw [at the time that the world was created] that twenty-six generations later, Israel would receive the Torah." Rabbi Scheinfeld points out in *Likutei Yehoshua* that this *Midrash* is hinted at in the word בְּרֵאשִׁית. The letters of בְּרֵאשִׁית can stand for בְּרֵאשִׁית רָאָה אֱלֹקִים שֶׁיְּקַבְּלוּ יִשְׂרָאֵל תּוֹרָה ("In the beginning, God saw that the Jews will accept the Torah").

The *Midrash Bereishis Rabbah* 1:7 also teaches that the sentence in *Tehillim* 119:160, רֹאשׁ דְּבָרְךָ אֱמֶת, *The beginning of your word is truth*, applies to the first sentence of the Torah. To help understand how this sentence in *Tehillim* relates to the beginning of the Torah, our Sages explain that the last letters of a few words *at the beginning of the Torah,* בְּרֵאשִׁית בָּרָא אֱלֹהִים אֵת, *In the beginning, God created the...,* spell the word אֱמֶת, which means truth. The Torah writes that *at the end of Creation*, God rested מִכָּל מְלַאכְתּוֹ אֲשֶׁר בָּרָא אֱלֹהִים לַעֲשׂוֹת, *from all His work which God created to make* (*Bereishis* 2:3). Here, once again, the last three words end with the letters of the word אֱמֶת, which means truth.

Itturei Torah is a magnificent collection of Torah insights by Rabbi Aharon Yaakov Greenberg published posthumously in 1965. *Itturei Torah* quotes Rabbi Simchah Bunim of Pshischa (1762–1837, a great Chasidic Rebbe) who explains the reason that the end of the words at the beginning and the conclusion of Creation spell אֱמֶת. This is because the *Gemaros* in *Sanhedrin* 64a and *Shabbos* 55a both quote Rabbi Chanina who teaches that the signature of God is אֱמֶת. Since it is customary for authors to affix their signatures to their writings, God attached His signature, which is אֱמֶת to the story of Creation at the beginning of the Torah, as described above.

Rabbi Lipman Podolsky was from Bangor, Maine, and became a beloved teacher at Yeshivat HaKotel in Jerusalem. I never met him, yet he made a long-lasting impression upon me with his excellent essays on the weekly Torah portions. Based entirely on *Gemara Shabbos* 104a, he wrote:

> The letters that comprise אֱמֶת (Truth) come from the beginning, middle, and the end of the *Alef-Beis* (Hebrew alphabet), respectively. This provides symbolic stability – an alphabetical tripod. The three letters comprising שֶׁקֶר (falsehood), though, are sequential. It cannot stand.
> Moreover, *each of the letters spelling the word* אֱמֶת *has two legs. It stands strong.* With שֶׁקֶר, each letter has only one leg, with the central "ק" longer then the others, שֶׁקֶר falters.

שֶׁקֶר is clearly unstable as each letter has only one leg, and the central "ק" that extends below the other letters creates instability (*Internet Parshah Sheet on Mishpatim*, 5760).

Itturei Torah also explains that the sentence in *Tehillim* 119:160, רֹאשׁ דְּבָרְךָ אֱמֶת (*The beginning of your word is truth*) hints to the beginnings of the Torah, *Mishnah*, and *Gemara*. The beginning of God's word is אֱמֶת because the first of The Ten Commandments begins with the letter א (אָנֹכִי); the *Mishnah* begins with the letter מ (מֵאֵימָתַי); and the *Gemara* begins with the letter ת (תָּנָא). Therefore, the word אֱמֶת alludes to the beginnings of both the Written and Oral Torah, suggested perhaps by the sentence רֹאשׁ דְּבָרְךָ אֱמֶת.

Our Sages have often taught, לֵיכָּא מִידֵי דְלֹא רְמִיזֵי בְּאוֹרַיְתָא, "There is nothing that is not hinted at in the Torah." This essay presents just a few of the numerous hints that are taught relating to the beginning of the Torah.

(If desired, see other essays that I have written, with God's help, that also discuss this principle on *Parshios Vayeitzei, Mishpatim, Tetzaveh, Shimini, Beha'aloscha, Re'eh, Ki Savo,* and *Vezos HaBerachah*.)

פרשת נח

Parshas Noach

> TRY HARD! DON'T BE AFRAID OF FAILURE

When the flood waters receded, God commanded Noach, in *Bereishis* 8:17, to take all the living creatures out of the ark. Rashi explains, based on *Midrash Bereishis Rabbah* 34:8, "If they don't want to go out, you take them out."

Rabbi Abraham J. Twerski, M.D., a contemporary Torah scholar and psychiatrist who has written many wonderful books, explains in *Living Each Week* that when the Torah records that Noach was commanded to take the animals out of the ark, the Torah is teaching an important lesson that is applicable to many human conditions. The Torah recognized that some animals would prefer to maintain the status quo and remain in an unnatural setting like the ark, which they had grown accustomed to, rather than to take a chance at having to find food and shelter in their natural habitat. Similarly, people have a tendency to maintain the status quo to which they have become accustomed, even if their current situation is less than optimal, rather than make the effort to improve their situation, which often requires hard work and could possibly result in failure. Many people have a tendency to maintain an undesirable situation because of laziness, or fear of failure. The

Torah doesn't approve of this attitude, and so commands Noach to take out any animals that may want to remain in the ark.

The Torah doesn't want us to be lazy or afraid of failure. Just as Noach was instructed not to allow the animals to remain in the ark and maintain their sub-optimal living conditions, which they had become accustomed to, people must make every effort to improve their status. Both the animals in the ark and people are instructed that *you can't succeed if you don't try*. If you don't make an effort, you are guaranteed to remain in your current situation and can't possibly improve.

This idea is closely related to the explanation offered by Rav Moshe Feinstein regarding the Torah's prohibition against building, מַצֵבוֹת (monuments). In the beginning of *Parshas Shoftim*, the Torah teaches, וְלֹא תָקִים לְךָ מַצֵבָה, *And you shall not erect for yourself a monument* (*Devarim* 16:22). The Jewish people are allowed and encouraged to build monuments only for the dead, and not for the living. Rav Moshe Feinstein explains that this is because a monument, which never changes, is not the ideal symbol for a living human being. The ideal symbol would convey activity and pursuit of spiritual improvement and not stasis, similar to a monument.

Rabbi Feinstein writes that the prohibition against building מַצֵבוֹת for the living teaches the following lesson:

> Since the Giving of the Torah, each Jew is required to strive constantly to raise himself to ever higher levels of observance of Torah and *mitzvos* (commandments)...Thus, the Torah prohibits a monolithic pillar because it suggests immutability, never accumulating further merits...Since the Giving of the Torah, however, we are obligated to do more than the minimum required by the Torah, to do as many *mitzvos* as we can and to strive to grow constantly, as we have described above. Therefore a pillar, which remains ever static, is as hateful to *Hashem* as a Jew who has given up trying to add to his store of *mitzvos* and good deeds...Since the Giving of

the Torah, however, a Jew is required to keep doing *mitzvos* until his last moment on earth, and is never allowed to rely on his past performance, as we explained above. After a person has departed this life, however, it is appropriate to erect a permanent monument to symbolize his reward for all the *mitzvos* and good deeds he performed during his lifetime, now that he cannot accumulate more.

Noach clearly wasn't as successful as Avraham. Avraham became the first forefather of the Jewish people, but Noach became an אִישׁ הָאֲדָמָה, man of the earth (*Bereishis* 9:20). Perhaps Noach wasn't as successful as Avraham because he didn't try hard enough. Rashi, based on the *Midrash Bereishis Rabbah* 30:7, explains in his commentary on *Bereishis* 6:14, that God had Noach labor to construct the ark for 120 years, even though God could have saved him in many different ways (i.e., by placing him on a mountaintop), so that people would wonder what he was building. Noach would easily be able to warn those who asked that God was going to cause a flood, in order for them to have the opportunity to repent. God put Noach in an ideal situation to warn everyone about the flood for 120 years. Despite this, Noach couldn't convince even one person, besides his own family, to join him in the ark! Perhaps Noach couldn't convince even one person because he didn't work hard enough to persuade others to live ethically and repent. This failure could be hinted at in Noach's name,(נֹחַ) which Rashi explains is derived from the Hebrew word, נוּחַ which means "rest" (commentary of Rashi on *Bereishis* 5:29).

Noach's name (נֹחַ), which is derived from the word "rest," may be related to his failure to save his generation and to become a forefather of the Jewish people. Noach's failure and God's command to force any animals that wanted to remain in the ark to return to their natural habitat teach us emphatically that one must be willing to make an effort, accept responsibility, not be lazy, and not be afraid to fail. *You can't succeed if you don't try.* You can't succeed if you are afraid of failure. If you don't make an effort, you are guaranteed to remain in your current situation and can't possibly improve. This is a crucial lesson that is applicable every day of our lives.

In contrast to Noach, whose name suggests "rest," the *Mishnah* in *Pirkei Avos* (*Ethics of the Fathers*) 5:4 teaches, "Our forefather Avraham was tested [by God] with ten trials, and he withstood them all..." Avraham didn't "rest." Our forefather Avraham repeatedly overcame difficult situations and grew spiritually.

The ideas presented in this essay may make it easier to gain a better understanding of a *Midrash* in *Bereishis Rabbah* 84:3 that discusses our forefather Yaakov. Rashi, in his commentary on *Bereishis* 37:2, quotes this *Midrash*, "Yaakov sought to live in tranquility, [when] the troubles of Yosef were sprung upon him..." This *Midrash* seems to suggest that it was inappropriate for our forefather Yaakov to want to live in tranquility. After many years of a very difficult relationship with his brother Eisav, and dealing with Lavan, who repeatedly attempted to deceive Yaakov, why does it seem that Yaakov was criticized for wanting to live in tranquility?

Perhaps this *Midrash* is teaching that just as God repeatedly challenged Avraham with difficult situations that were designed to help Avraham grow spiritually, God hadn't finished testing Yaakov. Instead of requesting to live in tranquility, perhaps Yaakov should have welcomed any other difficult situation that God was orchestrating for his benefit.

As described above, it seems that Noach didn't try hard enough to convince others to live ethically and repent. Noach is faulted, as his name implies, for too much "rest." Based on God's instructions to Noach regarding the animals that preferred to rest and remain in the ark, God wants us to avoid "rest," and to always strive to improve our status. As quoted above, Rav Moshe Feinstein writes, "Each Jew is required to strive constantly to raise himself to ever higher levels of observance of Torah and *mitzvos*..." Perhaps this is part of the reason that it seems that it was inappropriate for our forefather Yaakov to want to live in tranquility.

Many self-help books have been published in the last decade that are based on this fundamental principle – that you can't succeed if you don't try and are afraid to fail.

God taught this lesson to Noach when He told him to take all the animals out of the ark, even if they were afraid to return to their natural habitat. Our ancient Torah stresses this principle that is the basis of modern self-help psychology. The more one studies our ancient Torah, the more modern ideas one finds. As the last *Mishnah* in the fifth chapter of *Pirkei Avos* teaches, בֶּן בַּג בָּג אוֹמֵר הֲפָךְ בָּהּ וַהֲפָךְ בָּהּ דְּכֹלָּא בָהּ, "Ben Bag Bag says, 'Search in it and continue to search in it, for everything is in it.'"

(If desired, see related essay that I have written, with God's help, on *Parshas Vayeilech* entitled "Where Was Moshe Going?")

▸ THE FIRST COMMA

The Torah tells us that Noach and his family went into the ark מִפְּנֵי מֵי הַמַּבּוּל, *because of the waters of the flood* (*Bereishis* 7:7). Based on the *Midrash Bereishis Rabbah* 32:6, Rashi explains, אַף נֹחַ מִקְּטַנֵּי אֲמָנָה הָיָה, מַאֲמִין וְאֵינוֹ מַאֲמִין שֶׁיָּבֹא הַמַּבּוּל, וְלֹא נִכְנַס לַתֵּבָה עַד שֶׁדְּחָקוּהוּ הַמַּיִם, "Noach was also of those whose faith was weak; he believed and did not believe that the flood would come, and did not enter the ark until he was forced by the waters." According to this interpretation of Rashi, the Torah emphasizes that Noach went into the ark מִפְּנֵי מֵי הַמַּבּוּל, "when the waters forced him to," because Noach was מִקְּטַנֵּי אֲמָנָה (of those with little faith), and "he believed and did not believe that the flood would come."

There is a well-known argument concerning the character of Noach in the *Gemara Sanhedrin* 108a that Rashi paraphrases in his commentary on *Bereishis* 6:9. Rabbi Yochanan is of the opinion that Noach was only great in his generation, but had he lived in a better generation, he would not have been considered perfectly righteous. Reish Lakish disagrees and says that if Noach had lived in a better generation he would certainly have been considered perfectly righteous.

Can the opinion of Reish Lakish and all the Rabbis who say that Noach was righteous and would have been even greater had he lived in another generation, be reconciled with Rashi's explanation that Noach was מִקְטַנֵּי אֱמָנָה, and didn't enter the ark until the waters forced him? Rashi himself acknowledges Reish Lakish's opinion in his commentary at the beginning of this Torah portion (*Bereishis* 6:9), and writes יֵשׁ מֵרַבּוֹתֵינוּ דּוֹרְשִׁים אוֹתוֹ לְשֶׁבַח, "There are those among our Rabbis who infer from it to [Noach's] credit." How can Rashi seemingly contradict himself and write that Noach didn't enter the ark until the waters forced him, because he was מִקְטַנֵּי אֱמָנָה?

There is a beautiful solution to this problem, quoted in *Likutei Yehoshua* and *Itturei Torah*, which depends solely on where, in Rashi's explanation, the first comma is placed. If one places the first comma after the word מַאֲמִין, as opposed to the word הָיָה, Rashi's explanation reads entirely differently: אַף נֹחַ מִקְטַנֵּי אֱמָנָה הָיָה, מַאֲמִין, וְאֵינוֹ מַאֲמִין שֶׁיָּבֹא הַמַּבּוּל, וְלֹא נִכְנַס לַתֵּבָה עַד שֶׁדְּחָקוּהוּ הַמַּיִם, "Even Noach believed in those who were small in faith, and he did not believe that the flood would come, and [therefore] he didn't enter the ark until the waters forced him." Rashi explains in his commentary on *Bereishis* 6:14, based on the *Midrash Bereishis Rabbah* 30:7, that God had Noach labor to construct the ark for 120 years, even though God could have saved him in many different ways (i.e., by placing him on a mountaintop), so that people would ask Noach what he was building. Then Noach would have had the opportunity to explain that he was building an ark because God was going to cause a flood. Noach was in an ideal situation for 120 years, with the opportunity to warn everyone about the flood. Noach believed that some people of small faith, who had been warned about the flood for 120 years, would surely repent once the flood began, and that subsequently God would cancel the flood. Therefore, Noach didn't enter the ark until he was forced by the rising waters. Noach thought that people surely would repent when they saw with their own eyes that the forecast of the flood that he had been warning everyone about for 120 years was becoming a reality.

Rashi also teaches, based again on the *Midrash Bereishis Rabbah* 31:12, that God did not begin the flood with a huge deluge, but only with a more normal sort of rain so that people would have time to repent. Once people repented, God would cancel the flood, and then the rain that fell would be useful גִּשְׁמֵי בְרָכָה, rains of blessing (commentary of Rashi on *Bereishis* 7:12).

Thus, Rashi doesn't contradict his earlier opinion that some Sages teach that Noach would be considered very righteous in any generation, by writing וְלֹא נִכְנַס לַתֵּבָה עַד שֶׁדְּחָקוּהוּ הַמַּיִם (Rashi's commentary on *Bereishis* 7:7). **The intepretation of this comment by Rashi depends solely on the location of the first comma.** This comment by Rashi makes great sense according to both of the rabbis quoted in Rashi's earlier explanation, who disagree about the righteousness of Noach (Rashi's commentary on *Bereishis* 6:9). According to Reish Lakish and all those rabbis who say that Noach was righteous and would have been even greater had he lived in another generation, the first comma is after the word מַאֲמִין. According to Reish Lakish, Noach was extremely righteous and thought that some people of small faith, whom he had warned about the flood for 120 years, would surely repent once the flood began. Therefore Noach waited.

According to the other opinion quoted by Rashi in his commentary on *Bereishis* 6:9, based on Rabbi Yochanan and those Rabbis who taught that Noach would not have been considered to be exceptional in a more righteous generation, the first comma is placed after the word הָיָה. According to this interpretation of Rashi, Noach didn't enter the ark until the rising waters forced him to, because he wasn't very righteous, and he was "of those with little faith."

Thus, Rashi doesn't contradict his earlier statement about the character of Noach, because this comment by Rashi can easily be read according to either opinion, depending solely on the placement of the first comma. When the *Midrash Bereishis Rabbah* 32:6 discusses Noach's entrance into the ark, the *Midrash* writes, אָמַר רַבִּי יוֹחָנָן: נֹחַ מְחֻסַּר אֱמָנָה הָיָה, אִלּוּלֵי שֶׁהִגִּיעוּ הַמַּיִם עַד קַרְסֻלָּיו לֹא נִכְנַס לַתֵּבָה, "Rabbi Yochanan said: 'Noach lacked faith; had not the water reached his ankles, he would not have entered the ark.'" In this *Midrash*, Rabbi Yochanan is clearly consistent with his opinion that is taught in the *Gemara Sanhedrin* 108a, that Noach was only great in his generation, but had he lived in a better generation, he would not have been considered perfectly righteous.

Rashi expressed this thought in very different words than the *Midrash Bereishis Rabbah* and wrote, אַף נֹחַ מִקְּטַנֵּי אֱמָנָה הָיָה מַאֲמִין וְאֵינוֹ מַאֲמִין שֶׁיָּבֹא הַמַּבּוּל, וְלֹא נִכְנַס לַתֵּבָה עַד שֶׁדְּחָקוּהוּ הַמַּיִם. *Why does Rashi change the language of the Midrash so much?*

Perhaps Rashi chose to use these words, and not those of the *Midrash*, because depending on the location of the first comma, as described above, these words make sense according to either Reish Lakish or Rabbi Yochanan, who have different opinions regarding Noach's character. In his commentary on the first sentence of this *parshah* (Torah portion), Rashi explains that there is a disagreement regarding Noach's character. Therefore, later in his commentary on וַיָּבֹא נֹחַ...אֶל הַתֵּבָה מִפְּנֵי מֵי הַמַּבּוּל, *And Noach...went into the ark because of the waters of the flood* (*Bereishis* 7:7), Rashi is consistent and chooses words that agree with either opinion, depending on the location of the first comma. On the other hand, the *Midrash Bereishis Rabbah* 32:6 quoted above was taught by Rabbi Yochanan, and therefore uses words that make sense only according to Rabbi Yochanan's opinion that Noach would not have been considered perfectly righteous had he lived in a better generation.

Rashi's commentary on the Torah is famous for being very succinct, and there is no better example than Rashi's comment discussed above. In very few words, just depending on the placement of the first comma, Rashi offers an explanation as to why Noach didn't enter the ark until the waters forced him, which makes sense either according to the opinion of Reish Lakish or

Rabbi Yochanan. Either according to our Sages who teach that Noach was very righteous, or according to our Sages who teach that he was only considered righteous in his own generation, Rashi's comments fit perfectly, depending solely on the placement of the first comma.

פרשת לך לך
Parshas Lech Lecha

> THE HEIGHTS OF THE UNIVERSE

Most of the book of *Bereishis* (*Genesis*) relates the major events in the lives of our forefathers and the descent of Yaakov and his family to Egypt. In his commentary on the first sentence of the Torah, Rashi asks why the Torah starts with the story of creation, and not with the first commandment that was given to the Jewish nation. Since the purpose of the Torah is to teach the 613 commandments, Rashi wonders why the Torah doesn't begin with a commandment. Similarly, one can question why most of *Bereishis* relates the major events in the lives of our forefathers, instead of proceeding directly to teach the commandments. What is the purpose of the first book of the Torah which is devoted mostly to stories about the lives of our Patriarchs and Matriarchs?

The Ramban was one of the greatest biblical and Talmudic commentators, as well as a poet, philosopher, Kabbalist, and physician. He was born in Spain in 1194 and died in Israel in 1270. In 1263, he successfully defended Judaism in a public disputation for which King James I of Aragon presented the Ramban with a monetary award. After Pope Clement IV requested that the king penalize him, the Ramban escaped from Spain and immigrated to Israel.

In his commentary on the beginning of the Torah portion entitled *Lech Lecha*, the Ramban teaches a principle to help us understand the remainder of the book of *Bereishis*:

> *I will tell you a principle by which you will understand all the upcoming portions of the Torah* concerning Avraham, Yitzchak, and Yaakov. It is indeed a great matter which our Rabbis mentioned briefly, saying: "*Whatever has happened to the Patriarchs is a sign to the children*." It is for this reason that the verses narrate at great length the account of the journeys of the Patriarchs, the digging of the wells, and other events. Now someone may consider them unnecessary and of no useful purpose, but in truth they all serve as a lesson for the future: when an event happens to any one of the three Patriarchs, that which is decreed to happen to his children can be understood…It is for this reason that the Holy One, Blessed is He, caused Avraham to take possession of the Land [of Israel] and symbolically did to him all that was destined to happen in the future to his children. *Understand this principle*. (Based on the translation by Rabbi Dr. Charles B. Chavel. Italics are my emphasis.)

This principle is usually described in Hebrew as מַעֲשֵׂי אָבוֹת סִימָן לְבָנִים, "The happenings of the forefathers are a sign for the children," and is based on the *Midrash Tanchuma* (*Lech Lecha* 9). The Ramban writes that the Torah relates "at great length the account of the journeys of the Patriarchs" because they are a "sign for the children," and that we should "*understand this principle*." As the Ramban suggests, let us now try to understand this principle, which can be understood on several levels.

The simplest approach is that whatever happened to our forefathers predicts the future of the Jewish nation. For instance, Avraham left his birthplace to live in Israel, and eventually God will give the Land of Israel to the Jewish nation. Just as Avraham traveled to Egypt because of a famine in Israel, so too will the Jewish nation descend to Egypt because of a famine in Israel. Just as Yaakov fought with Eisav, so too will the Jewish nation fight with Eisav's descendants.

On a somewhat more complex level, מַעֲשֵׂי אָבוֹת סִימָן לְבָנִים may be teaching us that *whatever happened to our forefathers is an instructional guide for our future actions*. According to this approach, the actions of our forefathers not only predict the future, but they also serve as a guide for the current and future activities of all Jews. Just as Avraham was known for kindness, we too should try to be known for kindness. Just as Avraham left his birthplace to go to Israel, so too all of Avraham's descendants should do the same. The Ramban writes in his commentary on the beginning of *Parshas Vayishlach* that just as Yaakov utilized prayer, gifts, and military preparations in his confrontation with Eisav, so too the Jewish nation should use this multifaceted approach in its future confrontations.

Rabbi Eliyahu Eliezer Dessler (1892–1953) was one of the most profound Jewish thinkers of the last century. He was the *Rosh Yeshiva* (director) of the *Kollel* in Gateshead, England, and later *Mashgiach* (spiritual guide) of the Ponevezh Yeshiva in Israel. Rabbi Dessler's writings were published posthumously in a multivolume edition entitled *Michtav MiEliyahu*. The first volume of *Michtav MiEliyahu* has been translated into English by Rabbi Aryeh Carmell.

Rabbi Dessler was thrilled that he had acquired some insight into understanding מַעֲשֵׂי אָבוֹת סִימָן לְבָנִים from the commentary that Rabbi Chaim of Volozhin (1749–1821, the most prominent student of the Vilna Gaon and founder of the Yeshivah of Volozhin), wrote on *Pirkei Avos* (*Ethics of the Fathers*), Chapter 5, *Mishnah* 3.

Rabbi Dessler writes in *Michtav MiEliyahu*, Volume 1, in an essay on *The Attribute of Mercy*, "In this particular instance I am happy to say that *Hashem* has given me the merit to discover an important key which will help to elucidate the questions we referred to above..." Rabbi Dessler quotes Rabbi Chaim of Volozhin, "For there are many attributes which the *tzaddik* (the righteous man) labors hard and long to attain, while to his children they come *naturally* and they can achieve them with little effort." Regarding this brief comment by Rabbi Chaim of Volozhin, Rabbi Dessler writes that "one might see nothing special in these few words and pass them by hastily without realizing their true significance. *But no, my dear friends; these words stand at the very heights of the universe."*

Rabbi Dessler returns to the words of Rabbi Chaim of Volozhin:

> We have seen with our own eyes on many occasions how ignorant Jews who know nothing of Torah nevertheless readily give up their lives for the sanctification of the Divine Name [that is, they allow themselves to be killed rather than submit to conversion]. This is *ingrained in us* from Avraham, our father, who was ready to give up his life in the furnace of Ur Kasdim, for the sake of his faith (commentary of Rashi on *Bereishis* 11:28, quoting the *Midrash*). And so the purpose of all the ten tests [that God gave to Avraham] was to straighten the road for us [that is, to make it easier for us to arrive at certain spiritual levels]. Why do we find that a Jew is suddenly seized with a desire to immigrate to the Holy Land? This is derived from [Avraham's successful completion of] the test: "Go away from your land, your family and your father's house, to the land I will show you" (*Bereishis* 12:1).

Regarding this explanation by Rabbi Chaim of Volozhin, Rabbi Dessler teaches:

> It is indeed amazing, when we come to think of it, that we Jews should have retained our deep love for the Land of Israel after having been exiled from it for two thousand years.

The reason is that this attachment is, with us, not a matter of mere nationalism. If it had been only this, we should have forgotten about the Land of Israel many centuries ago. After all, other national groups, uprooted from their countries of origin, have adapted themselves completely to their new environment after two or three generations at the most...*It is a spiritual inheritance from Avraham*, our father, derived from the test of *Lech Lecha*. (This test, which required him to leave his birthplace and his old father for an unknown destination, called for much faith and self-sacrifice on his part.)

Thus, Rabbi Dessler explains, based on the comments of Rabbi Chaim of Volozhin, מַעֲשֵׂי אָבוֹת סִימָן לְבָנִים, "The happenings of the forefathers are a sign for the children," *because the attributes and spiritual greatness of the forefathers are ingrained in the nature of the Jewish nation.* The natural instincts of the Jewish nation are based on the מַעֲשֵׂי אָבוֹת. Because Avraham was willing to give up his life to sanctify God and leave his birthplace to move to Israel, *the personality of the Jew was modified so that it was less difficult for Jews over the centuries to do the same.*

The *Gemara* in *Yevamos* 79a teaches, שְׁלֹשָׁה סִימָנִים יֵשׁ בְּאוּמָה זוֹ הָרַחְמָנִים וְהַבַּיְישָׁנִין וְגוֹמְלֵי חֲסָדִים, "There are three signs [of the nature of the Jewish personality] in this nation: they are merciful, bashful, and they do acts of kindness." It's fascinating that this *Gemara* uses the word סִימָן, and not the word מִדּוֹת, which is the usual word for personality traits. The use of the word סִימָן in the *Gemara* in *Yevamos* 79a is reminiscent of the word סִימָן in מַעֲשֵׂי אָבוֹת סִימָן לְבָנִים, "The happenings of the forefathers are a sign for the children." This is easier to understand according to the theory of Rabbi Chaim of Volozhin discussed above, that the traits of the forefathers are ingrained in the nature of the Jewish nation. According to Rabbi Chaim of Volozhin, it's possible that the מַעֲשֵׂי אָבוֹת changed the סִימָנִים (signs or personality traits) of their בָּנִים (children) so that it is easier for them to be "merciful, bashful, and people who do acts of kindness."

Rabbi Chaim of Volozhin teaches that the מַעֲשֵׂי אָבוֹת changed the very essence of the Jewish people, so that certain difficult things, like moving to Israel or being prepared to give up everything to sanctify the name of God, will be less difficult for them in the future, because it is part of their nature.

The Ramban, quoted at the beginning of this essay, suggested that מַעֲשֵׂי אָבוֹת סִימָן לְבָנִים is an important principle that explains the purpose of most of the book of *Bereishis* and that we should try to "*understand this principle.*" Hopefully this essay, at least to some small degree, fulfills the suggestion of the Ramban, as it explains that this principle can be understood on at least three levels:

1) the most simplistic level is that the "happenings of the forefathers are a sign for the children" because they predict future events that will occur to their descendants, the Jewish nation.
2) on a somewhat more complex level, the "happenings of the forefathers are a sign for the children" because they are an instructional guide for the current and future activities of all Jews.
3) a third approach is suggested by Rabbi Dessler, based on the writings of Rabbi Chaim of Volozhin, who teaches that the "happenings of the forefathers are a sign for the children" because they changed the essence of the Jewish nation, so that following God's *mitzvos* will be easier because it is part of their nature.

As the Ramban writes, this is "*a principle by which you will understand all the*" stories in the book of *Bereishis*. As Rabbi Dessler teaches regarding Rabbi Chaim of Volozhin's explanation, "*these words stand at the very heights of the universe.*"

(If desired, see related essay on *Parshas Vayechi*, entitled "A Principle by Which You Will Understand the Book of *Bereishis*.")

▸ I WILL MAKE YOUR NAME GREAT

In the second sentence of the Torah portion entitled *Lech Lecha*, God tells Avraham, וַאֲגַדְּלָה שְׁמֶךָ, *And I will make your name great*. Rashi writes that "this is the basis for saying [in the beginning of the *Shemoneh Esrei* prayer] אֱלֹהֵי יַעֲקֹב, *God of Yaakov*." This seems difficult to understand and requires explanation. God tells Avraham, "I will make your name great," and Rashi says that this refers to the fact that we will continue to call Yaakov by his original name in the *Shemoneh Esrei* prayer. *How does calling Yaakov by his original name make Avraham's name great?*

Likutei Yehoshua and *Talilei Oros* quote a wonderful explanation for this that is attributed to Rabbi Shimshon Ostropoler. He was a prominent scholar and Kabbalist who, as the head of his community, died a martyr's death on July 22, 1648, during the Chmielnicki massacres (*Encyclopedia Judaica*).

Our four Matriarchs are שָׂרָה (Sarah), רִבְקָה (Rebecca), רָחֵל (Rachel), and לֵאָה (Leah). There are *thirteen* letters that make up the Hebrew names of our four Matriarchs. Unlike English letters, each letter of the Hebrew alphabet has its own unique numerical value. *Thirteen* is equivalent to the numerical value of the word אֶחָד, which means one (4=ד, 8=ח, 1=א). We have three forefathers, אַבְרָהָם (Avraham), יִצְחָק (Yitzchak) and יַעֲקֹב (Yaakov). אַבְרָהָם has five letters, יִצְחָק has four letters, and יַעֲקֹב has four letters. Similar to our four Matriarchs, this also adds up to *thirteen*, which as previously noted, adds up to the numerical value of the word אֶחָד, which means one. *Thirteen* also represents the 13 Attributes of God's Mercy that God revealed to Moshe (*Shemos* 34:6–7).

The Matriarchs' and Patriarchs' names, collectively, each have 13 letters. Thirteen plus thirteen equals twenty-six, which is equivalent to the numerical value of God's name (5=ה, 6=ו, 5=ה , 10=י). There are 26 total letters in the Hebrew names of our Patriarchs and Matriarchs, and this is the numerical equivalent of God's name. Through our Patriarchs and Matriarchs, God's name became one, and monotheism began to spread throughout the world.

After אַבְרָם's (Avram's) name was changed to אַבְרָהָם (Avraham), the Torah tells us in *Bereishis* 17:5 that he should only be called אַבְרָהָם (Avraham). After שָׂרַי's (Sarai's) name was changed to שָׂרָה (Sarah), the Torah tells us in *Bereishis* 17:15 that she should only be called שָׂרָה (Sarah). However, when Yaakov's name was changed to יִשְׂרָאֵל (Israel), the *Gemara* in *Berachos* 13a teaches that it is permissible to continue to use both names.

If we only called Yaakov by his new five-letter name, יִשְׂרָאֵל (Israel), there would be a total of fourteen letters in our forefathers' names, because the name אַבְרָם (Avram) has been permanently enlarged to the five letter אַבְרָהָם (Avraham). Rabbi Shimshon Ostropoler suggests that this is what Rashi is referring to, when Rashi explains that אַבְרָם (Avram) was told וַאֲגַדְּלָה שְׁמֶךָ, *And I will make your name larger* (לְגַדֵּל means to make bigger or enlarge), and that he will only be called by the larger five-letter name אַבְרָהָם (Avraham), because we say in the *Shemoneh Esrei* prayer אֱלֹהֵי יַעֲקֹב, *God of Yaakov*. Since the beginning of the *Shemoneh Esrei* prayer uses the four-letter name יַעֲקֹב (Yaakov), instead of the five-letter name יִשְׂרָאֵל (Israel), we can use the enlarged five-letter name אַבְרָהָם (Avraham), because the total letters of our forefathers' names will remain at 13, the numerical equivalent of אֶחָד. If we only called Yaakov by his new five-letter name, יִשְׂרָאֵל (Israel), there would be a total of fourteen letters in our forefathers' names, because the name אַבְרָם (Avram) has been permanently enlarged to the five letter אַבְרָהָם (Avraham).

Rabbi Shimshon Ostropoler explains that, according to Rashi, God tells Avraham, וַאֲגַדְּלָה שְׁמֶךָ, *And I will make your name great (enlarged)*, אַבְרָהָם (Avraham) instead of אַבְרָם (Avram), by continuing to use the original four-letter name of יַעֲקֹב (Yaakov) in the *Shemoneh Esrei* prayer. *This allows the total letters of our forefathers' names to still add up to thirteen.*

The cleverness of this Torah insight is typical of the other Torah thoughts that I have read by Rabbi Shimshon Ostropoler. The *Encyclopedia Judaica* also acknowledges that Rabbi Shimshon Ostropoler had the ability to find in the words of the Torah "extremely obscure hints which are so cleverly expounded."

(For other keen insights by Rabbi Shimshon Ostropoler, see related essays that I have written, with God's help, on *Parshas Beha'aloscha* and *Parshas Ki Savo*.)

פרשת וירא

Parshas Vayera

‣ THE FORMULA FOR A SUCCESSFUL MARRIAGE

The *Gemara* in *Shabbos* 55a and *Sanhedrin* 64a teaches, אָמַר רַבִּי חֲנִינָא, חוֹתָמוֹ שֶׁל הַקָּדוֹשׁ בָּרוּךְ הוּא אֱמֶת, "Rabbi Chanina said, 'The signature of the Holy One, Blessed is He, is [the word] 'truth.'" Even though God's signature is אֱמֶת (truth), God altered the truth so that Avraham would not get upset with his wife, Sarah. When Sarah heard the angel predict that she would have a son, she laughed in disbelief and said to herself, "and my husband is old" (*Bereishis* 18:12). In the next sentence, God asked Avraham, "Why did Sarah laugh saying, 'Can I really give birth when I am old?'" God told Avraham that Sarah laughed in disbelief because she was old, even though the truth is that she said that Avraham was old. God altered the truth to maintain שְׁלוֹם בַּיִת (domestic tranquility) between Avraham and his wife, Sarah. Rashi teaches, based on the *Gemara* and the *Midrash Bereishis Rabbah*, that "the Torah altered [its report of Sarah's words] for the sake of peace because she said 'and my husband is old.'" What an incredibly important lesson this must be, since God Himself teaches by His own example, towards the beginning of the Torah, that it is advisable to alter the truth to maintain שְׁלוֹם בַּיִת!

The *Gemara* teaches that we are commanded to emulate God. In *Shabbos* 133b, the *Gemara* tells us that the Jews are responsible to "be like Him. Just as [God] is gracious and compassionate, you also should be gracious and compassionate." This is also emphasized in the *Gemara Sotah* 14a, that just as it is written in the Torah that God provides clothes for the needy, visits the sick, comforts mourners, and buries the dead, we are commanded to emulate these attributes of God. Therefore, it follows that just as God altered the truth to maintain שְׁלוֹם בַּיִת between Avraham and Sarah, we should emulate God's example and make every effort to maintain שְׁלוֹם בַּיִת.

Perhaps because God Himself, towards the beginning of the Torah, teaches the importance of שְׁלוֹם בַּיִת, our Sages have emphasized the importance of mutual respect between husband and wife. Rabbi Yaakov Neuburger, who is the rabbi of the shul in which I pray, points out several of the examples from the writings of our Sages detailed below, relating to שְׁלוֹם בַּיִת. The *Gemara* in *Bava Metzia* 59a teaches that "Rabbi Chelbo said, 'A person must always be careful about his wife's honor, because blessing is found in a person's house only on account of his wife.'" The *Gemara* in *Bava Metzia* 59a also teaches that "Rav said, 'A person must always be wary of verbally wronging his wife…'" Rav Chisda teaches in the *Gemara Gittin* 6b, "A person should [be careful] never to instill excessive fear in his household…" The *Gemara* in *Yevamos* 62b teaches that a husband should love his wife like his own self and honor her more than his own self.

In the *Ketubah* (wedding contract) that every groom must give his bride at their wedding ceremony, the groom promises וַאֲנָא אֶפְלַח וְאוֹקִיר וְאֵיזוֹן וַאֲפַרְנֵס, "And I will *cherish*, *honor*, support and maintain." Every groom must promise not only to support his wife, but also to *cherish* and *honor* her. The obligation of the husband to *cherish* and *honor* his wife is so important that it *is mentioned first*, before the husband's promise to support her.

The Rambam was born in Spain, but when he was thirteen

years old, his family was forced to flee because of religious persecution. At the completion of his Commentary on the *Mishnah*, the Rambam notes that he began writing it at the age of 23, and completed it when he was 30 years old, and that these years can be described as a period "while my mind was troubled, and amid divinely ordained exiles, on journeys by land and tossed by the tempests at sea" (translation by the *Encyclopedia Judaica*). It is incredible that the Rambam became one of the greatest Jewish scholars of all time, even though he spent much of his youth wandering from place to place, which surely made it more difficult to study.

Based at least in part on the Talmudic sources outlined above, *the Rambam teaches the formula for a successful marriage* in his monumental code of Jewish Law, *The Mishneh Torah*, Laws of Marriage, 15:19-20. The Rambam writes:

> Similarly, our Sages have commanded that a man honor his wife more than his own person, and love her as he loves his own person…He should not cast an extra measure of fear over her. He should talk with her gently, being neither sad nor angry. And similarly, they commanded a woman to honor her husband exceedingly…She should follow the desires of his heart and distance herself from everything that he disdains.

The Rambam teaches that these measures of mutual respect between husband and wife that are taught by our Sages are the formula for a successful marriage. The Rambam concludes, "This is the custom of holy and pure Jewish women and men in their marriages. And these ways will make their marriage pleasant and praiseworthy."

Just as God altered the truth to maintain שָׁלוֹם בַּיִת between Avraham and Sarah, we must emulate God's example and make every effort to maintain שָׁלוֹם בַּיִת. Our Sages emphasize the tremendous importance of mutual respect between husband and wife, because as the Rambam teaches, it is of the essence to "make their marriage pleasant and praiseworthy."

> ### AN ESSENTIAL LESSON

The Torah portion entitled *Vayera* relates several events in the life of our forefather Avraham. In his commentary on the first sentence of the Torah, Rashi asks why the Torah starts with the story of creation, and not with the first commandment that was given to the Jewish nation. Since the purpose of the Torah is to teach the 613 commandments, Rashi wonders why the Torah doesn't begin with a commandment. Similarly, why does the Torah, whose main purpose is to teach the laws, devote a whole *parshah* to various events in the life of Avraham?

Our Sages teach, in *Midrash Vayikra Rabbah* 9:3, that ethical behavior preceded the giving of the Torah at Mount Sinai. Perhaps the Torah devotes an entire Torah portion to various events in the life of Avraham because דֶּרֶךְ אֶרֶץ קָדְמָה לַתּוֹרָה (ethical behavior precedes Torah) and there are numerous ethical lessons to be learned from the events related in *Parshas Vayera*.

One of the most important of these ethical lessons is taught when Avraham traveled to Gerar (*Bereishis* 20:1). In order to protect himself, Avraham lied to the inhabitants of Gerar, and told them that his wife, Sarah, was his sister (*Bereishis* 20:2). Later Avimelech, the king of Gerar, asked Avraham why he lied. Avraham responded, רַק אֵין יִרְאַת אֱלֹהִים בַּמָּקוֹם הַזֶּה וַהֲרָגוּנִי עַל דְּבַר אִשְׁתִּי, *There is only no fear of God in this place and they will kill me because of my wife* (*Bereishis* 20:11). Avraham tells Avimelech, the king of Gerar, that since the people in Gerar do not fear God, they would have killed him to have Sarah for themselves, had he told the truth that Sarah was his wife.

Avraham's actions teach us a fundamental and eternal ethical lesson. *Even if a society is scientifically, culturally, and ethically advanced, if* אִין יִרְאַת אֱלֹהִים בַּמָּקוֹם הַזֶּה רַק, *There is only no fear of God...*, *one needs to be afraid for his life*. Amalek is a nation that attacked the Jews immediately after their exodus from Egypt, even though they knew that God had performed incredible miracles for the Jews during their exodus. Considering the miraculous escape of the Jews from Egypt, Amalek's attack was completely illogical. The Torah testifies that Amalek attacked the Jews, despite the miracles that God performed for them, because וְלֹא יָרֵא אֱלֹהִים, *and he did not fear God* (*Devarim* 25:18). Amalek's attack is consistent with Avraham's response to Avimelech, that if fear of God is absent, one needs to be afraid for his own life.

Unfortunately, we have seen a powerful example of this in our times. Before World War II, the Germans were considered to be among the most advanced nations in the world, from every perspective. *The Germans were leaders philosophically, scientifically, and culturally.* Some of the world's best universities were found in pre-war Germany. *Yet, without fear of God, the Germans committed the most barbaric acts in the history of the world.*

Rav Elchanan Bunim Wasserman was born in 1875 and was one of the greatest Talmudic scholars and commmunal leaders in Europe at the beginning of World War II. He was the *Rosh Yeshiva* (director) of a Yeshiva in Baranowicze, Poland. *Peninim MiShulchan Gavoah* quotes Rav Elchanan Wasserman, who points out that the word רַק (only) seems superfluous. Why does the Torah say, רַק אֵין יִרְאַת אֱלֹהִים בַּמָּקוֹם הַזֶּה? The Torah could have just said, אֵין יִרְאַת אֱלֹהִים בַּמָּקוֹם הַזֶּה וַהֲרָגוּנִי עַל דְּבַר אִשְׁתִּי, *There is no fear of God in this place, and they will kill me because of my wife*. What is the purpose of the word רַק?

Rav Elchanan Wasserman suggests that the purpose of the word רַק is to teach that even if a society is advanced, as Avimelech's society was, if the *only* thing that is missing is fear of God, one needs to fear for his life. And indeed, in such a society, Avraham was afraid for his life. Even though Rav Elchanan clearly understood the danger that the Nazis posed, he chose to remain in Europe with his students. In June of 1941, Rav Elchanan Wasserman was arrested by the Nazis and tragically sent to his death.

The importance of this *fundamental and eternal lesson* taught by our forefather Avraham can not be underestimated. *Without* יִרְאַת אֱלֹקִים "fear of God," *the most scientifically, culturally, and ethically advanced person or nation is capable of the worst actions imaginable.* Perhaps, because דֶּרֶךְ אֶרֶץ קָדְמָה לַתּוֹרָה, "ethical behavior precedes Torah," the Torah teaches us important ethical lessons like this, prior to teaching all the laws.

In Rabbi Yehoshua Scheinfeld's magnificent collection of Torah insights entitled *Likutei Yehoshua* (*Collections of Yehoshua*), Rabbi Scheinfeld writes that the importance of fearing God is also taught in *Parshas Noach* 6:11, where the Torah writes, וַתִּשָּׁחֵת הָאָרֶץ לִפְנֵי הָאֱלֹהִים וַתִּמָּלֵא הָאָרֶץ חָמָס, *And the earth had become corrupt before God, and the earth had become filled with robbery*. According to Rabbi Scheinfeld, this sentence also teaches that robbery became prevalent because *the earth had become corrupt before God*, which suggests that there was a lack of יִרְאַת אֱלֹקִים. As Avraham told Avimelech, when there is no fear of God, a person or nation is capable of the worst actions imaginable.

Rabbi Herschel Schachter, a great contemporary Talmudic scholar and a *Rosh Yeshiva* at Yeshiva University, writes that this Torah portion, *Parshas Vayera*, emphasizes that even though Avraham is best known for the character traits of חֶסֶד (kindness), and אַהֲבַת יה־ה (love of God), he also mastered יִרְאַת אֱלֹקִים (fear of God) (from Torahweb.org, 11/16/2000).

Parshas Vayera begins with Avraham yearning to perform the commandment of הַכְנָסַת אוֹרְחִים (welcoming guests) (commentary of Rashi on *Bereishis* 18:1, based on the *Gemara* and *Midrash*). The *Midrash Bereishis Rabbah* 48:9 teaches that Avraham's tent had an opening on both sides to make it easier to welcome guests. Avraham's kindness extended to the evil people of Sodom for whom he fervently prayed (*Bereishis* 18:22–32). It is written in *Michah* 7:20, תִּתֵּן חֶסֶד לְאַבְרָהָם, *Give kindness to Avraham*. The Rambam writes in *Sefer HaMitzvos*, Positive Commandment 3, that Avraham is an example of someone who fulfilled the commandment to love God, and it is for this reason that it is written in *Isaiah* 41:8, אַבְרָהָם אֹהֲבִי, *Avraham, who loved me*.

Parshas Vayera teaches that despite the fact that Avraham is best known for the character traits of חֶסֶד and אַהֲבַת יְהֹוָה, Avraham also mastered יִרְאַת אֱלֹקִים. In *Parshas Vayera*, Avraham tells Avimelech, the king of Gerar, רַק אֵין יִרְאַת אֱלֹהִים בַּמָּקוֹם הַזֶּה וַהֲרָגוּנִי עַל דְּבַר אִשְׁתִּי, *There is only no fear of God in this place and they will kill me because of my wife* (Bereishis 20:11). And, toward the end of *Parshas Vayera*, after עֲקֵדַת יִצְחָק (the binding of Yitzchak on the altar) an angel testifies about Avraham, כִּי עַתָּה יָדַעְתִּי כִּי יְרֵא אֱלֹהִים אַתָּה, *For now I know that you are a God-fearing man* (Bereishis 22:12). Thus, *Parshas Vayera* emphasizes, both near the beginning and toward the end of the *parshah*, that Avraham, whose main attributes are kindness, and love of God, also mastered יִרְאַת אֱלֹקִים, fear of God.

The *Gemara Sotah* 31a acknowledges this and writes יְרֵא אֱלֹקִים הָאָמוּר בְּאַבְרָהָם מֵאַהֲבָה, "The fear of God that is stated regarding Avraham stems from his love [of God]." The ArtScroll commentary on the *Gemara Sotah* writes that Rabbi Yehuda Loewe (1526–1609, the great scholar known as the Maharal) explains that Avraham's fear of God wasn't related to a fear of punishment. Rather, Avraham loved God so much that it created the fear that "a misdeed might weaken the bond of love between them." Thus, this *Gemara* teaches that Avraham's fear of God grew from his great love of God. Consequently, Avraham is described in *Isaiah* 41:8, as אַבְרָהָם אֹהֲבִי, *Avraham, who loved me.*

Regarding "fear of God," King David writes in *Tehillim*, רֵאשִׁית חָכְמָה יִרְאַת יְהוָה, *The beginning of wisdom is the fear of God* (Psalms 111:10). The *Gemara Berachos* 33b teaches, "Everything is in the hands of Heaven, except for fear of Heaven." If fear of God is the beginning of wisdom, how does a person acquire it?

Rabbi Abraham J. Twerski, M.D., writes in his commentary on *Parshas Ki Sisa*, in *Living Each Week*, that Rabbi Aaron of Belz (1880–1957, prominent Chasidic Rebbe) said that his father explained, "One who observes the order of nature and the grandeur of nature should come to the realization of the existence of God, and develop a profound reverence for Him. *Failure to do so is not* due to lack of intellectual ability, but to one's desire to be free of the duties and responsibilities which awareness of God would impose."

Thus, the people of Gerar and Amalek, and the Nazis who lacked fear of God did not discern God's existence from "the order of nature and the grandeur of nature," because of their unwillingness to accept the obligations that the awareness of God would entail.

This concept that "One who observes the order of nature and the grandeur of nature should come to the realization of the existence of God" is taught by the Rambam in several places. The Rambam writes that not only fear of God, but also love of God is acquired "when a person contemplates His wondrous and great deeds and creations and appreciates His infinite wisdom…" (*Mishneh Torah, Sefer HaMada, Laws of Yesodi HaTorah*, 2:2). The Rambam repeats this concept later in the *Laws of Yesodei HaTorah*, 4:12. The Rambam concludes the Laws of Repentance by writing, "One can only love God [as an outgrowth] of the knowledge with which he knows Him…A greater amount of knowledge arouses a greater love. Therefore, it is necessary for a person…to [make every effort] to understand…concepts which make his Creator known to him…" In *SeferHaMitzvos*, Positive Commandment 3, the Rambam writes that the commandment to love God is achieved by thinking in depth about God's *mitzvos* (commandments) and about God's actions, such as creation and nature. In this manner, the Rambam teaches that a person learns to love God and will experience תַּכְלִית הַתַּעֲנוּג (*absolute joy*).

Parshas Vayera emphasizes that our forefather Avraham, the master of the character traits of חֶסֶד and אַהֲבַת יה־ה was also a master of יִרְאַת אֱלֹקִים (*Bereishis* 20:11 and 22:12). Avraham teaches the essential lesson that without יִרְאַת אֱלֹקִים, the most scientifically, culturally, and ethically advanced person or nation is capable of the worst actions imaginable.

(If desired, see related essay that I have written, with God's help, on *Parshas Yisro* entitled "What Did Yisro Hear?")

פרשת חיי שרה

Parshas Chayei Sarah

▸ A MARRIAGE MANUAL FOR ALL TIMES

The first twenty sentences of the Torah portion entitled *Chayei Sarah* describe Avraham's burial of his wife, Sarah. The next sixty-seven sentences are devoted to a detailed description of the process by which Avraham and his most trusted servant, Eliezer, find the proper wife for Avraham and Sarah's son, Yitzchak. As the beginning of the *parshah* describes Avraham's farewell to Sarah, and the next sixty-seven sentences describe the events that lead up to the initial stages of Yitzchak and Rivka's relationship, the first eighty-seven sentences of *Parshas Chayei Sarah* may be seen as being about the final and initial stages of marriage.

It's fascinating that the *Gemara*, at the very beginning of *Kiddushin* 2a, derives important laws dealing with the intricate legalities of the marriage process from Avraham's purchase of a burial plot for Sarah, from עֶפְרוֹן הַחִתִּי, Ephron the Hittite, which is described in the first twenty sentences of *Parshas Chayei Sarah*. *This Gemara teaches that the conclusion of Avraham and Sarah's relationship is relevant to the initial stage of all future marriages!* Is there any lesson to be learned from the *Gemara*'s association of the initial stage of all marriages with the conclusion of Avraham's marriage?

The *Gemara*, in *Menachos* 29b, teaches:

> Rav Yehuda said in the name of Rav, "When Moshe ascended to heaven, he found the Holy One, Blessed is He, sitting and tying crowns onto the letters. Moshe said, 'Lord of the Universe, is there anything lacking in the Torah that these additions are necessary?' God answered, 'There is one man who will live at the end of many generations, Akiva ben Yosef is his name, who will expound upon each and every point [of each letter in the Torah] heaps and heaps of laws...'"

Rabbi Akiva, who lived around 100 C.E. and was one of the foremost architects of the *Mishnah*, felt that each letter of the Torah is divinely endowed with so much purpose, that "heaps and heaps" of laws can be derived even from the crowns that are drawn on the top of individual letters.

Eighty-seven sentences are devoted to the end of Avraham's marriage and the beginning of Yitzchak's. If it is possible to derive important ideas even from the crowns that are drawn on the top of letters, what important ideas are we to derive from these eighty-seven sentences that discuss the end of Avraham's marriage and the beginning of Yitzchak's?

Rabbi Shlomo Riskin, a contemporary scholar, teacher, and communal leader, was a very popular rabbi of the Lincoln Square Synagogue in Manhattan. At the height of his popularity, Rabbi Riskin immigrated to Israel. He has achieved similar success in Israel as the rabbi of the community of Efrat and as Chancellor of the Ohr Torah Stone Institutions of Israel, which have an enrollment of over 2,000 students.

Rabbi Riskin points out (*Shabbat Shalom Sheets*, 11/2/02) that the Torah records very few important accomplishments by Avraham after Sarah passed away. The binding of Yitzchak and all of Avraham's other great accomplishments occurred during Sarah's lifetime. According to Rabbi Riskin, "Apparently Avraham was the *Rav* in no small measure because Sarah was the *Rebbetzin*." The Torah is emphasizing the crucial role that a wife plays in her husband's accomplishments.

The obvious lesson that the Torah teaches from Rivka's giving water to Eliezer and his ten camels is that willingness to perform acts of *chesed* (kindness) is the most important attribute that one should seek when looking for a wife. Rabbi Zvi Sobolofsky, a contemporary scholar, communal leader, and teacher, explains that the first twenty sentences of *Parshas Chayei Sarah* teach that the kindness that a husband and wife show to each other should be similar to the kindness displayed by Avraham when he buried Sarah (*torahweb*.org, 2002). Rashi explains in his commentary on *Bereishis* 47:29, that *chesed* that is done for the dead is considered חֶסֶד שֶׁל אֱמֶת, true kindness, for one does not expect to be paid back. Just as Avraham's effort to purchase a burial plot for Sarah was חֶסֶד שֶׁל אֱמֶת, true kindness, for which Sarah could not pay Avraham back, so too all kindness within a marital relationship should be performed without the expectation to be paid back. Avraham teaches that a spouse should not be kind with the purpose that the other partner in marriage be kind in return, but that acts of kindness within a marital relationship should be performed just for the sake of being kind, without any expectation of being paid back.

Rabbi Sobolofsky suggests that this is the reason that the *Gemara* at the beginning of *Kiddushin* associates the legalities of the initial stage of all marriages with Avraham's acquistion of a burial plot for Sarah, at the conclusion of their marriage. The *Gemara* is suggesting that all marriages, from their inception, should be based on the performance of חֶסֶד שֶׁל אֱמֶת similar to that which Avraham exhibited towards Sarah at the conclusion of their marriage. **Avraham teaches that the foundation of a successful marriage is for each spouse to be looking actively to perform acts of chesed for the other, without any expectation of being paid back.**

The first eighty-seven sentences of *Parshas Chayei Sarah* are not just a long story about the end of one marriage and the beginning of another. These sentences are a marriage manual for all people and all times concerning the importance of חֶסֶד שֶׁל אֱמֶת, true kindness – the performance of acts of kindness, by each spouse for the other, without expecting repayment in kind.

▸ GOD'S LANGUAGE

After Avraham buried his wife Sarah, he sent his servant Eliezer to search for a wife for their son, Yitzchak, among his relatives who lived in Aram Naharaim. Eliezer himself was a Canaanite, and Avraham made Eliezer swear that *you not take a wife for my son from the daughters of the Canaanites* (Bereishis 24:3). Eliezer asked Avraham what to do if, אוּלַי לֹא תֹאבֶה הָאִשָּׁה לָלֶכֶת אַחֲרָי, *Perhaps the woman shall not wish to follow me* (Bereishis 24:5). In the next sentence, Avraham responded, *Beware not to return my son there.*

When Eliezer met Rivka's father, Besuel, and her evil brother, Lavan, Eliezer told them everything that Avraham instructed him and everything that happened after he left Avraham's house. Rashi notes that when Eliezer repeats to Besuel and Lavan that he questioned Avraham, אֻלַי לֹא תֵלֵךְ הָאִשָּׁה אַחֲרָי, *Perhaps the woman shall not wish to follow me* (Bereishis 24:39), the word *perhaps*, which was originally spelled אוּלַי, is spelled אֻלַי. The letter "ו" is omitted when Eliezer recounts what happened to Besuel and Lavan. Rashi, based on the *Midrash Bereishis Rabbah*, explains that without the letter "ו," אוּלַי becomes אֻלַי, which is the exact same spelling as the word אֵלַי, which means *to me*.

Rashi explains that Eliezer "had a daughter, and he was looking for an excuse…to allow his daughter to marry" Yitzchak. Eliezer really had hoped that, *Perhaps the woman shall not wish to follow me;* then he would be able to have Yitzchok אֵלַי, which means *to me*, for his own daughter.

One can ask: If Eliezer really wanted Yitzchak for his own daughter, why did he say אוּלַי *perhaps*, and not אֵלַי (that is the same spelling as the word אֵלַי, which means *to me*) when he originally asked Avraham, אוּלַי לֹא תֹאבֶה הָאִשָּׁה לָלֶכֶת אַחֲרָי (*Bereishis* 24:5)? Why is the word אולי (perhaps) spelled with a "ו" when Eliezer spoke to Avraham, and without a "ו" when he spoke to Besuel and Lavan?

The Vilna Gaon explains that even though Eliezer said אוּלַי, *perhaps*, with a "ו", which *does not* suggest אֵלַי, which means "to me," when he spoke to Avraham, it is still clear that Eliezer really hoped that, אֵלַי לֹא תֵלֵךְ הָאִשָּׁה אַחֲרָי, *Perhaps the woman shall not wish to follow me...*(*Bereishis* 24:5), and then Yitzchak could marry Eliezer's own daughter.

The Vilna Gaon points out that although there are two words that mean "perhaps" in Hebrew, אולי and פֶּן, they have different connotations. The word פֶּן means *perhaps in a situation that one hopes will not happen*. For instance, פֶּן יִפְתֶּה לְבַבְכֶם, *perhaps your heart will be seduced* (*Devarim* 11:16) and ...פֶּן יֵשׁ בָּכֶם אִישׁ אוֹ אִשָּׁה אֲשֶׁר לְבָבוֹ פֹנֶה, *Perhaps there is among you a man or a woman... whose heart turns away* (*Devarim* 29:17). The word אולי means *perhaps in a situation that one hopes will happen*. For instance, Avraham said regarding Sodom אוּלַי יֵשׁ חֲמִשִּׁים צַדִּיקִם, *Perhaps there are fifty righteous people* (*Bereishi*s 18:24), and Sarah said regarding her maidservant, Hagar, אוּלַי אִבָּנֶה מִמֶּנָּה, *Perhaps I will be built up through her* (*Bereishis* 16:2). The word פֶּן is *perhaps with a negative connotation*, and the word אולי is *perhaps with a positive connotation*. Even though Eliezer used the word אוּלַי, and not אֵלַי (which is the same spelling as the word אֵלַי, which means *to me*) when he initially spoke to Avraham, *since Eliezer used the word אולי, which has a positive connotation, and not פֶּן* it is still clear that he hoped that Rivka would not want to travel back with him, so that his own daughter could marry Yitzchak.

אולי and פֶּן both mean *perhaps*, but they are not synonymous. As the Vilna Gaon explains, אולי has a positive connotation, and פֶּן has a negative connotation. The *Mishnah*, which was redacted by Rabbi Yehuda *HaNasi* around 200 C.E., calls the Hebrew language

לָשׁוֹן הַקֹּדֶשׁ, the "Holy Language" (*Sotah* 7:1). Perhaps because Hebrew is לָשׁוֹן הַקֹּדֶשׁ there are no exact synonyms, and each and every word has a different meaning.

The Ramban elaborates on the holiness of Hebrew in his commentary on *Shemos* 30:13. The Ramban writes that our Rabbis call Hebrew the "Holy Language" because:

> The words of the Torah and the prophecies...were all expressed in that language. It is thus the language in which the Holy One, Blessed is He, spoke with His prophets, and with His congregation [when he said] אָנֹכִי יְהֹוָה אֱלֹהֶיךָ ("I am *Hashem*, your God") and לֹא יִהְיֶה לְךָ אֱלֹהִים אֲחֵרִים עַל פָּנָי ("You shall have no other gods before Me") (*Shemos* 20:2–3) and in that tongue He created His world...In that language He called the names of Avraham, Yitzchak, Yaakov, and Solomon and others. (Adapted from the translation by Rabbi Dr. Charles B. Chavel.)

This idea is based on the *Midrash Bereishis Rabbah* 18:4 which teaches: "Just as the Torah was given in לָשׁוֹן הַקֹּדֶשׁ, so was the world created with לָשׁוֹן הַקֹּדֶשׁ." Since Hebrew is the language that God used to create the world and the language that God used to speak to His prophets, it is likely that each word is unique, and that there are no exact synonyms.

To describe Eliezer's initial converstaion with Avraham, the Torah uses the word אוּלַי, which has a positive connotation, and not פֶּן, which has a negative connotation, because Eliezer hoped that, אוּלַי לֹא תֹאבֶה הָאִשָּׁה לָלֶכֶת אַחֲרַי (*Bereishis* 24:5), so that Yitzchak could marry his own daughter. When Eliezer later retells his conversation with Avraham to Besuel and Lavan, אוּלַי is spelled אֻלַי (*Bereishis* 24:39), and the letter "ו" is omitted. According to Rashi's commentary described above, based on the *Midrash*, the Torah leaves out the letter "ו" because אֻלַי has the exact same spelling as the word אֵלַי, which means "to me," and Eliezer really wanted Yitzchak to marry his own daughter. Why does the Torah need to omit the "ו" to emphasize אֵלַי only when Eliezer is talking to Besuel and Lavan? According to the Vilna Gaon, from the use of the word אוּלַי, and not פֶּן, we already know that Eliezer is hoping that Rivka won't accompany him back to Avraham's house. Why is the "ו" left out of the word אוּלַי only when Eliezer speaks to Besuel and Lavan (*Bereishis* 24:39), and not when Eliezer speaks to Avraham (*Bereishis* 24:5)? In both instances, Eliezer is hoping that Rivka won't return with him, so that Yitzchak will be אֵלַי, "to me," for Eliezer's daughter.

Rabbi Zalman Sorotzkin (1881–1966, a great scholar and communal leader in pre-World War II Europe and later in Israel) explains that after Eliezer saw the evil and idolatrous habits of Besuel and Lavan, he was prompted to suggest אֵלַי, meaning that Yitzchok would be better off marrying Eliezer's own daughter. Alternatively, Rav Sorotzkin explains that when Eliezer was speaking to Besuel and Lavan, in order to persuade them to allow Rivka to leave, Eliezer suggested אֵלַי, meaning that he would love to have Yitzchak for his own daughter.

Itturei Torah is a magnificent collection of Torah insights by Rabbi Aharon Yaakov Greenberg, which was published posthumously in 1965. *Itturei Torah* quotes the Gerrer Rebbe, Rabbi Avraham Mordechai Alter (1866–1948) on this question. The Gerrer Rebbe explains that when Eliezer was in the presence of our righteous forefather Avraham, Eliezer was influenced by Avraham's righteousness and didn't acknowledge that he truly hoped that Yitzchak would marry Eliezer's own daughter. Only later, when Eliezer was in the presence of the evil Lavan and Besuel, he was influenced by them and said אֵלַי without the letter "ו", which is the same spelling as the word אֵלַי, implying "to me," and thereby revealed his true desire, that Yitzchak would marry his own daughter. This is an example of the principle taught in *Pirkei Avos* (*Ethics of the Fathers*) 2:13 and 6:9), that it is very important to have good neighbors, because people are influenced by their surroundings.

Rabbi Abraham J. Twerski, M.D., a contemporary scholar and

psychiatrist, quotes Rabbi Menachem Mendel of Kotzk (1787–1859, one of the foremost Chasidic Rebbes of his era) who explains that initially, when Eliezer was talking to Avraham, his true feelings were hidden deeply and repressed in his subconscious. Only later, when Eliezer realized that Rivka was meant for Yitzchak, did Eliezer's true feelings surface. Only then did Eliezer omit the letter "ו" and suggest אֵלַי, meaning that he would prefer to have Yitzchak for his own daughter. Rabbi Twerski points out that the Kotzker Rebbe "lived many decades before Sigmund Freud proposed… that forbidden wishes may be repressed and remain in a person's subconscious mind. Clearly, the Rabbi of Kotzk knew of this."

As described above, the Vilna Gaon emphasizes the uniqueness of לָשׁוֹן הַקֹּדֶשׁ and that the two Hebrew words for "perhaps" are different. אוּלַי has a positive connotation, and פֶּן has a negative connotation. As the Ramban teaches based on the *Midrash*, Hebrew is the language that God used to create the world and the language that God used to speak to His prophets. Therefore, it is likely that each word is unique, and that there are no exact synonyms.

The Vilna Gaon explains that even when Eliezer is speaking to Avraham, the word אוּלַי (perhaps) has a positive connotation and suggests that Eliezer is really hoping that Rivka won't agree to accompany him back to Avraham's house, so that Yitzchak can marry his own daughter. Only later, when Eliezer is talking to Besuel and Lavan, does the Torah actually omit the letter "ו", and write אֵלַי which is the same spelling as the word אֵלַי, which means "to me." *Only then does the Torah emphasize Eliezer's true feelings*, because of the reasons offered by Rabbi Zalman Sorotzkin, and the Gerrer and the Kotzker Rebbes.

(I am thankful to Rabbi Elozor Preil who taught me some of the ideas that are discussed in this essay.)

פרשת תולדת

Parshas Toldos

▸ WHOEVER HONORS THE TORAH

The *Mishnah* teaches, רַבִּי יוֹסֵי אוֹמֵר כָּל הַמְכַבֵּד אֶת הַתּוֹרָה גּוּפוֹ מְכֻבָּד עַל הַבְּרִיּוֹת, "Rabbi Yose says, 'Whoever honors the Torah is himself honored by people'" (*Pirkei Avos* 4:8). Rabbi Ovadiah of Bartenura wrote a classic and indispensable commentary on the *Mishnah*. He was born in Italy in approximately 1450 and died in Israel in approximately 1515. Rabbi Ovadiah of Bartenura explains that *one of the best ways to honor the Torah*, according to the *Mishnah* quoted above, is הַדּוֹרֵשׁ הַחֲסֵרוֹת וְהַיְתֵרוֹת שֶׁבַּתּוֹרָה...שֶׁאֵין בָּהּ דָּבָר לְבַטָּלָה, "He who expounds [upon words] that are spelled with missing letters or [upon words] that are spelled with extra letters...because there is nothing in the Torah without a purpose." Since everything in the Torah has a purpose, it is important to try to understand why some words are spelled מָלֵא (complete) with extra letters, and some words חָסֵר (missing) certain letters. Rabbi Ovadiah of Bartenura adds, אֵין לְךָ כָּבוֹד תּוֹרָה גָּדוֹל מִזֶּה, "You don't have a greater honor for the Torah than this." A person who expounds upon missing letters or extra letters honors the Torah, because by doing so, that person is displaying his belief that every letter in the Torah has a purpose, because the Torah was created by God. To honor the Torah, I'll relate two such examples in the Torah portion of *Toldos*.

The Torah tells us that, at the request of his mother, Rivka, Yaakov impersonated Eisav to receive Yitzchak's blessing, wearing goat skin in order to appear similar to Eisav, who was hairy (*Bereishis* 27:16). When Yitzchak, whose vision was poor, listened to and felt Yaakov, Yitzchak said, הַקֹּל קוֹל יַעֲקֹב וְהַיָּדַיִם יְדֵי עֵשָׂו, *The voice is the voice of Yaakov, and the hands are the hands of Eisav* (*Bereishis* 27:22).

Based on this sentence, the *Midrash Bereishis Rabbah* 65:20 teaches that when the voice of Yaakov is strong, in the synagogue and in schools, then the hands of Eisav will have no power, but if Yaakov's voice weakens, then the hands of Eisav will have power.

This *Midrash* seems difficult to understand because the sentence appears to state exactly the opposite. The Torah seems to be telling us that when הַקֹּל קוֹל יַעֲקֹב, when *the voice is the voice of Yaakov*, then הַיָּדַיִם יְדֵי עֵשָׂו, *the hands are the hands of Eisav*. The Torah seems to be telling us that when the voice of Yaakov is strong, then the hands of Eisav will be strong, God forbid. How does the *Midrash* derive the opposite from this text – that when the voice of Yaakov is strong, then the hands of Eisav will have no power?

In his commentary on the *Midrash*, Rashi points out that the word קוֹל, which means "voice," appears twice in this sentence and is spelled differently each time. The first time the word קֹל appears, it is spelled without the letter "ו", and therefore can be taken to mean "קַל", which means "not heavy, light." Based on Rashi's explanation of the *Midrash*, this sentence means, הַקֹּל קוֹל יַעֲקֹב, that when the voice of Yaakov is light, הַיָּדַיִם יְדֵי עֵשָׂו, then "the hands of Eisav will be strong." Since the first קֹל is missing the letter "ו" and can therefore mean "light," the *Midrash* teaches that when the voice of Yaakov is light, in the synagogues and in the schools, then the hands of Eisav will be strong. This *Midrash honors the Torah* by deriving an important principle based on a single missing letter. This is based on recognizing that the first word קֹל is spelled without a "ו", and can be translated to mean "light," rather than "voice."

Rabbi Baruch HaLevi Epstein (1860–1942) "declined offers to occupy rabbinical positions in such great communities as Pinsk, Moscow, and Petrograd, preferring to work in a bank and to devote all his spare time to his studies. Rabbi Epstein is best known for his [commentary on the Torah] *Torah Temimah*...which attests to his vast and profound knowledge of Talmud" (*Encyclopedia Judaica*).

During World War I, the German army captured Rabbi Epstein's hometown of Pinsk. Rabbi Epstein writes in his preface to *Mekor Baruch* that this "effectively cut Pinsk off from the outside world...I soon learned that this was not the time or the place for serious intellectual pursuits..." During the years that Pinsk was occupied by the Germans, Rabbi Epstein wrote *Mekor Baruch*, which is a historical work that contains his recollections of the great Torah scholars that he knew while growing up. Rabbi Epstein wanted to "give the people of his tortured generation a clear picture of the lives of our forefathers in the previous generation, in order to appreciate what we have lost."

After writing *Torah Temimah*, Rabbi Baruch HaLevi Epstein wrote another commentary on the Torah entitled *Tosefes Berachah*. In *Tosefes Berachah*, Rabbi Epstein *honors the Torah* by explaining the importance of "missing and extra letters" in the word תוֹלְדוֹת, which means "descendants" or "history." Rabbi Epstein points out that the word תוֹלְדוֹת appears in the Torah with three different spellings, depending on how many times the letter "ו" appears in the word.

The first spelling occurs in *Bereishis* 2:4, אֵלֶּה תוֹלְדוֹת הַשָּׁמַיִם וְהָאָרֶץ, *This is the history of the heaven and the earth*. In this sentence the word תוֹלְדוֹת is spelled מָלֵא, complete, with a "ו" at the beginning and at the end, because, as the *Midrash Bereishis Rabbah* 12:6 comments, "God's creation was complete."

In *Bereishis* 25:12, the second variation of this spelling is found, וְאֵלֶּה תֹּלְדֹת יִשְׁמָעֵאל, *And these are the descendants of Yishmael*. In this sentence, the word "תֹּלְדֹת" is חָסֵר, missing, and is spelled without the letter "ו" at the beginning and at the end. Rabbi

Epstein explains that this is because Yishmael's descendants are unsatisfactory since they have caused the Jewish people considerable pain (commentary of Rashi on *Bereishis* 21:17, quoting the *Midrash*).

The third variation in the spelling of this word occurs in the beginning of *Parshas Toldos* where it is spelled with only one "וֹ." The Torah writes, וְאֵלֶּה תּוֹלְדֹת יִצְחָק, *And these are the descendants of Yitzchak* (*Bereishis* 25:19). Why does the Torah choose to spell the word תּוֹלְדוֹת differently, with only one "וֹ", in the beginning of *Parshas Toldos*?

Rashi explains, *And these are the descendants of Yitzchak* refers to "Yaakov and Eisav who are spoken of [later] in this Torah portion." Rabbi Baruch HaLevi Epstein asks, "What is Rashi adding to our understanding of this sentence? Doesn't everyone who reads the Torah already know that Yaakov and Eisav are the descendants of Yitzchak?"

Rabbi Epstein explains that Rashi was bothered by the fact that in the sentence וְאֵלֶּה תּוֹלְדֹת יִצְחָק the word תּוֹלְדוֹת has only one "וֹ." Therefore, Rashi comments that the word תּוֹלְדוֹת (descendants) refers to "Yaakov and Eisav who are spoken of [later] in this Torah portion." The word תּוֹלְדוֹת is spelled with one "וֹ" at the beginning because of the completeness of our forefather Yaakov, and it is missing the second "וֹ" because the evil Eisav, like Yishmael, was an unsatisfactory creation.

Rabbi Ovadiah of Bartenura explains that the *Mishnah* in *Pirkei Avos* (*Ethics of the Fathers*) 4:8 teaches that *one of the best ways to honor the Torah* is to "expound [upon words] that are spelled with missing letters or [upon words] that are spelled with extra letters...because there is nothing in the Torah without a purpose..." The *Midrash Bereishis Rabbah* 65:20, according to Rashi's explanation discussed above, *honors the Torah* by deriving an important principle based on a missing "וֹ", in the first קֹל, in the sentence הַקֹּל קוֹל יַעֲקֹב וְהַיָּדַיִם יְדֵי עֵשָׂו (*Bereishis* 27:22). Rabbi Baruch HaLevi Epstein *honors the Torah* by explaining the significance of the three different ways the word תּוֹלְדוֹת is spelled in the Torah, depending on how many times the letter "ו" appears in the word. Hopefully, this essay *honors the Torah* by presenting two different examples, based on the teachings of our Sages, of the significance of missing letters and extra letters in *Parshas Toldos*.

▸ LET'S TRY TO SOLVE THE GREAT MYSTERY

One of the greatest mysteries in the entire Torah is the preference of our forefather Yitzchak to bless Eisav over Yaakov. Prior to Yitzchak's decision to bless Eisav, the Torah relates in *Bereishis* 25:27 that Eisav was a אִישׁ שָׂדֶה (man of the field) and that Yaakov was אִישׁ תָּם יֹשֵׁב אֹהָלִים (a wholesome man, living in tents). Rashi explains, based on the *Midrash Bereishis Rabbah*, that Yaakov dwelled in the tents of the Yeshiva of Shem and Ever studying Torah. Why does Yitzchak attempt to bless Eisav, who was a "man of the field," and not Yaakov, who was devoted to the study of Torah? Furthermore, the sentence that *immediately precedes* Chapter 27, which describes Yitzchak's attempt to bless Eisav, tells us that Eisav married two women who *were a source of spiritual rebellion to Yitzchak and Rivka* (*Bereishis* 26:35). Rashi quotes the *Midrash* that "all the actions [of Eisav's wives] caused anguish to Yitzchak and Rivka because they worshiped idols." Thus, prior to Yitzchak's blessing, the Torah relates that Eisav was clearly involved in nothing but trouble, and Yaakov was sitting and studying in Yeshiva. Why then does Yitzchak prefer to bless Eisav?

The Torah portion *Toldos* begins by telling us, וְאֵלֶּה תּוֹלְדֹת יִצְחָק בֶּן אַבְרָהָם אַבְרָהָם הוֹלִיד אֶת יִצְחָק, *And these are the offspring of Yitzchak the son of Avraham; Avraham gave birth to Yitzchak* (*Bereishis* 25:19). At first glance, this sentence seems superfluous because we have already been told that Avraham is Yitzchak's father (*Bereishis* 21:3). This sentence also seems inaccurate because it begins by describing the offspring of Yitzchak, but doesn't mention Yaakov and Eisav. Rashi explains that *And these are the offspring of Yitzchak* refers to "Yaakov and Eisav who are spoken of [later] in this *parshah*." What is Rashi adding to our understanding of this sentence?

Perhaps the first sentence in this *parshah* serves as an introduction to this Torah portion, because it can help explain the great mystery of *Parshas Toldos* – Yitzchak's preference to bless Eisav over Yaakov. This sentence can help us to understand, as Rashi teaches, what happens to "Yaakov and Eisav who are spoken of [later] in this *parshah*." Perhaps this sentence is teaching that since אַבְרָהָם הוֹלִיד אֶת יִצְחָק, *Avraham gave birth to Yitzchak*, Yitzchak wanted to bless his more outgoing son, Eisav, since he seemed best fit to follow in Avraham's footsteps, because Avraham was an outgoing person whose main attribute was חֶסֶד (showing kindness to others).

Avraham's expertise in חֶסֶד is acknowledged in *Michah* 7:20, where it is written, תִּתֵּן חֶסֶד לְאַבְרָהָם, *Give kindness to Avraham*. This character trait found expression in Avraham's love for the *mitzvah* (commandment) of הַכְנָסַת אוֹרְחִים (welcoming guests) (commentary of Rashi on *Bereishis* 18:1, based on the *Gemara* and *Midrash*). The *Midrash Bereishis Rabbah* 48:9 teaches that Avraham's tent had an opening on both sides to make it easier to welcome guests. Avraham's kindness extended to the evil people of Sodom for whom he fervently prayed (*Bereishis* 18:22–32). The Torah tells us about Avraham's ability to convince people to believe in God (*Bereishis* 12:5). To optimally perform acts of חֶסֶד, it is beneficial to have an *outgoing* personality that is interested in the well-being of others.

Perhaps Yitzchak thought that since Yaakov seemed introverted and spent most of his time in the tents of the Yeshiva of Shem and Ever, he would not be suited to follow in Avraham's path of reaching out to teach others about God. Maybe Yitzchak thought that Eisav, who was outgoing and an אִישׁ שָׂדֶה would be better suited to follow in Avraham's outgoing lifestyle of חֶסֶד.

Therefore, the first sentence of *Parshas Toldos* is not superfluous at all. It explains the great mystery of our *parshah* – the reason that Yitzchak preferred to bless Eisav over Yaakov. Perhaps Yitzchak preferred to bless Eisav because, as this sentence emphasizes, *Avraham gave birth to Yitzchak,* and Yitzchak thought that

Eisav's outgoing personality would make it easier for him to adopt Avraham's character trait of חֶסֶד.

Perhaps this is what Rashi taught when he explained that the first sentence of *Parshas Toldos*, *And these are the offspring of Yitzchak*, refers to "Yaakov and Eisav who are spoken of [later] in this *parshah*." Rashi is saying that this first sentence explains the great mystery of the story of "Yaakov and Eisav who are spoken of [later] in this *parshah*"; *that Yitzchak preferred to bless Eisav because* אַבְרָהָם הוֹלִיד אֶת יִצְחָק, *Avraham gave birth to Yitzchak*. Perhaps Yitzchak thought that Eisav's outgoing personality would make it easier for Eisav to follow in Avraham's footsteps.

Rivka wanted Yaakov to receive Yitzchak's blessing because she understood that the Torah knowledge that Yaakov acquired in the tents of the Yeshiva of Shem and Ever would enable him to follow in the footsteps of Avraham, and to become more outgoing and master Avraham's trait of חֶסֶד. Rabbi Shlomo Riskin, a contemporary communal leader and teacher, writes that Rivka "understood the real world because she came from the house of Lavan and Besuel, masters of deceit and treachery." Because she was an expert at dealing with the real world, Rivka was confident that Yaakov would be able to become more like Avraham, since he had acquired much Torah knowledge in the tents of the Yeshiva of Shem and Ever. She therefore thought that her righteous son Yaakov should receive Yitzchak's blessing. (*www.jpost.com*, 11/30/2000)

The second sentence in *Parshas Toldos* reminds us that Rivka is the בַּת בְּתוּאֵל הָאֲרַמִּי מִפַּדַּן אֲרָם אֲחוֹת לָבָן הָאֲרַמִּי, *daughter of Besuel, the Aramean from Paddan Aram, [and the] sister of Lavan the Aramean*. Since the Torah has already told us in great detail about Rivka's father and brother in Chapter 24, why is this information repeated again in the second sentence of *Parshas Toldos*? Rashi explains, based on the *Midrash*, that the Torah reminds us about her evil father and brother to "relate Rivka's praise that she was the daughter of a wicked person, and the sister of a wicked person…and she did not learn from their deeds."

One can also suggest that the Torah reminds us of Rivka's evil family *specifically in the second sentence* of *Parshas Toldos*, because this fact is essential to understanding the great mystery of *Parshas Toldos* – that Rivka differed with her husband, Yitzchak, and suggested that Yaakov impersonate Eisav to receive Yitzchak's blessing. The *second sentence* of *Parshas Toldos* is an introductory sentence that helps explain the great mystery of *Parshas Toldos* by teaching us that Rivka had a different approach than Yitzchak, because she learned how to deal with the real world growing up in the house of the evil Besuel and Lavan.

Thus, the first sentence of *Parshas Toldos* is an introductory sentence that helps to explain the great mystery of *Parshas Toldos* from *Yitzchak*'s point of view – that Yitzchak preferred to bless Eisav because *Avraham gave birth to Yitzchak*, and Yitzchak felt that Eisav's outgoing nature would enable him to follow in Avraham's footsteps. The second sentence is also an introductory sentence that helps to explain the great mystery of *Parshas Toldos* from *Rivka*'s point of view – that Rivka disagreed with Yitzchak, because she learned how to deal with the problems of the real world growing up among an evil father and brother. She understood that Yaakov should receive Yitzchak's blessing, since the knowledge that Yaakov acquired in the tents of the Yeshiva of Shem and Ever was the main ingredient he needed to follow in Avraham's path.

Rivka showed Yitzchak that their introverted son Yaakov, who specialized in studying Torah, could also learn to become an אִישׁ שָׂדֶה who could deal with the challenges of the real world, by having him successfully impersonate Eisav to receive the blessings. Rivka was clearly correct, and Yaakov continued to develop the outgoing facet of his personality and his ability to deal with problems outside of the walls of the Yeshiva, when he worked for the evil Lavan for twenty years (*Bereishis* 31:38), and in his confrontation with Eisav, who wanted to kill him (*Bereishis* 27:41). Just like his mother, Rivka, Yaakov became an expert at dealing with the real world. Rivka understood that if one first acquires a strong foundation in the Torah, as Yaakov did, then one can learn to be outgoing and master Avraham's trait of חֶסֶד.

Rivka is teaching all Jews in every generation that the best preparation for dealing with real world problems is to approach life as did our forefather Yaakov. Before attempting to confront the challenges of modern life, the best preparation is to obtain a strong foundation in Torah study and become a יֹשֵׁב אֹהָלִים (living in the tents) of the Yeshiva, studying Torah.

(I am thankful to Rabbi Menachem Leibtag for some of the ideas in this essay, which are based on his thoughts at *www.tanach.org*.)

פרשת ויצא

Parshas Vayeitzei

▸ ANCIENT AND INVALUABLE ADVICE FOR EVERY HUSBAND AND FATHER

The Torah tells us וַיַּרְא יְהֹוָה כִּי שְׂנוּאָה לֵאָה, *And God saw that Leah was hated* (Bereishis 29:31). Is this really true? Just one sentence earlier, it is written, וַיֶּאֱהַב גַּם אֶת רָחֵל מִלֵּאָה, *and he [Yaakov] loved Rachel even more than Leah*. This clearly implies that Yaakov loved Leah also, but that he loved Rachel more. Why, then, does the Torah write in the very next sentence that Yaakov hated Leah?

Rabbi Yaakov Neuburger is a *Rosh Yeshiva* at Yeshiva University and the rabbi of the shul in which I pray. Rabbi Neuburger relates a clever psychological insight made by the Ramban to explain these two apparently contradictory sentences. The Ramban quotes Rabbi David Kimchi (c.1160–c.1235, biblical commentator and grammarian, who is known as the Radak), who explains that if one wife is loved more than the other, then the second wife will feel hated, even though she is not. Therefore, even though the Torah tells us that Yaakov loved Rachel more than Leah, the Torah records that Leah felt as if she was actually hated. The Torah is teaching us that in a spousal relationship, if one wife is loved less, she will feel hated.

The Radak teaches that this principle also applies to a sentence that appears much later in the Torah, in *Parshas Ki Seitzei*, כִּי תִהְיֶיןָ לְאִישׁ שְׁתֵּי נָשִׁים הָאַחַת אֲהוּבָה וְהָאַחַת שְׂנוּאָה, *If a man will have two wives, one beloved and one hated* (*Devarim* 21:15). The Radak suggests that this applies even if the second wife is not truly hated. If the husband loves one wife more than the other, then the second wife will feel hated, similar to Leah's situation.

Rabbi Neuburger suggests that, according to this explanation of the Ramban quoting the Radak, the Torah is trying to teach all husbands in every generation the importance of making one's wife feel central in a relationship. If a husband makes his wife feel even slightly unloved, as Yaakov did to Leah because of his greater love for Rachel, then she might feel hated. As Rabbi Neuburger writes, "Whereas other relationships can weather orbits of varying strengths and closeness, marriage is a center-or-nothing matter. Either spouses are central to each other or they will feel distanced" (*torahweb.org*, 2002).

The Rambam also emphasizes that it is crucial for a husband always to make his wife feel central in their relationship. The Rambam writes, based on the *Gemara Yevamos* 62b, "Similarly, our Sages have commanded that a man honor his wife more than his own person, and love her as he loves his own person" (*Mishneh Torah*, Laws of Marriage 15:19).

Towards the end of *Parshas Vayeitzei*, the Torah teaches husbands and fathers another invaluable lesson. After Yaakov works twenty years for Lavan, God clearly tells him that he should return to the Land of Israel (*Bereishis* 31:3). In the next ten sentences that follow, Yaakov summons his wives and offers them a fairly lengthy explanation as to why they should leave their father and their birthplace to travel with him to Israel. Yaakov persuades them by saying, *And your father mocked me and changed my wage a hundred times* (*Bereishis* 31:7), *And God took away your father's livestock and gave them to me* (*Bereishis* 31:9).

Many commentators wonder why Yaakov did not just tell his wives that God said that it was time to return to Israel. Why does the Torah record Yaakov's lengthy explanation as to why they should be willing to travel with him to Israel? Why didn't Yaakov just tell them that God had commanded them to travel to Israel?

Rabbi Yeshayah Horowitz (c.1560–1630) is known as the Sh'lah HaKadosh, the Holy Sh'lah, from the initials of the title of his major work, *Shnei Luchos Habris*. He was *Av Bet Din* (director of the Jewish Court) in Frankfurt on the Main until the expulsion of the Jews in 1614. In 1621, he immigrated to Israel and became the rabbi of the Ashkenazi community. He was imprisoned by the ruling authorities in 1625, until he was ransomed. The Sh'lah HaKadosh, the Holy Sh'lah, was a very influential figure. The *Encyclopedia Judaica* acknowledges that "generations of Jews in Central and Eastern Europe until the end of the 18th century walked in the light of the Holy Sh'lah." Avraham Yaakov Finkel writes in *The Great Torah Commentators* that the Holy *Sh'lah* is one of only four works in all of Jewish literature that are usually referred to as *Kadosh* (Holy): the *Zohar HaKadosh*, the *Or HaChayim Hakadosh*, the *Alshich HaKadosh*, and the *Sh'lah HaKadosh*.

The *Sh'lah HaKadosh* offers a wonderful reason to explain why the Torah relates Yaakov's lengthy persuasive efforts. The *Sh'lah* explains:

> A husband, although he is head of the household, should not wield his authority or use intimidation on his wife and family. Rather, he should use persuasion and gentle reasoning to induce them to follow his suggestions. This mild and amiable approach was used by Yaakov as he spoke to his wives. He had the clearly expressed mandate of God "to return to the land of your fathers" (*Bereishis* 31:3). Yet, broaching the subject of returning, he gradually introduced the idea to Rachel and Leah, reviewing the entire history of his stay with Lavan, devoting ten verses to the process (*Bereishis* 31:4–13). All this, in order to make them amenable to his proposed plan. (Translation is by Avraham Yaakov Finkel.)

The Torah records Yaakov's lengthy, persuasive explanation to teach husbands in every generation not to impose their will on their wives and children, but to explain gently the reason for their decisions.

This insight of the *Sh'lah HaKadosh* is also quoted in *Itturei Torah* (a magnificent collection of Torah insights by Rabbi Aharon Yaakov Greenberg, published posthumously in 1965) and by Rabbi Yissocher Frand (a contemporary scholar and teacher who is the author of many magnificent Torah thoughts). As Rabbi Frand writes:

> This means that a person can feel very strongly about a certain household decision. He may have no doubt in his mind at all. And, he can be capable of enforcing that decision. "This is the way it's going to be." The *Sh'lah* teaches us: Do not do it that way. *Convince, cajole, persuade, but do not impose.* (ryfrand@torah.org)

Towards the beginning of *Parshas Vayeitzei*, according to the commentary of the Ramban written more than 700 years ago, quoting the Radak, the Torah teaches husbands in every generation that they must always make their wives feel important in their relationship. If a husband makes his wife feel even slightly unloved, then she might feel hated. Towards the end of *Parshas Vayeitzei*, the Torah teaches, according to the explanation of the *Sh'lah HaKadosh* written approximately 400 years ago, that a husband or father should gently explain his decisions and not impose his will on his wife and children. **These psychological insights as to how a husband or father should conduct himself are clearly as valuable today as the day they were written hundreds of years ago.**

▸ **EVERYTHING IS HINTED AT IN THE TORAH – TWO MAGNIFICENT ABBREVIATIONS**

The Torah describes how our forefather Yaakov reacted after meeting his future wife, Rachel. The Torah says that one of Yaakov's reactions was, וַיִּשָּׂא אֶת קֹלוֹ וַיֵּבְךְּ, *And he raised his voice and cried*

(*Bereishis* 29:11). In his commentary on this sentence, Rashi offers two reasons that Yaakov cried almost immediately after meeting his beloved wife to be. One of these reasons is based on an elaborate story that doesn't appear anywhere in the Torah. According to Rashi, Yaakov cried because all his possessions had been stolen by Eisav's son Elifaz, and consequently, Yaakov cried because he didn't have any gifts for Rachel. Rashi explains:

> Yaakov said, 'Eliezer, my paternal grandfather's [Avraham's] slave, had in his hands…bracelets and delicacies [when he went to find a wife for Yitzchak] (see *Bereishis* 24:10 and 22). But, I have nothing with me.' Because Elifaz, the son of Eisav, pursued Yaakov, by order of his father, in order to kill him, and [Elifaz] overtook him. But, since Elifaz was raised on Yitzchak's lap, he refrained from killing him [Yaakov]. Elifaz said to Yaakov, 'What should I do about my father's order?' Yaakov replied to him, 'Take whatever I have with me, because a poor person is considered as dead.'

Rabbi Zev Wolf Einhorn's commentary on the *Midrash Rabbah* is extraordinary because it attempts to explain the uncomplicated, true meaning of the *Midrash*. The commentary is known, by the initials of his name, as the פֵּרוּשׁ מַהַרְזַ"וּ. Yonah Frankel writes in דַּרְכֵי הָאַגָּדָה וְהַמִּדְרָשׁ, *The Ways of the Aggadah and Midrash*, that Rabbi Zev Wolf Einhorn's birthdate is not known and that he died in Vilna in 1862. In his commentary on *Devarim Rabbah* 2:20, Rabbi Einhorn cites Rashi's source for this story as the *Midrash, Sefer HaYashar.*

Elifaz was concerned about fulfilling his father's command to kill Yaakov. This seems strange because Elifaz clearly wasn't permitted ethically to fulfill such an evil command. Perhaps Elifaz was so concerned about fulfilling the command of his father because כַּבֵּד אֶת אָבִיךָ, *Honor your father* (*Shemos* 20:12), was the only commandment that Eisav excelled at, and Elifaz learned the importance of this commandment from his father. *Midrash*

Devarim Rabbah 1:15 teaches that "Rabbi Shimon ben Gamliel says, 'No son has ever honored his parents as I have done, and yet I find that Eisav honored his father even more than I…'" Similarly, the *Midrash Yalkut Shimoni* (*Bereishis* 115) teaches, "Rabbi Shimon ben Gamliel says, 'All the days that I served my father, I didn't serve him 1/100th of how the evil Eisav served his father. When I served my father, I wore dirty clothes and when I went to the market, I wore clean clothes. But, when Eisav served his father, he wore only clothes fit for royalty" (as is described in *Bereishis* 27:15). Since Eisav was a specialist only in the commandment of כַּבֵּד אֶת אָבִיךָ, his son Elifaz, understood the importance of this commandment and wanted to fulfill his father's command to kill Yaakov. Therefore, the *Midrash* relates, as quoted by Rashi above, that "Elifaz said to Yaakov, 'What should I do about my father's order?' Yaakov replied to him, 'Take whatever I have with me, because a poor person is considered as dead.'" The Torah tells us that when Yaakov met Rachel's father, Lavan, וַיְסַפֵּר לְלָבָן אֵת כָּל הַדְּבָרִים הָאֵלֶּה, *And he [Yaakov] told Lavan all these events* (*Bereishis* 29:13). Once again, Rashi explains that Yaakov told Lavan that he has no gifts for him because "all his money was taken from him [by Elifaz]."

Rashi teaches that the two sentences quoted above, *Bereishis* 29:11 and 13, are understood based on an elaborate story that is recorded in *Midrash Sefer HaYashar*, but isn't written anywhere in the Torah, relating that Elifaz stole all of Yaakov's possessions. *Isn't it surprising that such an elaborate story doesn't appear anywhere in the Torah?* our Sages have taught, לֵיכָּא מִידֵי דְּלֹא רְמִיזֵי בְּאוֹרָיְתָא, "There is nothing that is not hinted at in the Torah." The source for this teaching is not entirely clear, as this exact phrase does not appear in the *Gemara* or *Midrash*. A similar but more limited idea appears in *Gemara Ta'anis* 9a, where the *Gemara* teaches that everything written in the נְבִיאִים (*Prophets*) and כְּתוּבִים (*Writings*) is hinted at in the Torah. Perhaps this principle is also based on the last *Mishnah* in the fifth chapter of *Pirkei Avos* (*Ethics of the Fathers*) that teaches, בֶּן בַּג בַּג אוֹמֵר הֲפָךְ בָּהּ וַהֲפָךְ בָּהּ דְּכֹלָּא בָהּ, "Ben Bag

Bag says, 'Search in it and continue to search in it, for everything is in it.'" Since we have been taught, לֵיכָּא מִידֵי דְלֹא רְמִיזֵי בְּאוֹרַיְתָא, "There is nothing that is not hinted at in the Torah," where is this elaborate story about Elifaz stealing all of Yaakov's possessions hinted at in the Torah?

Over thirty years ago, when I was a high school student, my *rebbe*, Rav Shmuel Scheinberg, taught that this story about Elifaz is hinted at in the first sentence of the Torah portion entitled *Vayeitzei*. This sentence says, וַיֵּצֵא יַעֲקֹב מִבְּאֵר שָׁבַע וַיֵּלֶךְ חָרָנָה, *And Yaakov went out from Beer-Sheva and went toward Charan* (Bereishis 28:10). Rav Shmuel Scheinberg taught that *the letters of* מִבְּאֵר שָׁבַע וַיֵּלֶךְ חָרָנָה *are an abbreviation for* מִיָּד בָּא אֱלִיפָז רָשָׁע שֶׁהוּא בֶּן עֵשָׂו וְיִתֵּן יַעֲקֹב לוֹ כָּל חֵילוֹ רַק נִשְׁאַר הַמַּקֵּל, "Immediately the evil Elifaz came, who is the son of Eisav, and Yaakov gave him all his possessions. Only his walking staff remained." The first sentence in *Parshas Vayeitzei* teaches that וַיֵּצֵא יַעֲקֹב, *And Yaakov went out* and then "immediately the evil Elifaz came, who is the son of Eisav, and Yaakov gave him all his possessions. Only his walking staff remained." The fact that "only his walking staff remained" alludes to the sentence in the next Torah portion, *Vayishlach*, where Yaakov said כִּי בְמַקְלִי עָבַרְתִּי אֶת הַיַּרְדֵּן, *for with my staff I crossed the Jordan* (Bereishis 32:11). This sentence also hints to the story that Elifaz stole all of Yaakov's possessions, and all that remained was Yaakov's walking staff.

In the *Gemara*, this sort of abbreviation is called נוֹטָרִיקוֹן. The *Gemara* in *Shabbos* 105a teaches that נוֹטָרִיקוֹן (abbreviations) are found in the Torah. This נוֹטָרִיקוֹן (abbreviation) that my *rebbe*, Rav Shmuel Scheinberg, taught our high school class is also quoted in *Torah Ladaas* by Rabbi Matis Blum, a contemporary scholar and author, in the name of Rabbi Y. Assad.

Interestingly, my daughter's fourth grade teacher, Rebbetzin Ancselovits, taught her class that this abbreviation extends to the beginning of the sentence and includes the words "...וַיֵּצֵא יַעֲקֹב", which stand for וַיֵּצֵא יַעֲקֹב צַדִּיק; אָז יִשָּׂא עֵשָׂו קוֹל בִּבְכִי, "And the righteous Yaakov went out; then Eisav raised his voice in tears." This alludes to the sentence that tells us that when Eisav found out that Yaakov received Yitzchak's blessing, וַיִּשָּׂא עֵשָׂו קֹלוֹ וַיֵּבְךְּ, *And Eisav raised his voice and cried* (*Bereishis* 27:38). Thus, the נוֹטָרִיקוֹן (abbreviation) that hints at the entire story described by Rashi, that Elifaz stole all of Yaakov's possessions, is found in the entire first sentence in *Parshas Vayeitzei.* וַיֵּצֵא יַעֲקֹב מִבְּאֵר שָׁבַע וַיֵּלֶךְ חָרָנָה stands for וַיֵּצֵא יַעֲקֹב צַדִּיק אָז יִשָּׂא עֵשָׂו קוֹל בַּבְּכִי מִיָּד בָּא אֱלִיפָז רָשָׁע שֶׁהוּא בֶּן עֵשָׂו וְיִתֵּן יַעֲקֹב לוֹ כָּל חֵילוֹ רַק נִשְׁאַר הַמַּקֵּל, "And the righteous Yaakov went out; then Eisav raised his voice in tears. Immediately the evil Elifaz came, who is the son of Eisav, and Yaakov gave him all his possessions. Only his walking staff remained."

Torah Ladaas, by Rabbi Matis Blum, quotes a book entitled תּוֹסֶפֶת דָּבָר (*Tosefes Davar*), which points out that there is another נוֹטָרִיקוֹן (abbreviation) that hints at the story that Elifaz took all of Yaakov's possessions. This abbreviation is found in another sentence that refers to Elifaz's thievery, וַיְסַפֵּר לְלָבָן אֵת כָּל הַדְּבָרִים הָאֵלֶּה, *And he [Yaakov] told Lavan all these events* (*Bereishis* 29:13). As described above, Rashi explains that Yaakov told Lavan that he had no gifts for him because "all his money was taken from him [by Elifaz]." The words אֵת כָּל הַדְּבָרִים הָאֵלֶּה, *all these events,* which describe what Yaakov told to Lavan, stand for אַל תֹּאמַר כִּי לֹא הֵבֵאתִי דָּבָר בְּרַב רְכוּשׁ יָצָאתִי מִבֵּיתִי הָלַךְ אֱלִיפָז לָקַח הַכֹּל, "Don't say that I didn't bring anything. With a lot of possessions I left my house. Elifaz came and took everything."

As described above, Rashi explains that two sentences in the Torah (*Bereishis* 29:11 and 13) refer to an elaborate story, described in *Midrash Sefer HaYashar,* that Elifaz stole all of Yaakov's possessions. At first glance, it is surprising that such an elaborate story doesn't appear anywhere in the Torah. The two abbreviations in two separate sentences of the Torah, describing in detail Elifaz's encounter with Yaakov, are a wonderful example of the principle that our Sages have taught, לֵיכָּא מִידֵי דְּלֹא רְמִיזֵי בְּאוֹרַיְתָא "There is nothing that is not hinted at in the Torah."

(If desired, see other essays that I have written, with God's help, on *Parshios Bereishis, Mishpatim, Tetzaveh, Shimini, Beha'aloscha, Re'eh, Ki Savo,* and *Vezos HaBerachah,* that also discuss this principle.)

פרשת וישלח

Parshas Vayishlach

> THE IMAGE ON GOD'S THRONE

In the Torah portion entitled *Vayishlach*, our forefather Yaakov was given a new name, יִשְׂרָאֵל (Israel), first by an angel (*Bereishis* 32:29) and later by God Himself (*Bereishis* 35:10). Our Sages tell us that Yaakov is the בָּחוּר שֶׁבָּאָבוֹת, "chosen one of the Patriarchs" (*Midrash Bereishis Rabbah* 76:1), and that when the angels in Yaakov's dream (*Bereishis* 28:12) went up the ladder, they saw Yaakov's image engraved on God's throne (*Gemara Chullin* 91b, *Bereishis Rabbah* 68:12 & 82:2). It seems that the principle quoted by Rashi in his commentary on *Vayishlach* 33:2, אַחֲרוֹן אַחֲרוֹן חָבִיב, "The last is the most beloved," might also apply to Yaakov, since he was the last of the Patriarchs and also the בָּחוּר שֶׁבָּאָבוֹת.

Rabbi Eliyahu Eliezer Dessler (1892–1953) was one of the most profound Jewish thinkers of the last century. He was the *Rosh Yeshiva* (director) of the *Kollel* in Gateshead, England, and later *Mashgiach* (spiritual guide) of the Ponevezh Yeshiva in Israel. Rabbi Dessler's writings were edited and published posthumously in a multivolume edition entitled *Michtav MiEliyahu*.

In an essay on the Torah portion entitled *Lech Lecha*, Rabbi Dessler discusses the main character traits of the Patriarchs:

Avraham, Yitzchak, and Yaakov. Rabbi Dessler explains that Yaakov's personality incorporated the best character traits of Avraham and Yitzchak. Perhaps this is the reason that Yaakov is the בָּחוּר שֶׁבָּאָבוֹת.

Avraham is known for the character trait of חֶסֶד (kindness) This character trait found expression in Avraham's love for the *mitzvah* (commandment) of הַכְנָסַת אוֹרְחִים (welcoming guests) (commentary of Rashi on *Bereishis* 18:1, based on the *Gemara* and *Midrash*). The *Midrash Bereishis Rabbah* 48:9 teaches that Avraham's tent had an opening on both sides to make it easier to welcome guests. Avraham's kindness extended to the evil people of Sodom for whom he fervently prayed (*Bereishis* 18:22–32). The Torah tells us about Avraham's ability to convince people to believe in God (*Bereishis* 12:5). חֶסֶד requires an *outgoing* personality that is interested in the well-being of others. Avraham's expertise in חֶסֶד is acknowledged in *Micah* 7:20, where it is written, תִּתֵּן... חֶסֶד לְאַבְרָהָם, *Give...kindness to Avraham*.

Yitzchak's outstanding character trait was פַּחַד (fear of God). Yitzchak focused *inwardly* and perfected his own fear of God. Yaakov acknowledged his father Yitzchak's outstanding character trait in *Bereishis* 31:42, לוּלֵי אֱלֹהֵי אָבִי אֱלֹהֵי אַבְרָהָם וּפַחַד יִצְחָק הָיָה לִי, *Had not the God of my father, the God of Avraham, and the fear of Yitzchak been with me*. Yitzchak's outstanding character trait found expression in עֲקֵדַת יִצְחָק (the binding of Yitzchak). Yitzchak's outstanding פַּחַד enabled him to allow his father, Avraham, to tie him up, without hesitation, to be sacrificed (*Bereishis* 22:8–9).

Rabbi Dessler explains that Yaakov incorporated Yitzchak's and Avraham's attributes into his personality. At first, Yaakov is described in *Bereishis* 25:27 as אִישׁ תָּם יֹשֵׁב אֹהָלִים, *a wholesome man, living in tents*. Rashi explains, based on the *Midrash Bereishis Rabbah*, that Yaakov dwelled in the tents of the Yeshiva of Shem and Ever, studying Torah. At first, Yaakov was *inwardly* focused, similar to Yitzchak, and spent his time improving his own personality by learning Torah in the Yeshiva of Shem and Ever. Later, Yaakov worked for the evil Lavan for twenty years

(*Bereishis* 31:38) and was forced to confront his brother, Eisav, who wanted to kill him (*Bereishis* 27:41). These experiences enabled Yaakov to develop the *outgoing* aspect of his personality, and taught Yaakov how to live according to the precepts of the Torah in the "real world," away from the Yeshiva of Shem and Ever. Thus, Yaakov combined Yitzchak's *inwardly* focused attribute of פַּחַד, which he mastered by spending many years studying in yeshiva, and Avraham's *outwardly* focused attribute of חֶסֶד by learning how to apply the principles of the Torah in his dealings with Lavan and Eisav.

Our Sages define Yaakov's outstanding character trait as אֱמֶת (truth). Rabbi Dessler explains that אֱמֶת is based on the unification of Avraham's חֶסֶד and Yitzchak's פַּחַד. The Prophet, Micah, acknowledged this, as it is written תִּתֵּן אֱמֶת לְיַעֲקֹב, *Give truth to Yaakov* (Micah 7:20).

Rabbi Dessler teaches that the Torah is referred to as תּוֹרַת אֱמֶת ("Torah of truth") (*Malachi* 2:6, *Nechmiah* 9:13, and in the Blessings on the Torah), because אֱמֶת is the culmination of Avraham's *outward* focus on doing kindness and Yitzchak's *inward* focus on self-improvement. Rabbi Dessler writes that "a person whose desire is אֱמֶת will never stumble." Rabbi Dessler suggests that *Yaakov*, whose main character trait is אֱמֶת, *is the only one of our forefathers to have all righteous children*, because אֱמֶת is more balanced than Avraham's *outwardly* focused חֶסֶד and Yitzchak's *inwardly* focused פַּחַד.

The word אֱמֶת begins with the first letter of the alphabet and ends with the last letter. In the middle of the word אֱמֶת is the letter מ, which occurs at approximately the middle of the alphabet. Thus the word אֱמֶת seems to encompass the entire alphabet, just as the meaning of the word אֱמֶת is all-inclusive.

Rabbi Lipman Podolsky, was from Bangor, Maine, and became a beloved teacher at Yeshivat HaKotel in Jerusalem. I never met him, yet he made a long-lasting impression upon me with his excellent essays on the weekly Torah portions. He wrote, based entirely on *Gemara Shabbos* 104a:

The letters that comprise אֱמֶת (Truth) come from the beginning, middle, and the end of the *Alef-Beis* (Hebrew alphabet), respectively. This provides symbolic stability – an alphabetical tripod. The three letters comprising שֶׁקֶר (falsehood), though, are sequential. It cannot stand.

Moreover, *each of the letters spelling the word* אֱמֶת (Truth) *has two legs. It stands strong.* With שֶׁקֶר (falsehood), each letter has only one leg, with the central "ק" longer then the others. שֶׁקֶר falters.

שֶׁקֶר (falsehood) is clearly unstable as each letter has only one leg, and the central "ק" that extends below the other letters creates instability (*Internet Parshah Sheet on Mishpatim*, 5760).

Rabbi Yitzchak Luria (1534–1572) is known as the Ari HaKadosh and is one of the foremost Kabbalists. As mentioned above, Yaakov was given a new name, יִשְׂרָאֵל (Israel), first by an angel (*Bereishis* 32:29) and later by God Himself (*Bereishis* 35:10). *Talelei Oros*, which was published in 1992, is an excellent collection of Torah insights by Rabbi Yissachar Dov Rubin. In *Talelei Oros*, Rabbi Rubin quotes the Ari HaKadosh, who teaches that there is a fascinating hint in the name יִשְׂרָאֵל (Israel) to indicate that Yaakov represents the בָּחוּר שֶׁבָּאָבוֹת, "chosen one of the Patriarchs." The Ari HaKadosh explains that the name יִשְׂרָאֵל contains the names of all of the Matriarchs and Patriarchs: "י" stands for יִצְחָק (Yitzchak) and יַעֲקֹב (Yaakov), the "שׂ" stands for שָׂרָה (Sarah), the "ר" stands for רִבְקָה (Rebecca) and רָחֵל (Rachel), the "א" stands for אַבְרָהָם (Avraham), and the "ל" stands for לֵאָה (Leah). Perhaps the name יִשְׂרָאֵל (Israel) hints at all the Matriarchs and Patriarchs, because Yaakov learned from their personalities and completed the character development of all the Matriarchs and Patriarchs. Yaakov developed the character trait of אֱמֶת, which incorporated and refined the attributes of all the Matriarchs and Patriarchs.

According to Rabbi Dessler, Yaakov "completed the work" that Avraham and Yitzchak started. Yaakov represents the culmination of the work of the אָבוֹת (Patriarchs), but Yaakov could not have completed the task without the preparation of Avraham and Yitzchak. Perhaps this is the reason that Yaakov is the בָּחוּר שֶׁבְּאָבוֹת and the one whose image appears on God's throne.

▸ MASTERS OF SILENCE

The Torah tells us that after Rachel's death, וַיֵּלֶךְ רְאוּבֵן וַיִּשְׁכַּב אֶת בִּלְהָה פִּילֶגֶשׁ אָבִיו, *Reuven went and lay with Bilhah, his father's concubine* (Bereishis 35:22). In the same sentence, the Torah tells us that Yaakov's reaction to this was, וַיִּשְׁמַע יִשְׂרָאֵל, *and Yisrael heard*. At this point, there is a surprising interruption in the middle of this sentence. In the Torah scroll, after the words וַיִּשְׁמַע יִשְׂרָאֵל, *even though it is in the middle of the sentence*, there is an empty space, and *the last five words of this sentence start a new line, as if to begin a new paragraph*. In the Torah scroll, the last five words of this sentence, וַיִּהְיוּ בְנֵי יַעֲקֹב שְׁנֵים עָשָׂר, *The sons of Yaakov were twelve*, begin a new paragraph. To the best of my knowledge, this is the only time in the Torah that there is an interruption like this in the middle of a sentence.

Rabbi Yaakov Neuburger is a *Rosh Yeshiva* at Yeshiva University and the rabbi of the shul in which I pray. Rabbi Neuburger explains this sentence beautifully by referring to Rashi's commentary on the sentence. Rashi explains, based on the *Gemara Shabbos* 55b, that Reuven didn't actually lay with Bilhah. According to Rashi, "when Rachel died, Yaakov took his bed, which was always located in Rachel's tent…and placed it in Bilhah's tent [Bilhah was Rachel's maidservant]. Reuven then came and protested his mother's [Leah's] humiliation. For this reason, he disturbed [Yaakov's sleeping arrangement]." According to this, all Reuven did was move Yaakov's bed from Bilhah's tent into the tent of his mother, Leah.

This angered Yaakov, but the Torah doesn't tell us at this point what Yaakov said. The Torah does mention that many years later, close to Yaakov's death (*Bereishis* 49:4), Yaakov rebukes Reuven for his actions. But at this point the Torah just says, וַיִּשְׁמַע יִשְׂרָאֵל, *and Yisrael heard*. This is where the interruption, an empty space in the middle of the sentence, occurs, as if Yaakov thought about this for quite some time. But all we are told of his reaction, according to the Torah, is that he heard. At this point, he did not rebuke Reuven. *Yaakov heard, and he thought about it. He understood it, and he was silent.*

Yaakov did not want to lose Reuven by rebuking him and upsetting him too much. He was angry at him, but he did not feel that this was the proper time to rebuke him. Therefore he heard, and he was silent. After the empty space alluding to Yaakov's silence, the continuation of this sentence is, וַיִּהְיוּ בְנֵי יַעֲקֹב שְׁנֵים עָשָׂר, *The sons of Yaakov were twelve.*

Yaakov is the only forefather who had only righteous children. Yaakov was afraid that if he rebuked Reuven at this point, he could possibly upset him, and Reuven might rebel. Therefore, Yaakov was quiet. His reaction was limited to וַיִּשְׁמַע יִשְׂרָאֵל.

Rashi, in his commentary on *Devarim* 1:3, quotes a *Midrash Sifre* that summarizes this as follows: "…He [Yaakov] said, 'Reuven, my son, I will tell you why I did not admonish you during all these years; because I did not want you to desert me and join my brother Eisav…'" The Torah tells us that, because Yaakov initially listened and did not rebuke Reuven until Yaakov was near death, Reuven didn't rebel and Yaakov's children remained twelve – "all equal and righteous" (commentary of Rashi on *Bereishis* 35:22).

The Torah, according to Rabbi Neuburger, is teaching a lesson for all generations. There is a time when it is proper to rebuke children, and a time when one must not rebuke. Clearly it takes a great deal of wisdom to understand when to rebuke and when not to rebuke. But there is a place for *silence*, and this is what Yaakov is teaching us.

It is interesting to note that earlier in this Torah portion, *Parshas Vayishlach*, after Shechem defiled Yaakov's daughter, the Torah also emphasizes Yaakov's ability to show restraint and to be silent. The Torah says, וְיַעֲקֹב שָׁמַע כִּי טִמֵּא אֶת דִּינָה בִתּוֹ וּבָנָיו הָיוּ אֶת מִקְנֵהוּ בַּשָּׂדֶה וְהֶחֱרִשׁ יַעֲקֹב עַד בֹּאָם, *And Yaakov heard that he had defiled his daughter, Deenah, while his sons were with his cattle in the field; and Yaakov remained silent until they returned* (*Bereishis* 34:5).

Perhaps Yaakov learned the importance of silence from his beloved wife, Rachel. In last week's Torah portion, Rachel was the *paradigm of silence*, when she allowed her older sister to marry Yaakov, so as not to embarrass her. Rashi, in his commentary on *Bereishis* 29:25, quotes the *Gemara* (*Megillah* 13a, *Bava Basra* 123a) that says, "…Yaakov had given Rachel signs, and when Rachel saw that Leah was being brought to him [to marry Yaakov], she said, 'My sister may now be humiliated,' whereupon she readily transmitted those signs to her." Yaakov had given Rachel special signs to give to him on their marriage night, so that even if Rachel's father, Lavan, would try to trick Yaakov into marrying someone else, he would know the difference. When Rachel saw that her sister would be embarrassed, Rachel didn't protest and was *silent*, and she gave the signs to her sister.

Rabbi Lipman Podolsky points out that Rachel did not know that Yaakov would eventually marry her also (*Internet Parshah Sheet on Vayeitzei*, 5761). As a matter of fact, there was good reason to think that she would never get to marry Yaakov, since it is forbidden to marry two sisters. Therefore, when Rachel was *silent* and gave the signs to her sister, she was, as far as she knew, giving up the chance to marry her beloved. She was also giving up the chance to be one of the mothers of the Jewish tribes. In addition, since some people thought that Leah was supposed to marry Eisav (commentary of Rashi on *Bereishis* 29:17), Leah's marriage to Yaakov could possibly mean that Rachel would now have to marry Eisav. Nevertheless, so as not to embarrass her sister, Rachel was *silent* and gave the signs to her sister.

Rachel's greatness was her *silence*. Through her silence she became the *model of human sensitivity*. She was willing to give up her chance to marry her beloved and be a mother of the Jewish tribes, just to avoid embarrassing her sister. Rachel's *silence* now became the *model of human sensitivity* for all times. In *Parshas Vayeitzei*, Rachel became the *paradigm of silence* (based on an essay by Rabbi Dovid Siegel, *Internet Parshah Sheet on Vayeitzei*, 5760).

It seems that Yaakov learned the importance of silence from his beloved wife, Rachel. In *Parshas Vayeitzei*, Rachel teaches us the merits of silence. Yaakov does the same in the *parshah* that follows, *Parshas Vayishlach*, when Yaakov is silent and does not rebuke Reuven, after Reuven angers him by moving his bed.

The *Midrash Tanchuma*, which is ascribed to Tanchuma bar Abba, who lived in the second half of the fourth century C.E., states, רָחֵל תָּפְשָׂה בִּשְׁתִיקָה עָמְדָה זַרְעָהּ בִּשְׁתִיקָה, "Rachel grabbed the trait of silence; [consequently] her children stood with silence" (*Midrash Tanchuma, Parshas Vayeitzei*, section 6). Rachel had two sons, Yosef and Binyamin. Yosef was clearly an expert at silence. Not only did he not try to contact his father during the twenty-two years that he was separated from him in Egypt, but he clearly knew how to be silent when he met his brothers after their long separation. Binyamin also knew how to be quiet. According to this same *Midrash Tanchuma*, Binyamin knew about the sale of Yosef and was silent about it. It seems that Yosef and Binyamin learned to become experts on silence from their parents, Yaakov and Rachel, who were *masters of silence*.

Rabbi Abraham J. Twerski, M.D., writes in *Living Each Week* that in *Parshas Mikeitz*, Rachel teaches a great practical lesson in parenting from her ability to transmit the trait of silence to Yosef and Binyamin. According to Rabbi Twerski, "Rachel did not need to lecture her children…Rachel taught by her own actions and by how she lived and this is why her teachings were so effective." *Rachel's silence on Leah's wedding night, so as not to embarrass her, was a great heroic act*. Rachel taught Yosef and Binyamin by example how to exercise silence and self-restraint. According to Rabbi Twerski, Rachel teaches an important lesson in parenting – that it is best to teach children by behavior and actions, and not just through verbal instruction.

Many of the major personalities of the second half of the Book of *Bereishis* – Rachel, Yaakov, and their sons Yosef and Binyamin, were masters of the trait of silence. *Mastering the trait of silence may be one of the important themes of the second half of the Book of Bereishis.*

Our Sages learned this lesson well and emphasized the importance of silence. King Solomon writes in *Mishlei* 10:19, וְחוֹשֵׂךְ שְׂפָתָיו מַשְׂכִּיל, *and he who restrains his lips is wise.* The *Mishnah* in *Pirkei Avos* 1:17 states, וְכָל הַמַּרְבֶּה דְבָרִים מֵבִיא חֵטְא, "and whoever talks excessively brings on sin." Rabbi Akiva teaches in *Pirkei Avos* 3:17, סְיָג לַחָכְמָה שְׁתִיקָה, "a fence for wisdom is silence."

The *Gemara* in *Eruchin* 15b teaches, "The Holy One, Blessed is He, said to the tongue, 'All human limbs are on the outside, and you are inside [the mouth]; and not only that, but I surrounded you with two walls, one of bone [the teeth], and one of flesh [the lips].'"

Irving Bunim (1903–1980, a businessman who worked tirelessly for the Jewish community, a founder of the Young Israel movement, and right-hand man of Rabbi Aharon Kotler) explains this *Gemara* in his classic commentary on *Pirkei Avos, Ethics from Sinai* (1:17), "Knowing the lethal power of the tongue, the Almighty enclosed it within two gates. First are the hard teeth which one can lock tight. Should the tongue attempt to squeeze through…the teeth, we have as the next line of defense the soft but airtight lips."

The *Midrash Tehillim* (16:11) and *Yalkut Shimoni* (*Tehillim* 669) teach, "Anyone who listens to insults and is silent is called a חָסִיד (pious)." Simcha Groffman (*Internet Parshah Sheet on Vayeitzei*, 5760) explains that the best way to end an argument is to be silent because the other person cannot continue arguing with himself. The *Gemara* in *Megillah* 18a writes, "The best medicine of all is silence…If a word is worth a *sela*, silence is worth two." The *Gemara* in *Pesachim* 99a states, יָפֶה שְׁתִיקָה לַחֲכָמִים קַל וָחוֹמֶר לַטִּפְּשִׁים, "Silence is fitting for the wise and all the more so for fools."

Similarly, the Rambam writes:

One should always cultivate silence and refrain from speaking, except with regard to matters of wisdom or things that are necessary for one's physical welfare. It was said that Rav, the disciple of our saintly teacher [Rabbi Yehuda HaNasi], never said an idle word in all his days…Therefore, one should not hasten to answer, nor speak at length. He should teach his students in calm and tranquility…This is what Solomon stated, דִּבְרֵי חֲכָמִים בְּנַחַת נִשְׁמָעִים, *The words of the wise are heard in tranquility* (Koheles 9:17). A Torah Sage…should speak gently to all people…He should greet all men [before they greet him], so that they be pleased with him. He should judge everyone in a good light, speak favorably of his fellow man, [never mentioning] anything that is shameful to him, love peace and pursue it. If he sees that his words will be effective and will be given attention, he should speak; if not, he should keep silent…The guiding rule is that he should speak only about wisdom or acts of kindness. (*Mishneh Torah*, Laws of *De'os*, chapters 2:4–5 & 5:7, italics are my emphasis.)

The Torah commands in *Devarim* 6:7, וְשִׁנַּנְתָּם לְבָנֶיךָ, *And you shall teach them [the words of the Torah] to your children*. In addition, our Sages teach, based on the *Midrash Tanchuma* (*Lech Lecha* 9), מַעֲשֵׂי אָבוֹת סִימָן לְבָנִים, "The happenings of the forefathers are a sign for the children." Rachel, Yaakov, Yosef, and Binyamin were *masters of silence*, and, as the above examples indicate, they taught this lesson well to their descendants.

פרשת וישב

Parshas Vayeshev

> **THE TORAH OF THE YESHIVA OF SHEM AND EVER**

The Torah tells us in *Bereishis* 37:3 that Yaakov loved Yosef מִכָּל בָּנָיו כִּי בֶן זְקֻנִים הוּא לוֹ, *more than all his sons because he was a son of his old age.* Rashi refers to the *Midrash Bereishis Rabbah* 84:8 that explains, "Rabbi Nechemiah said, 'All the laws that Shem and Ever transmitted to Yaakov, he transmitted to Yosef.'"

After Yaakov received the blessings from Yitzchak, his brother Eisav hated him and planned to kill him. Their mother, Rivka, advised Yaakov to leave the Land of Israel and flee to her brother, Lavan, to escape Eisav's jealous anger (*Bereishis* 27:41–43). Yaakov lived with Lavan, who was an evil idolater, for twenty years (*Bereishis* 31:38), and married his daughters, Leah and Rachel. Rashi, based on the *Gemara Megillah* 17a and the *Midrash Bereishis Rabbah* 68:11, teaches in his commentary on *Bereishis* 28:11, that Yaakov learned Torah in the Yeshiva of Ever for fourteen years between the time he left his parents' house and the time that he arrived at Lavan's house. Rabbi Nechemiah teaches, as quoted above, that it is this knowledge, acquired by Yaakov in the Yeshiva of Shem and Ever, that Yaakov transmitted especially to Yosef, more than to Yosef's brothers.

Does this mean that Yaakov did not teach Yosef all the Torah that he learned from his father, Yitzchak, or anything else that he knew, for that matter? Does this mean that he only taught him the Torah that he learned from Shem and Ever? Why did Yaakov teach the knowledge of the Yeshiva of Shem and Ever to Yosef especially, and not to his other children?

Rav Yaakov Kamenetzky (1891–1986) was the dean of Mesivta Torah Vodaath and one of the foremost leaders of his era. His commentary on *Chumash* was published posthumously and is entitled *Emes LeYaakov*. Rav Kamenetzky explains that the Torah that Yaakov learned in the Yeshiva of Shem and Ever prepared him for exile. It prepared him for leaving the Land of Israel and for living with the evil idolater, Lavan.

Shem, who was the son of Noach, learned how to be righteous even while living among the evil generation of the Flood. Similarly, Ever, who was the great-great-grandson of Noach (*Bereishis* 10:24), learned how to be righteous even while living among the evil generation of the Dispersion, which rebelled against God and built the Tower of Babel (*Bereishis* 11:1–9). Therefore, Rav Kamenetzky explains that Shem and Ever, who were experts at maintaining righteousness even while living among evil people, were best able to prepare Yaakov for his twenty-year sojurn in exile, living with the evil idolater, Lavan. Yaakov learned Torah in the Yeshiva of Shem and Ever for fourteen years before traveling outside of Israel to Lavan's house, to prepare himself spiritually for exile and for living in the house of idolaters (*Emes LeYaakov*, *Bereishis* 28:11).

God told Yaakov's grandfather, Avraham, that his descendants would be slaves בְּאֶרֶץ לֹא לָהֶם, *in a land that is not theirs*, for 400 years (*Bereishis* 15:13). Rav Yaakov Kamenetzky explains that the reason God told Avraham about this was in order to give Avraham and his descendants the opportunity to prepare for life in exile. In order to educate Yosef for the task of living "in a land that is not theirs," Yaakov taught Yosef the Torah of the Yeshiva of Shem and Ever, which specialized in preparing a person to live among evildoers. Yaakov knew that Yosef would be the leader of his brothers, and therefore prepared him to lead the Jewish nation in exile among evil idolaters.

Interestingly, Rabbi Nechemiah emphasizes the importance of עֵבֶר (Ever) in Avraham's life, as well as in the lives of Yaakov and Yosef. It is the same Rabbi Nechemiah who teaches in *Bereishis Rabbah* 84:8 the importance of the knowledge of the Yeshiva of Shem and Ever that Yaakov transmitted to Yosef, who also teaches in *Bereishis Rabbah* 42:8 that the Torah names Avraham אַבְרָם הָעִבְרִי ("Avram, the *Hebrew*") (*Bereishis* 14:13), because Avraham is descended from עֵבֶר. Rav Yaakov Kamenetzky writes that *Avraham is called אַבְרָם הָעִבְרִי because Avraham popularized the teachings of the Yeshiva of עֵבֶר* (*Emes LeYaakov, Bereishis* 40:15). Similarly, Rav Yaakov suggests that the Jewish people are called עִבְרִים ("Hebrews") (*Bereishis* 40:15 & 43:32, *Shemos* 2:6 & 5:3) because the Torah of the Yeshiva of עֵבֶר was also transmitted to the Jewish people (*Emes LeYaakov, Bereishis* 10:21).

Thus, the name of the Jewish people, הָעָם עִבְרִי *("the Hebrew nation") even in modern times, is derived from Ever, the great-great-grandson of Noach (Bereishis 10:24) and the leader of the Yeshiva of Ever, where our forefathers studied.*

Yaakov realized that Yosef, as the leader of his brothers, would carry forth the tradition of the Jew in exile. Therefore, Yaakov taught him the knowledge that he acquired from Shem and Ever, knowledge that specializes in maintaining righteousness even while living among evil people. This helps us better understand why the brothers were jealous of Yosef. They saw that Yaakov was teaching Yosef, and not them, certain specialized aspects of the Torah. Rabbi Meir Leibush ben Yechiel Michal (1809–1879, who is known by his initials as the Malbim) explains that the brothers were afraid that, just as Avraham chose Yitzchak over Yishmael, and Yitzchak chose Yaakov over Eisav, that Yaakov would choose Yosef over them. In actuality, Yaakov only taught Yosef the Torah of the Yeshiva of Shem and Ever in order to prepare him for the eventual exile of the Jewish nation. Yaakov did not choose Yosef over his brothers for the reason that Avraham chose Yitzchak over Yishmael, because, as Rashi writes in his commentary on *Bereishis* 35:22, all of Yaakov's children were considered righteous.

Yaakov taught Yosef the Torah of the Yeshiva of Shem and Ever, because this knowledge explains how to remain righteous even while living among evil idolaters outside the Land of Israel. Rashi, in his commentary on *Bereishis* 37:3, based on the *Midrash Bereishis Rabbah* 84:8, teaches that Yosef's appearance resembled Yaakov's.

Perhaps the point of this *Midrash* is that Yosef resembled Yaakov because they had similar roles. Yaakov was able to give rise to the future Jewish nation while living in exile with the evil idolater, Lavan. All of Yaakov's sons, the fathers of the Jewish Tribes, were born while Yaakov was living with Lavan, except for Binyamin. Yaakov specialized in living successfully as a Jew in exile among evil idolaters. Yaakov learned this from the Torah of the Yeshiva of Shem and Ever and taught this to Yosef, who also specialized in living successfully as a Jew in exile.

Yosef is the role model for all future generations, showing how to succeed as a Jew while living among gentiles in exile. Even though Yosef was sold into exile by his own God-fearing brothers, he never rejected his family's religion. If he had sinned while living in Egypt, none of his family would have known. After Potiphar's wife attempted to seduce Yosef, he was imprisoned (*Bereishis* 39:20). Despite being sold by his own "God-fearing" family, being thrown into prison, and being the only Jew in Egypt, Yosef remained righteous. Yosef became the role model, showing how a Jew should behave during difficult times in exile. Perhaps it is for this reason that our Sages refer to Yosef as יוֹסֵף הַצַּדִּיק, "Yosef, the Righteous" (*Bereishis Rabbah* 93:7; *Zohar, Parshas Vayeshev* 189b; see also *Megillah* 13b and *Kesuvos* 111a).

The Ramban teaches in his commentary on *Bereishis* 12:6, "I will tell you a principle by which you will understand all the upcoming portions of scripture…It is indeed a great matter which our Rabbis mentioned briefly, saying: 'Whatever has happened to the Patriarchs is a *sign to the children.*" This principle is usually described as מַעֲשֵׂי אָבוֹת סִימָן לְבָנִים, "The happenings of the forefathers are a *sign to the children,*" and is based on *Midrash Tanchuma, Lech Lecha* 9. Yosef became the role model for all future generations of Jews. Yosef's life is a *sign to the children* for all generations as to how to succeed as a Jew while living in exile among gentiles.

The Torah of the Yeshiva of Shem and Ever taught Yaakov how to remain righteous, even while living among evil idolaters outside of the Land of Israel. Yaakov taught this specialized aspect of the Torah to Yosef, who needed this knowledge to remain a righteous Jew in Egypt and to become the role model for a Jew in exile. According to Rav Yaakov Kamenetzky, Jews are also called עִבְרִים because the knowledge of the Yeshiva of עֵבֶר was transmitted to the Jewish people. If life in exile is very difficult and, as a result, a person begins to question his or her belief in God, Yosef's example will hopefully remind that person to remain "righteous." Yosef became the paradigm of the optimal behavior of a Jew in exile for all future generations.

▸ YOSEF AND CHANUKAH

The *Shulchan Aruch* is the classic Code of Jewish Law written by Rabbi Yosef Karo, who lived from 1488–1575. The *Shulchan Aruch* teaches that certain specific Torah portions are always read in close proximity to certain holidays (*Orach Chayim* 428:4). The Torah portion entitled *Vayeshev* is usually read near the holiday of Chanukah.

Most of *Parshas Vayeshev* discusses Yosef and the beginning of his life in Egypt. This suggests that there may be a relationship between Yosef and Chanukah. This essay will explore this relationship and some interesting ideas that are related to the word חֲנוּכָּה (Chanukah).

Chanukah commemorates the victory of the Jews over the Syrian-Greeks in 165 B.C.E. According to the Rambam, the "Greek kingdom issued decrees against the Jewish people, [attempting to] nullify their faith and refusing to allow them to observe the Torah and its commandments" (*Mishneh Torah*, Laws of Chanukah 3:1). Similarly, the *Al Hanisim* prayer that is recited on Chanukah relates that "...the wicked Greek kingdom rose up against Your people Israel to make them forget Your Torah and compel them to stray from the statutes." The aim of the Greeks was not the physical destruction of the Jews, like Haman's intention in the days of Mordechai and Esther, but rather their spiritual demise.

The Greeks sought to annihilate the Jews spiritually. For example, the *Midrash Bereishis Rabbah* (2:4) relates that the Greeks ordered the Jews to write that they have "no portion in the God of Israel." The Greeks sought to annul *Shabbos*, circumcision, and the sanctification of the months (*Megillas Antiochus* 1:9). Interestingly, the desire of the Greeks to abolish the sanctification of the months, may relate to the fact that Chanukah is the only Jewish holiday, besides Rosh HaShanah, that includes a רֹאשׁ חֹדֶשׁ, the beginning of a new month. Rashi tells us that the Greeks decreed that every Jewish bride must first have sexual relations with the local Greek commander (commentary of Rashi on *Shabbos* 23a). The Rambam teaches that the Greeks "entered the Sanctuary, wrought havoc within, and made the pure become impure" (*Mishneh Torah*, Laws of Chanukah 3:1).

Yosef is the role model for all generations, showing how to succeed as a Jew while living among gentiles outside of the Land of Israel. Even though Yosef was sold into exile by his own "God-fearing" brothers, he never rejected his family's religion. If he had sinned while living in Egypt, none of his family would have known. After Potiphar's wife attempted to seduce Yosef, he was imprisoned (*Bereishis* 39:20). **Despite being sold by his own God-fearing family, being thrown into prison, and being the only Jew in Egypt, Yosef remained righteous.** Perhaps it is for this reason that our Sages refer to Yosef as יוֹסֵף הַצַּדִּיק ("Yosef, the Righteous") (*Bereishis Rabbah* 93:7; *Zohar, Parshas Vayeshev* 189b).

Yosef is the role model for the Jew in exile. If life in exile is very difficult and, as a result, a person begins to question his or her belief in God, Yosef's example will hopefully remind that person to remain "righteous." our Sages have taught, based on the *Midrash Tanchuma, Lech Lecha* 9, מַעֲשֵׂי אָבוֹת סִימָן לְבָנִים, "The happenings of the forefathers are a *sign to the children*." Yosef's life is a *sign to the children* for all generations as to how to succeed as a Jew while living among gentiles in exile.

Similar to Yosef, who suffered the hardships of a Jew in exile and still earned the title יוֹסֵף הַצַּדִּיק, the Jews triumphed over the Greeks and remained righteous. The life of יוֹסֵף הַצַּדִּיק is a *sign to the children,* for all generations, that the Jews have the strength not to assimilate. **Just as Yosef remained righteous and didn't assimilate despite having been sold by his own family, and being the Viceroy of Egypt, so too the Jews withstood the Greek attempt to destroy Jewish culture and religion.**

Since Yosef is the role model for all generations of a Jew who doesn't assimilate despite external pressure to do so, the story of Yosef coincides with the holiday of Chanukah. Perhaps this is one of the reasons that *Parshas Vayeshev,* which discusses Yosef's descent to Egypt, is usually read near the holiday of Chanukah.

Rabbi Shlomo Ganzfried (1804–1886) discusses the meaning of the name חֲנוּכָּה (Chanukah) in the *Kitzur Shulchan Aruch* (139:1). Rabbi Ganzfried explains that "the name חֲנוּכָּה can be divided into חָנוּ כ"ה ('They rested from their enemies on the twenty-fifth' [day of the month of Kislev, which is the day that Chanukah begins]). Also, the word חֲנוּכָּה is derived from 'חנכ' ('dedicate') for it was at that time that the Jews rededicated the Temple after their foes had defiled it."

Some of the other major laws of Chanukah are hinted at in the word חֲנוּכָּה. There is a well-known argument, quoted in *Gemara Shabbos* 21b, that is essential to candle lighting on Chanukah. The School of Shammai teaches that on the first night of Chanukah one kindles eight lights, and on each successive night the number of lights continuously decreases. The School of Hillel teaches that on the first night, the obligation is to kindle one light, and on each successive night the number of lights continuously increases.

The law is followed according to the School of Hillel, and that is our current practice.

Rabbi Yosef Karo (1488–1575) is best known for three major works: 1) the *Shulchan Aruch* – the classic Code of Jewish Law. 2) the *Beis Yosef* – a commentary on the *Tur Shulchan Aruch*. 3) the *Kesef Mishneh* – a commentary on the Rambam's *Mishneh Torah*. In the *Beis Yosef* (*Orach Chayim* 670), Rabbi Yosef Karo asks why is it that we celebrate Chanukah for eight days? Since there was enough oil for one day, and the oil only burned miraculously for seven days, why isn't the holiday observed for only seven days?

This is a well-known question that many of our Sages have addressed. The *Beis Yosef* himself offers three answers for this question. The *Book of Our Heritage* by Rabbi Eliyahu Kitov (1912–1976, born in Poland and immigrated to Israel where he first worked as a constuction worker before writing several important scholarly books) offers ten answers to explain why we celebrate Chanukah for eight days and not seven. (I will not present these answers because they are somewhat lengthy and not directly pertinent to this essay.)

Rabbi Benjamin Blech is a communal leader, teacher, and author of *The Secrets of Hebrew Words*. Rabbi Blech points out that *these two major laws of Chanukah are hinted at in the word* חֲנוּכָה, which is an abbreviation for ח׳ נֵרוֹת וַהֲלָכָה כְּבֵית הִלֵּל ("Eight candles and the law is according to the School of Hillel.")

There are two other major laws of Chanukah that are beautifully hinted at in the word חֲנוּכָה. Even though it is our practice to light the menorah inside the house, the *Gemara* in *Shabbos* 21b clearly states, "The requirement is to place the Chanukah light outside (מִבַּחוּץ) the doorway of one's house." Rabbi Shlomo Ganzfried writes in the *Kitzur Shulchan Aruch* 139:7, "This was the practice in the era of the *Mishnah* and the *Gemara*." (*Moadim U'Zemanim Hashalem*, volume 2 – entry 140, presents an extensive discussion as to why we no longer follow the law as stated in the *Gemara*, to light outside the doorway.)

Another important law described by Rabbi Yosef Karo in

the *Shulchan Aruch* (*Orach Chayim* 672:1–2) is that the Chanukah light should optimally be kindled at the end of sunset, "but if this time happened to pass…, he may perform the kindling of lights all night" (see the commentary of the *Mishnah Berurah* that discusses under what circumstances one may say a blessing, if one is lighting late).

Rabbi Benjamin Blech also points out that *these two laws – that the Chanukah lights should be kindled outside, and that the lights can be kindled all night, are hinted at in the word* חֲנוּכָּה, which is also an abbreviation for חוּצָה נִדְלָקִים וּזְמַנָּם כָּל הַלַּיְלָה, "Outside they are lit and their time is all night."

Thus, the word חֲנוּכָּה is not only an abbreviation for חָנוּ כ"ה, "They rested [from their enemies] on the twenty-fifth [day of the month of Kislev]," but also for four of the major laws of Chanukah: 1) Chanukah is to be celebrated for eight days. 2) The law is according to the School of Hillel regarding the number of lights that are kindled each night. 3) The Chanukah lights should be kindled outside. 4) The Chanukah lights may be kindled all night.

פרשת מקץ

Parshas Mikeitz

> **COULDN'T YOSEF HAVE BEEN A LITTLE NICER?**

After not seeing his brothers for twenty-two years, Yosef hid his identity from them and וַיְדַבֵּר אִתָּם קָשׁוֹת, *And he spoke with them harshly* (*Bereishis* 42:7). Instead of greeting them warmly, Yosef devised an elaborate scheme that included slandering his brothers as spies, imprisoning Shimon, and framing Binyamin by planting his goblet in Binyamin's sack. Yosef's scheme caused his elderly father, Yaakov, much anguish, since it delayed the return of Yaakov's children and left Yaakov alone at home worrying what happened to them.

Our Sages refer to Yosef as יוֹסֵף הַצַּדִּיק, "Yosef the Righteous" (*Bereishis Rabbah* 93:7; *Zohar, Parshas Vayeshev* 189b). How could "Yosef the Righteous" devise a false scheme that would cause his elderly father and brothers so much anguish? Many of the great and holy biblical commentators have asked this question. In the words of Rabbi Shlomo Ephraim of Luntshitz (1550–1619, rabbi of Prague and author of the biblical commentary *Kli Yakar*), יִשְׁתּוֹמֵם כָּל מַשְׂכִּיל מַה רָאָה יוֹסֵף עַל כָּכָה לְצַעֵר אֶת אָבִיו וְאֶת אֶחָיו חִנָּם, "Every intelligent person should be astonished why Yosef [devised a scheme] that caused his father and brothers pain for no reason."

The Ramban, in his commentary on *Bereishis* 42:9, explains that "[Yosef] conceived of the strategy of devising a charge against them so that they would also bring his brother Binyamin to him, in order to fulfill the first dream [which is described in *Bereishis* 37:7]. It is for this reason that he did not wish to tell them at this time 'I am Yosef, your brother.'" According to the Ramban, Yosef devised this entire elaborate false scheme and caused his brothers and elderly father much grief, in order to fulfill his dreams.

Rabbi Yitzchak Arama lived from approximately 1420–1494, and is the author of the biblical commentary entitled *Akeidas Yitzchak*. He also wrote a commentary on Aristotle's *Ethics*. Both the *Kli Yakar* and Rabbi Yitzchak Arama find the same difficulty with the Ramban's explanation. Rabbi Yitzchak Arama writes, "I am astonished at the Ramban's explanation...As for the dreams, leave it to Him who sends them to make them come true. It seems infinitely foolish for a man to strive to fulfill his dreams, which are matters beyond his control" (quoted in commentary of Professor Nechama Leibowitz on *Parshas Mikeitz*).

Professor Nechama Leibowitz (1905–1997) wrote a widely studied "teach-yourself" commentary on each of the weekly Torah portions. She ended each chapter with questions for further study and remarked that she received hundreds of thousands of responses to these questions. She wrote, "I am enthralled...for our joint studies involved no certificates, examinations, marks, prizes; no credits, scholarships, income-tax rebates but simply the joy so deep of the one who studies Torah" (quoted in *Introduction to Studies in Bereishit*, English edition).

Rabbi Don Yitzchak Abarbanel (1437–1508) was a biblical commentator, statesman, and philosopher. He was the Treasurer of Portugal. Because of the expulsion of the Jews from Spain and Portugal, both the Abarbanel and Rabbi Yitzchak Arama resettled in Italy.

Professor Nechama Leibowitz quotes Rabbi Yitzchak Arama and Rabbi Don Yitzchak Abarbanel, who offer an alternative explantion for the false and elaborate scheme that Yosef devised. The

Gemara in *Yuma* 86b teaches that to accomplish תְּשׁוּבָה (repentance) one must succeed in not committing the same sin again when given the opportunity. The *Gemara* adds that the opportunity must be identical, בְּאוֹתָהּ אִשָּׁה בְּאוֹתוֹ פֶּרֶק בְּאוֹתוֹ מָקוֹם, "with that same woman, at that same time, and at that same place." Therefore, in order to make it possible for his brothers to truly repent for what they did to him, Yosef needed to create a similar set of circumstances so that the brothers could prove that they would be willing to give their lives to protect Binyamin, Rachel's other son.

Subsequently, Yosef slandered his brothers by calling them מְרַגְּלִים (spies), and held Shimon hostage in prison, so that the brothers would bring Binyamin to Egypt. He then framed Binyamin by putting his goblet in his sack, so that the brothers would then have an opportunity to truly repent for the way they treated him, Rachel's oldest son. They would show that they would give their lives to protect Rachel's other son, Binyamin. When Yehuda, as spokesman for Yosef's other brothers, makes it clear that he is willing to give his life to protect Binyamin and to spare Yaakov the anguish of losing another child of Rachel's (*Bereishis* 44:31–34), the brothers achieve complete repentance for the way they treated Yosef.

At that point the Torah says, וְלֹא יָכֹל יוֹסֵף לְהִתְאַפֵּק... וַיֹּאמֶר יוֹסֵף אֶל אֶחָיו אֲנִי יוֹסֵף, "Now Yosef could not restrain himself…And Yosef said to his brothers, 'I am Yosef'" (*Bereishis* 45:1, 3). A simple understanding of this is that Yosef emotionally could no longer restrain himself and therefore finally admitted his true identity. Rabbi Shmuel Bornstein, the Rebbe of Sochaczev (1855–1927, author of the biblical commentary *Shem MiShmuel*), as quoted in *Likutei Yehoshua* and *Itturei Torah*, explains that Yosef could no longer restrain himself because he had achieved the objective of creating a scenario whereby the brothers could achieve complete repentance. Once Yehuda, as spokesman for his brothers, achieved complete repentance, Yosef couldn't restrain himself because he no longer had any reason to conceal his identity.

Rabbi Moshe Green, in *Impressions on the Heart*, which is a book that is culled from the thoughts of Rabbi Shlomo Freifeld (founder of Yeshiva Sh'or Yoshuv in 1967), summarizes the above and writes that Yosef "proved to be a master educator...He created a set of circumstances that would touch the hearts of his brothers. He put them in a situation that would simultaneously make crystal clear the mistake they had made by selling him, yet draw them near at the same time."

Rabbi Yehoshua Scheinfeld discusses the ideas described above in *Likutei Yehoshua*, which was published around 1958. Rabbi Scheinfeld explains that Yosef created an elaborate, slanderous scheme and accused his brothers of being spies, because he could not admit his identity immediately to his brothers. If he had told his brothers when they first arrived in Egypt that he was Yosef, it would have been impossible for them to repent properly. Had they apologized to Yosef after learning that he was the Prime Minister of Egypt, this would not have been an acceptable apology, as people tend to be intimidated by powerful people. In addition, how sorry could they be for selling him, if they knew that their sale led to Yosef becoming the Prime Minister? By concealing his identity from his brothers when they first arrived in Egypt, he made it possible for them to properly repent for their actions. As discussed above, Yosef created a set of circumstances whereby Yehuda, speaking for Yosef's other brothers, made it clear that he was willing to give his life to protect Binyamin and to spare Yaakov the anguish of losing another of Rachel's children (*Bereishis* 44:31–34). The *Kli Yakar* adds that Yosef specifically chose to accuse his brothers of being מְרַגְּלִים (*Bereishis* 42:9), as opposed to some other profession, because he wanted to prevent his brothers from "snooping around" and asking a lot of questions. The Egyptians knew that Yosef was a "Hebrew" (see *Bereishis* 41:12). Yosef was afraid that his brothers might be looking for their long lost brother, since the caravans of Yishmaelites and Midianites to whom Yosef was sold frequently travelled to Egypt. **To prevent his brothers from asking a lot of questions and discovering that the Prime Minister was a Hebrew, Yosef accused them of being spies.**

The Torah teaches, מִדְּבַר שֶׁקֶר תִּרְחָק, "Distance yourself from a false word" (*Shemos* 23:7). The first Gerrer Rebbe, Rabbi Yitzchak Meir Alter (1799–1866), teaches that this is the only instance in which the Torah commands us to distance ourselves from a sin. God dislikes falsehood so much that He commands us to distance ourselves from it. **There is no biblical command to distance ourselves from any specific sin, except for falsehood.** The *Gemara* teaches in *Sanhedrin* 64a and in *Shabbos* 55a that אֱמֶת (truth) is the signature of God. Therefore, some of our Sages have suggested that there must be some truth hidden in the words of יוֹסֵף הַצַּדִּיק when he accused his brothers of being מְרַגְּלִים (*Bereishis* 42:9). Rabbi Matis Blum, contemporary scholar and author of *Torah LaDaas*, quotes the author of *Shevet Mussar*, who points out that the word מְרַגְּלִים is also an abbreviation for מִזֶּרַע רָחֵל גְּנַבְתֶּם לְאָרְחַת יִשְׁמְעֵאלִים מְכַרְתֶּם, "From the seed of Rachel you have stolen, to caravans of Yishmaelites you have sold him." This is reminiscent of the brothers' sale of Yosef, וַיַּשְׁלִכוּ אֹתוֹ הַבֹּרָה... וְהִנֵּה אֹרְחַת יִשְׁמְעֵאלִים בָּאָה, *and they threw him into the pit…and, behold, a caravan of Yishmaelites was coming* (*Bereishis* 37:24–25). Based on this abbreviation, a great deal of truth is hidden in Yosef's accusation that his brothers are מְרַגְּלִים.

Therefore, when Yosef called his brothers מְרַגְּלִים, it wasn't as blatant a lie as it appeared to be, and Yosef began to orchestrate a scenario, whereby his brothers were able to achieve complete repentance for having sold him. Perhaps this is another reason that our Sages call Yosef יוֹסֵף הַצַּדִּיק, "Yosef the Righteous," *because the ultimate righteousness is to help others be righteous.* Yosef worked diligently and successfully to enable his brothers to achieve complete repentance for having sold him, and thus, regain their *righteousness*.

▸ THE AMAZING VISION OF THE VILNA GAON

When Yosef's brothers returned from their first trip to buy food in Egypt, they told their father, Yaakov, that the Lord of Egypt insisted that they return with their brother Binyamin, and that

Shimon was being held hostage until their return. Yaakov replied, יוֹסֵף אֵינֶנּוּ וְשִׁמְעוֹן אֵינֶנּוּ וְאֶת בִּנְיָמִן תִּקָּחוּ עָלַי הָיוּ כֻלָּנָה, *Yosef is gone, Shimon is gone, and now you would take away Binyamin? Upon me all this has happened* (*Bereishis* 42:36). The words עָלַי הָיוּ כֻלָּנָה, *Upon me all this has happened*, seem superfluous. Why does the Torah record that Yaakov said this?

The *Gemara* in *Menachos* 29b teaches that God told Moshe, "There is one man who will live at the end of many generations, Akiva ben Yosef is his name, who will expound upon each and every point [of each letter in the Torah] heaps and heaps of laws." Rabbi Akiva, who lived around 100 C.E. and was one of the foremost architects of the *Mishnah*, felt that each letter of the Torah is divinely endowed with so much purpose that "heaps and heaps" of laws can be derived even from the crowns that are drawn on the tops of individual letters. If even the crowns that are drawn on the tops of letters are important, certainly there are no extra words in the Torah. For what purpose does the Torah tell us that Yaakov said עָלַי הָיוּ כֻלָּנָה?

Over thirty years ago, my *rebbe* Rabbi Shmuel Scheinberg taught my high-school class a wonderful explanation by the Vilna Gaon that clarifies the purpose of these words. The Vilna Gaon, Rabbi Eliyahu ben Shlomo Zalman, lived from 1720–1797 and was one of the greatest Torah scholars of the last few centuries. According to the *Encyclopedia Judaica*, the Vilna Gaon was a "semi-legendary figure of saint and intellectual giant, [who] towered over Lithuanian Jewry and influenced its cultural life in the 19th and into the 20th centuries." **The Vilna Gaon had amazing insight and often revealed wonderful explanations that were previously not apparent.** The Vilna Gaon taught that it is possible to understand the purpose of the words עָלַי הָיוּ כֻלָּנָה by understanding a similar phrase in an earlier *parshah*.

Earlier in the Book of *Bereishis*, Rivka told her son, Yaakov, to impersonate Eisav, whom their father Yitzchak was planning to bless. Yaakov told Rivka that he was afraid that Yitzchak would find out that he was an impostor and would curse him. Rivka replied to Yaakov, עָלַי קִלְלָתְךָ בְּנִי, *your curse will be upon me, my son* (*Bereishis* 27:13). Rivka's response is difficult to understand. If Yitzchak found out that Yaakov was an impostor and cursed Yaakov, could Rivka easily transfer this curse onto herself? Also, Rivka could have just said simply, "Don't worry, Yaakov, I promise you that I know that Yitzchak will not curse you." Why does Rivka say, עָלַי קִלְלָתְךָ בְּנִי?

The Vilna *Gaon* explains that the letters in the word עָלַי stand for עֵשָׂו, לָבָן, יוֹסֵף (Eisav, Lavan, and Yosef). The first letters of the words עֵשָׂו, לָבָן, יוֹסֵף, spell עָלַי. Therefore, Rivka told Yaakov, עָלַי קִלְלָתְךָ בְּנִי, *your curses are* עָלַי (which is an abbreviation for עֵשָׂו, לָבָן, יוֹסֵף – Eisav, Lavan, and Yosef). Rivka told Yaakov that Yitzchak would not curse him, because she knew that Yaakov's curses, during his entire lifetime, would be limited to those contained in the word עָלַי, which stands for עֵשָׂו, לָבָן, יוֹסֵף – Eisav, Lavan, and Yosef.

Eisav was one of Yaakov's curses because he wanted to kill Yaakov (*Bereishis* 27:41). Lavan was one of Yaakov's curses because he made Yaakov work for him for fourteen years so that Yaakov could marry Leah and Rachel (*Bereishis* 29:27), and he changed Yaakov's salary repeatedly (*Bereishis* 31:41). Yosef was one of Yaakov's curses because of the anguish that Yaakov suffered when Yosef disappeared, as he was led to believe that Yosef had been eaten by a wild animal (*Bereishis* 37:33).

With this in mind, the Vilna Gaon explains what Yaakov meant later when he told Yosef's brothers in the Torah portion entitled *Mikeitz*, עָלַי הָיוּ כֻלָּנָה, "*Upon me all this has happened*" (*Bereishis* 42:36). When Yaakov was told by Yosef's brothers that the Lord of Egypt insisted that they return with their brother, Binyamin, Yaakov told them, עָלַי "עָלַי הָיוּ כֻלָּנָה, [which stands for the curses of עֵשָׂו, לָבָן, יוֹסֵף – Eisav, Lavan, and Yosef] have all happened." Yaakov couldn't understand how he could possibly lose Binyamin, since Rivka had promised him that his curses would be limited to עָלַי, which stands for the curses of עֵשָׂו, לָבָן, יוֹסֵף – Eisav, Lavan, and Yosef. Thus, the Vilna Gaon explains that the phrase

עָלַי הָיוּ כֻלָּנָה (*Bereishis* 42:36) is very meaningful and not at all superfluous, and is based on the meaning of the word עָלַי earlier in the Book of *Bereishis* when Rivka told Yaakov, עָלַי קִלְלָתְךָ בְּנִי, *your curse will be upon me, my son.*

The word עָלַי appears again later in the Book of *Bereishis*, in *Parshas Vayechi*, when Yaakov apologizes to Yosef for burying his mother Rachel outside of the Cave of Machpela, where Avraham and Sarah were buried. Yaakov told Yosef, מֵתָה עָלַי רָחֵל, *Rachel died upon me* (*Bereishis* 48:7). Once again, at first glance, עָלַי seems superfluous. What is the reason that the Torah tells us that Yaakov said, מֵתָה עָלַי רָחֵל?

This is once again understood, based on the explanation of the Vilna Gaon, that עָלַי stands for the curses of עֵשָׂו, לָבָן, יוֹסֵף – Eisav, Lavan, and Yosef. Thus, Yaakov told Yosef, מֵתָה עָלַי רָחֵל, *Rachel's death is part of the curses of* עָלַי (which is an abbreviation for עֵשָׂו, לָבָן, יוֹסֵף – Eisav, Lavan, and Yosef). In his commentary on *Vayikra* 18:25, the Ramban discusses Rachel's premature death. The Ramban explains that Rachel died when Yaakov returned from Lavan's house to the Land of Israel, because Yaakov observed all the laws of the Torah only in Israel, and therefore could no longer be married to two sisters. The Ramban adds, in his commentary on *Bereishis* 48:7, that this is also one of the reasons that Rachel was not buried in the Cave of Machpela with Yaakov and Leah. Since Lavan tricked Yaakov into marrying two sisters, and Yaakov couldn't be married to two sisters when he was in the Land of Israel, Lavan bore a major portion of the responsibility for Rachel's premature death. Consequently, Yaakov told Yosef, מֵתָה עָלַי רָחֵל, *Rachel's death is part of the curses of* עָלַי (which is an abbreviation for עֵשָׂו, לָבָן, יוֹסֵף – Eisav, Lavan, and Yosef), because, according to the Ramban's explanation, Lavan is at least partially responsible for Rachel's premature death.

The Vilna Gaon had amazing insight. *The Vilna Gaon explains two difficult, seemingly unrelated phrases, by pointing out that they both contain the word* עָלַי, *which is an abbreviation for the names of those who caused the major problems that Yaakov* had in his lifetime: עֵשָׂו, לָבָן, יוֹסֵף. This idea also helps to clarify the purpose of the word עָלַי in a third seemingly unrelated phrase, when Yaakov told Yosef, regarding Rachel's premature death, מֵתָה עָלַי רָחֵל, *Rachel died upon me* (*Bereishis* 48:7). Perhaps as explained above, since Lavan is at least partially responsible for Rachel's premature death, Yaakov told Yosef, מֵתָה עָלַי רָחֵל, which, as the Vilna Gaon explains, is an abbreviation for עֵשָׂו, לָבָן, יוֹסֵף – Eisav, Lavan, and Yosef.

פרשת ויגש

Parshas Vayigash

> KIND WORDS – A TRIBUTE TO
> RABBI SHLOMO FREIFELD

Yosef tells his brothers in *Bereishis* 45:5, "And now, do not be sad, and do not be angry with yourselves, that you have sold me here, for it was to preserve life that *God sent me before you.*" Within the next few sentences, Yosef repeats this idea two more times. In *Bereishis* 45:7, Yosef says, "*God sent me before you* to insure your survival in the land and to keep you alive for a great deliverance." In the very next sentence, Yosef says once again, "And now, *it was not you that sent me here, but God*; and He has made me as a father to Pharaoh, and master of all his house, and ruler over all the land of Egypt." *Within four sentences, Yosef repeats three times that God sent him to Egypt,* to insure that his brothers not be sad or angry with themselves, because God sent him to Egypt, and not them.

Rabbi Moshe Green, in *Impressions on the Heart*, a book culled from the thoughts of Rabbi Shlomo Freifeld (1923–1988, beloved teacher and founder of Yeshiva Sh'or Yoshuv), points out that Yosef was very careful to say words of encouragement to his brothers so that they would not be sad. This is probably the reason that

Yosef, in *Parshas Vayigash*, repeated to his brothers three times within four sentences that God sent him to Egypt, and not them. At the end of *Parshas Vayechi*, after Yaakov's passing, Yosef once again reassures his brothers, "God meant it for good…to preserve the lives of a great people" (*Bereishis* 50:20). In the next sentence, the Torah confirms that through Yosef's words of encouragement "…he comforted them and spoke to their hearts." Yosef's kind words made all the difference in his brothers' happiness.

Rabbi Moshe Green quotes the *Gemara* in *Shabbos* 89a that makes a similar point. Rabbi Yehoshua ben Levi said, "When Moshe ascended to the heavenly heights, he found the Holy One, Blessed is He, attaching crowns to the letters" of the Torah. Moshe was filled with awe by the sight and unable to speak. Upset by Moshe's silence, God remarked, "Moshe, is it not the custom to offer greetings in your town?" Moshe answered that he was silent because it is improper for a servant to initiate a conversation with his master. To this God responded, הָיָה לְךָ לְעָזְרֵנִי, "You should have [at least] offered Me support." Rashi explains that God suggested that Moshe offer helpful words of encouragement. Moshe agreed and immediately said to God, "And now, may the strength of my Lord be magnified as You have spoken."

According to this *Gemara*, when Moshe saw God attaching crowns to the letters of the Torah, Moshe was quiet until God urged him, הָיָה לְךָ לְעָזְרֵנִי. Perhaps this *Gemara* is teaching us that if God, who clearly doesn't need our support, wants words of encouragement, that it is crucial to offer kind words of encouragement to our fellow human beings who might benefit from our support.

Yosef was a master of this trait. He repeated over and over to his brothers that it was not their fault that he was in Egypt, but that God had sent him there. As the Torah tells us in *Parshas Vayechi* (*Bereishis* 50:21), these kind words of encouragement comforted Yosef's brothers.

This is a magnificent lesson that emphasizes the importance of speech and that *kind words make all the difference*. It is fascinating that Rabbi Moshe Green quotes this idea in a book culled from the teachings of Rabbi Shlomo Freifeld. I was privileged to have met Rabbi Freifeld, and to have been in his presence on many occasions. It seems to me that one of the most important reasons that Rabbi Freifeld was beloved by those who met him was his ability and willingness to offer kind words of encouragement and support. Rabbi Freifeld personified the lessons taught by this *Gemara* in *Shabbos*. Rabbi Freifeld had a heartfelt and warm greeting for everyone that he met and was always looking to offer kind words of encouragement. These words of support were carefully chosen for each individual in order to boost his or her self-esteem, so that each individual would be optimistic about the possibility of reaching his or her potential. Even to a teenager like myself, Rabbi Freifeld's warm personality radiated his attitude that each person has magnificent potential, no matter what station of life one is currently at. Rabbi Freifeld was often able to choose just the right words of encouragement for each individual to help lift that person from his or her current level, increase his or her feelings of self-worth, and start that individual on the road to fulfilling his or her potential. After just a very short time with Rabbi Freifeld, each person received an injection of self-esteem through Rabbi Freifeld's words of encouragement.

I remember that one of the items on the wall of Rabbi Freifeld's study was a sign, written in Hebrew, that I think was attributed to Rabbi Nachman of Breslov (1772–1811, a great Chasidic Rebbe), that to the best of my recollection said, "A person should have patience, especially with himself." Even for himself, a person needs kind words of encouragement. Rabbi Freifeld even had words of encouragement hanging on the wall of his study.

In 1967 Rabbi Freifeld founded Yeshiva Sh'or Yoshuv in Far Rockaway, New York City. The Yeshiva and entire community have been thriving since that time and continue to flourish over fifteen years since Rabbi Freifeld's passing. Perhaps this is because of the Yeshiva's continued commitment to Rabbi Freifeld's love for each person and desire to offer individually-chosen kind words of encouragement to boost each person's self-esteem, in order to help each person fulfill his or her potential.

The *Gemara* in *Shabbos* 133b teaches us to emulate God's attributes: אַבָּא שָׁאוּל אוֹמֵר... הֱוֵי דּוֹמֶה לוֹ מַה הוּא חַנּוּן וְרַחוּם אַף אַתָּה הֱיֵה חַנּוּן וְרַחוּם, "Abba Shaul said... 'Be similar to Him. Just as He is kind and merciful, so you should be kind and merciful.'" The *Gemara* in *Sotah* 14a also teaches that it is our responsibility to emulate God's attributes. Just as God provides clothes for the needy, visits the sick, comforts mourners, and buries the dead, the *Gemara* in *Sotah* 14a teaches that we should emulate these attributes.

The *Gemara* in *Shabbos* 89a quoted above teaches that God urged Moshe to offer a greeting and words of encouragement. Yosef understood this and repeated words of encouragement over and over again to his brothers. Rabbi Freifeld was a master at emulating God's suggestion to Moshe that it is always proper to offer a greeting and kind words of encouragement. This is one of the reasons that Rabbi Freifeld was so beloved and able to build a Yeshiva and community that continue to flourish and emulate these principles.

▸ YEHUDA, JEWS, AND JUDAISM

In the Torah portion entitled *Vayigash*, Yehuda approaches Yosef and attempts to persuade him to release Binyamin, who was being held captive. There is an amazing *Midrash* about Yehuda that correctly predicts the future. The *Midrash* is a compilation of early rabbinic literature that forms a commentary on specific books of the *Tanach* (which consists of the Torah, Prophets, and Writings). This *Midrash* is written in *Bereishis Rabbah*, which is one of the earliest *Midrashim* dating from 400–500 C.E.

The *Midrash* in *Bereishis Rabbah* 98:6 teaches that Rabbi Shimon bar Yochai said regarding Yehuda, "All your brothers will be called by your name. A man does not say 'I am a *Reuveni*' or 'I am a *Shimoni*,' but 'I am a יְהוּדִי (*Yehudi*).'" Rabbi Shimon bar Yochai was one of the most prominent Rabbis of his era. His teacher was Rabbi Akiva, and one of his pupils, according to *Gemara Eruvin*

91a, was Rabbi Yehuda HaNasi, who edited and arranged the *Mishnah* in its current format. According to tradition, Rabbi Shimon bar Yochai is the author of the *Zohar*.

It is amazing that Rabbi Shimon bar Yochai, who lived in approximately 150 C.E., correctly predicted that, in the future, the Hebrew nation would not primarily be known as Hebrews or Israelites, but as Jews. Our religion is usually known as Judaism (יַהֲדוּת) and we are most often known as Jews (יְהוּדִים). "In modern Hebrew the term for a Jew is *Yehudi*, in German *Jude*, its Yiddish counterpart is *Yid*, and even the English Jew and Judaism are all obvious variations of the name *Yehuda*, or Judah" (a quote from an essay by Aaron Feigenbaum, *Internet Parshah Sheet on Vayechi*, 5763).

According to rabbinic teaching, names have great significance. The Torah often explains the meaning of names, as in the following examples related to our Forefathers. The Torah tells us regarding Avraham's name, וְהָיָה שִׁמְךָ אַבְרָהָם כִּי אַב הֲמוֹן גּוֹיִם נְתַתִּיךָ, *and your name shall be Avraham for I have made you the father of a multitude of nations* (Bereishis 17:5). The Torah tells us regarding Yitzchak's name, וַתֹּאמֶר שָׂרָה כָּל הַשֹּׁמֵעַ יִצְחַק לִי, *And Sarah said "Whoever hears will laugh for me"* (Bereishis 21:6). The Torah tells us regarding Yaakov's name, וְיָדוֹ אֹחֶזֶת בַּעֲקֵב עֵשָׂו וַיִּקְרָא שְׁמוֹ יַעֲקֹב, *and his hand was grasping on to the heel of Eisav; so he called his name Yaakov* (Bereishis 25:26).

The *Gemara* discusses the importance of names, and teaches in *Berachos* 7b, דִּשְׁמָא גָרִים that a name is the cause of future occurrences. Rabbi Yaakov ben Solomon Ibn Chaviv (c.1445-c.1515) explains in his classic commentary, *Ein Yaakov*:

> A parent naming a child does not receive a prophecy; however, God inspires him or her to select a particular name that has significance unbeknown to the parent. Many years later the significance of the name may become apparent to all. *Of course, a name does not determine good or bad: a name does not preclude free will.* Despite the fact that it is a major

principle of our faith that God knows everything that will happen, each person is given free choice to choose good. (This translation is adapted from the ArtScroll commentary on *Gemara Berachos* 7b.)

Rabbi Shimon bar Yochai correctly predicted that Jews of every tribe would forever be known as *Yehudim*, after the fourth son of Yaakov, Yehuda. Mordechai, who was from the tribe of Binyamin, is known as מָרְדֳּכַי הַיְהוּדִי (Mordechai, the *Yehudi*) (*Megillas Esther* 2:5, 9:29,10:3). Since names have profound significance, we should try to understand why we are, even in our own era, named after Yehuda. Several explanations are suggested.

1) The same Rabbi Shimon bar Yochai, who taught us in the *Midrash* quoted above that the Israelites will always be known as *Yehudim*, also teaches in *Gemara Berachos* 7b the reason that the name Yehuda is so extraordinary: "From the day the Holy One, Blessed is He, created His world, there was no person who offered thanks…until Leah came and thanked Him, as it is stated [regarding the naming of Yehuda in *Bereishis* 29:35] 'this time let me *thank* God.'" Rashi explains that Leah thanked God *because she was given more than her share* when her fourth son, Yehuda, was born. Since Yaakov had four wives and 12 sons, three would have been an equal share. When her fourth son Yehuda was born, and she realized that she was given more than her share, she thanked God with the name Yehuda, which is related to the word לְהוֹדוֹת, which means *to thank*.

Rabbi Yitzchak Meir Alter (1799–1866), the first *Gerrer Rebbe* (Ger is a city in Poland), writes in his commentary on *Bereishis* 29:35 that we are named after Yehuda until this day because every Jew is supposed to feel like Leah, and that *we need to express our thanks to God for giving us more than our share*. Rabbi Yaakov Asher Sinclair, a contemporary scholar, writes (*Internet Parshah Sheet on Vayigash*, 5760), "We are not called Jews by coincidence. In Hebrew, a name defines the very essence of a thing. **If the name Yehuda means to thank, then that must be the essence of being**

Jewish. We are 'the Thankers.'" The Jewish nation until this day is usually called *Yehudim* ("*the Thankers*"), rather than Hebrews or Israelites. That is because, as the first *Gerrer Rebbe* quoted above explains, we need to express our thanks to God for giving us more than our share. That is why the first prayer of the morning is מוֹדֶה אֲנִי, thanking God for "returning my soul within me with compassion." Since we are *Yehudim* or "*the Thankers*," we have two prayers in the *Shemoneh Esrei* (Silent *Amidah*) beginning with the words מוֹדִים אֲנַחְנוּ לָךְ, which thank God for His abundant blessings.

Perhaps this is why bringing the first fruits (בִּכּוּרִים) to Jerusalem and thanking God for the first fruits (*Devarim* 26:2) is such an important commandment, because it is part of the essence of our being, which is to thank God. The *Midrash Bereishis Rabbah* 1:4 tells us that one of the things for which the world was created is the *mitzvah* (commandment) of first fruits (בִּכּוּרִים). The first sentence in the Torah says, בְּרֵאשִׁית בָּרָא אֱלֹהִים אֵת הַשָּׁמַיִם וְאֵת הָאָרֶץ, *In the beginning, God created the heavens and the earth*. The *Midrash* interprets this to mean "With רֵאשִׁית God created the heavens and the earth," and רֵאשִׁית, which means *first*, refers to the *mitzvah* of בִּכּוּרִים (*first* fruits), which in *Shemos* 23:19 is called רֵאשִׁית. Perhaps this *Midrash* emphasizes the importance of the *mitzvah* of בִּכּוּרִים, because as the name *Yehudim* implies, expressing our thanks to God is one of the main responsibilities of the Jews.

As noted above, יְהוּדָה is directly related to the word לְהוֹדוֹת, which means *to thank*. It is fascinating that the word לְהוֹדוֹת has two additional meanings. לְהוֹדוֹת also means *to praise*, similar to הוֹדוּ לַיהוָה כִּי טוֹב, *Praise God for He is good* (*Tehillim* 136:1). In addition, לְהוֹדוֹת also means *to admit*, similar to וְהִתְוַדָּה עָלָיו, *and admit upon it* (*Vayikra* 16:21). Thus, the word לְהוֹדוֹת has three meanings: "to thank," "to praise," and "to admit."

Rabbi Yaakov Asher Sinclair explains that another reason Jews are called יְהוּדִים is related to all three meanings of the word לְהוֹדוֹת. Rabbi Sinclair writes, "A Jew *admits* that everything comes from God…The foundation of all belief in God is to *admit* that life is one gigantic gift." If a person *admits* that life is one gigantic gift, then that person will look to *praise* and to *thank* God, just as Leah did when she named Yehuda, **to thank God for giving her more than her share.** This is the essence of the Jewish nation, and this is why the Jewish nation is called יְהוּדִים, which means "*the Thankers*" or "*the Admitters.*"

Rabbi Shimon bar Yochai, in the *Midrash Bereishis Rabbah* quoted above, teaches that Jews will always be called *Yehudim*. The same Rabbi Shimon bar Yochai teaches in *Gemara Berachos* 7b that Leah named her fourth son Yehuda, to *thank* God for giving her more than her share. The word *Yehudim* also implies that we are supposed to *admit* that life is one gigantic gift, and to *praise* God for that.

2) Yehuda guaranteed Binyamin's return to Yaakov by saying, אָנֹכִי אֶעֶרְבֶנּוּ, *I will guarantee him* (*Bereishis* 43:9). Yehuda helped to establish the crucial concept כָּל יִשְׂרָאֵל עֲרֵבִים זֶה לָזֶה, "All of Israel are responsible for each other (*Gemara Shevuos* 39a). It is possible that we are called Jews (after Yehuda) until this day because Yehuda established the concept of עֲרֵבוּת (responsibility for each other), which has always been crucial for the existence of the Jewish people.

3) Rabbi Yehuda Aryeh Leib Alter (1847–1905) is the grandson of the first *Gerrer Rebbe* quoted above and is known as the *Sefas Emes*. The *Sefas Emes* offers another reason that we are still called *Yehudim*, a name derived from Yaakov's fourth son, Yehuda. The *Sefas Emes* teaches that Yehuda (יְהוּדָה) is derived from לְהוֹדוֹת which, among its several meanings as described above, is "to admit." One of Yehuda's greatest deeds was admitting that he was wrong regarding his relationship with his daughter-in-law Tamar and that she was right (*Bereishis* 38:26). This caused him great embarrassment, but it saved her life.

According to the *Sefas Emes*, **admitting the truth when one is wrong is so important that we are still called Yehudim** (the Admitters), in remembrance of Yehuda's great deed when he confessed to Tamar (commentary by the *Sefas Emes* on *Parshas Vayechi*, תרנ"ז and תרס"ב).

The *Gemara Zevachim* 101b teaches that Moshe wasn't ashamed to admit his error and say, "I heard it and forgot." Similarly, the *Mishnah* in *Pirkei Avos* (*Ethics of the Fathers*) 5:9 teaches that one of the traits of a wise person is מוֹדֶה עַל הָאֱמֶת, "He admits the truth." The *Sefas Emes* adds that admitting the truth, which is one of the main attributes of Yehuda, allows a person to come closer to God, whose signature, according to the *Gemaros* in *Shabbos* 55a and *Sanhedrin* 64a, is truth.

As quoted by the *Midrash*, Rabbi Shimon bar Yochai, who lived in approximately 150 C.E., correctly predicted that approximately 1850 years later, the Hebrew nation would still be called "Yehudim"(Jews). As Yehuda was responsible for Binyamin, God wants us to be עֲרֵבִים זֶה לָזֶה (responsible for each other). *Yehudim* or Jews is the eternal name for the Jewish nation because the Jews are "*the Thankers*" and "*the Admitters.*" As the first *Gerrer Rebbe* taught, Jews are usually called "*Yehudim*," "*the Thankers*," rather than Hebrews or Israelites, because *we need to express our thanks to God for giving us more than our share.* As the *Sefas Emes* taught, *admitting the truth when one is wrong is so important that we are still called Yehudim, "the Admitters," in remembrance of Yehuda's great deed when he admitted his relationship with Tamar.* Admitting the truth brings the Jews closer to God, whose signature, according to the *Gemaros* in *Shabbos* 55a and *Sanhedrin* 64a, is "truth."

פרשת ויחי

Parshas Vayechi

> **THE BRILLIANCE OF THE BA'AL HATURIM**

Our Sages have pointed out the similarity between the Torah portion entitled וַיְחִי (*Vayechi*) and the Torah portion entitled חַיֵּי שָׂרָה (*Chayei Sarah*). These portions describe the deaths of two great righteous people, Yaakov and Sarah, but both are described using the Hebrew word for life, חַיִּים. This may be because our Rabbis tell us in *Gemara Berachos* 18b and *Midrash Tanchuma, Zos HaBeracha* 7, צַדִּיקִים בְּמִיתָתָן קְרוּיִין חַיִּים, "The righteous are considered alive even after they have passed away." This is even truer regarding Yaakov, because the *Gemara Ta'anis* 5a teaches, יַעֲקֹב אָבִינוּ לֹא מֵת, "Yaakov, our father, never died."

Rabbi Yaakov ben Asher (c.1269–c.1343) was born in Germany and was the third son of the great Talmudist, Rabbi Asher ben Yechiel (c.1250–1327), who is known as the Rosh, an abridgement of his name, Rabbeinu Asher. Because of pogroms, the Rosh and his family fled Germany in 1303 and eventually settled in Spain.

Rabbi Yaakov ben Asher knew the intricacies of the Talmud and its commentaries so well that he was able to organize Jewish law and write a monumental codification of all the laws, entitled

אַרְבָּעָה הַטּוּרִים (*Four Rows*). Rabbi Yosef Karo (1488–1575) later based the *Shulchan Aruch*, which is the foundation for *Halachah* (Jewish law) until today, on the אַרְבָּעָה הַטּוּרִים. Because of the importance of the אַרְבָּעָה הַטּוּרִים, Rabbi Yaakov ben Asher became known as the בַּעַל הַטּוּרִים (Ba'al HaTurim). Despite his immense scholarship, the Ba'al HaTurim never accepted any salaried rabbinical position or payment for his services to the community.

The Ba'al HaTurim also wrote a commentary on the Torah in two parts: a shorter one which he described as containing "…appetizers, numerical calculations, and interpretations of masoretic notes to attract [the reader's] heart," and a comprehensive and much longer commentary. Despite the fact that the Ba'al HaTurim had a magnificent grasp of the entire Talmud and its commentaries and wrote a monumental codification of all the laws, the Ba'al HaTurim seems also to have enjoyed explanations that revolve around the numerical value of words (גִּימַטְרִיָּא), ideas that come from the letters that make up a particular word (רָאשֵׁי תֵּבוֹת, נוֹטָרִיקוֹן), and other similar explanations. This shorter commentary, written "to attract [the reader's] heart," has been very popular and has recently been translated into English.

Parshas Vayechi begins with the words, וַיְחִי יַעֲקֹב בְּאֶרֶץ מִצְרַיִם שְׁבַע עֶשְׂרֵה שָׁנָה, *And Yaakov lived in the land of Egypt seventeen years*. The letters of the Hebrew alphabet, unlike English, are each assigned a specific numerical value. The Ba'al HaTurim points out that the numerical value of the first word in this Torah portion, וַיְחִי, which means *And [Yaakov] lived*, adds up to thirty-four (ו=6, י=10, ח=8, י=10; 6+10+8+10=34). Thirty-four equals the number of years that Yaakov lived with his son Yosef. Yosef was sold by his brothers when he was seventeen years old (*Bereishis* 37:2), and Yaakov lived in Egypt for seventeen years with Yosef (*Bereishis* 47:28). Therefore, Yaakov spent a total of thirty-four years with Yosef, which is the numerical value of the first word in this Torah portion, וַיְחִי, which means, *And [Yaakov] lived*. This alludes to the fact that the "best" life that Yaakov had was the 34 years that he spent with Yosef. During these 34 years, Yaakov "truly lived."

Perhaps these 34 years that Yaakov and Yosef were together were so special because, as the Torah tells us, וְיִשְׂרָאֵל אָהַב אֶת יוֹסֵף מִכָּל בָּנָיו, *And Yisrael* [another name for Yaakov] *loved Yosef more than all his sons.* (*Bereishis* 37:3). Our Rabbis teach that Yaakov was very similar to Yosef. In his commentary on this sentence, Rashi quotes the *Midrash Bereishis Rabbah* 84:8, that Yosef looked like Yaakov. The *Midrash Bereishis Rabbah* 84:6 lists more than fifteen other similarities that Yaakov and Yosef shared, such as:

> Just as Yaakov emigrated from the Land of Israel, Yosef emigrated from the Land of Israel; Just as Yaakov took a wife outside of the Land, Yosef took a wife outside of the Land; Just as Yaakov begot children outside of the Land, Yosef begot children outside of the Land; …Just as one went down to Egypt, the other one went down to Egypt…

Perhaps Yaakov loved Yosef more than his other sons, and shared so many similarites with Yosef, because they shared a similar spiritual goal, which Yaakov taught to him. Yaakov and Yosef both showed through the manner in which they lived that one can remain Jewish and flourish spiritually, even if one needs to live outside of the Land of Israel among gentiles. Yaakov forged the way when he lived with Lavan for many years and succeeded in remaining righteous and raising a large successful Jewish family, even while living with the evil idolator Lavan. This set a precedent for Jews in all generations, that it is possible to raise righteous Jewish families even in exile. Yosef clearly pursued this same tradition, and was able to raise a righteous Jewish family, even though for many years his was the only Jewish family in Egypt. The Torah tells us that Yaakov's spirit was alive only during the 34 years that he lived with Yosef (*Bereishis* 45:27). Perhaps these are the reasons that the Ba'al HaTurim points out that the numerical value of וַיְחִי, which means, *And [Yaakov] lived*, is thirty-four, which are the years that Yaakov "truly lived" because Yosef was with him.

Parshas Chayei Sarah begins with the words וַיִּהְיוּ חַיֵּי שָׂרָה, *And the life of Sarah* was 127 years. As he commented on the first word in *Parshas Vayechi*, the Ba'al HaTurim also comments on the first word of *Parshas Chayei Sarah*, and points out that the numerical value of וַיְהִי equals thirty-seven (6+10+5+10+6=37). This is the number of years that Sarah lived with her only son, Yitzchak. Sarah gave birth to Yitzchak when she was ninety (*Bereishis* 17:17), and as the Torah says at the very beginning of *Parshas Chayei Sarah*, she died at the age of 127. Therefore, Sarah lived thirty-seven years with Yitzchak, and those were the most important, and probably the happiest years of her life.

Accordingly, the Ba'al HaTurim teaches that the numerical value of the first word of *Parshas Chayei Sarah*, וַיְהִי, equals thirty-seven, because the חַיֵּי שָׂרָה (life of Sarah) was the 37 years that she lived with Yitzchak.

The *Gemara* in *Nedarim 64b* teaches that a person who has no children is considered, in some sense, as if he or she were dead. Therefore, the years that Sarah "truly lived" are the numerical value of the first word of *Parshas Chayei Sarah*, וַיְהִי, which equals 37, because that is the number of years that she had a child.

Parshas Vayechi, וַיְחִי, and *Parshas Chayei Sarah*, חַיֵּי שָׂרָה, are similar in that they describe the deaths of two great righteous people, Yaakov and Sarah, in terms of life, חַיִּים, because צַדִּיקִים בְּמִיתָתָן קְרוּיִין חַיִּים, "The righteous are considered alive even after they have passed away" (*Gemara Berachos* 18b). In addition, the Ba'al HaTurim teaches another amazing similarity between these Torah portions. The first word of *Parshas Vayechi*, וַיְחִי, adds up to 34, which is the number of years that Yaakov lived with Yosef; and the first word of *Parshas Chayei Sarah*, וַיְהִי, adds up to 37, which is the number of years that Sarah lived with Yitzchak. Yitzchak and Sarah are intimately connected because Yitzchak is Sarah's only son and spiritual heir. Yaakov and Yosef are intimately connected, because Yaakov specialized in remaining righteous even while living among gentiles. Yaakov transmitted this specialty specifically to Yosef, who required this knowledge because for many years he was the only Jew in Egypt.

(I am indebted to my *rebbe*, Rabbi Shmuel Scheinberg, who taught this *Ba'al HaTurim* to my high school class over thirty years ago.)

‣ A PRINCIPLE BY WHICH YOU WILL UNDERSTAND THE BOOK OF BEREISHIS

The Ramban was one of the greatest biblical and Talmudic commentators, as well as a poet, philosopher, Kabbalist, and physician. He was born in Spain in 1194, and died in Israel in 1270. In 1263, he successfully defended Judaism in a public disputation for which King James I of Aragon presented the Ramban with a monetary award. After Pope Clement IV requested that the king penalize him instead, the Ramban escaped from Spain and immigrated to Israel.

In his commentary on the beginning of the Torah portion entitled *Lech Lecha*, the Ramban teaches a principle to help understand the Book of *Bereishis* (*Genesis*). The Ramban writes:

> I will tell you a principle by which you will understand all the upcoming portions of the Torah concerning Avraham, Yitzchak, and Yaakov. It is indeed a great matter which our Rabbis mentioned briefly, saying: *"Whatever has happened to the Patriarchs is a sign to the children."* It is for this reason that the verses narrate at great length the account of the journeys of the Patriarchs…and other events. Now someone may consider them unnecessary and of no useful purpose, but in truth *they all serve as a lesson for the future*: when an event happens to any one of the three Patriarchs, that which is decreed to happen to his children can be understood. (Based on the translation by Rabbi Dr. Charles B. Chavel.)

This principle is usually described as מַעֲשֵׂי אָבוֹת סִימָן לְבָנִים, "The happenings of the forefathers are a sign for the children," and is based on the *Midrash Tanchuma* (*Lech Lecha* 9). The last fourteen chapters of the Book of *Bereishis* (*Genesis*), chapters 37–50, relate in detail the story of Yosef's sale by his brothers to the Ishmaelites, Yosef's advancement to become the Viceroy of Egypt, and the descent to Egypt by Yaakov and his family. In the second Book of the Torah, *Shemos* (*Exodus*), the Jewish people are enslaved in Egypt and God's promise to Avraham, יָדֹעַ תֵּדַע כִּי גֵר יִהְיֶה זַרְעֲךָ בְּאֶרֶץ לֹא לָהֶם, *Know with certainty that your offspring shall be aliens in a land that is not theirs* (*Bereishis* 15:13) is fulfilled. The Jewish nation was molded in Egypt and exited miraculously to receive the Torah at Mount Sinai. According to the Ramban quoted above, all of the stories in the Book of *Bereishis* are recorded to "serve as a lesson for the future." What important lessons are we to derive from the last fourteen chapters of the Book of *Bereishis*, which describe in great detail the story of the descent of Yaakov and his family to Egypt?

Perhaps one of the major lessons of chapters 37–50, approximately the last quarter of the Book of *Bereishis*, is summarized by Yosef toward the end of the last Torah portion of the Book of *Bereishis*, *Parshas Vayechi*, when he tells his brothers, וְאַתֶּם חֲשַׁבְתֶּם עָלַי רָעָה אֱלֹהִים חֲשָׁבָהּ לְטֹבָה, *And you intended to hurt me, but God meant it for good* (*Bereishis* 50:20). In the preceding Torah portion, *Parshas Vayigash*, when Yosef first revealed his identity to his brothers, Yosef also emphasizes, *And now, don't be sad, and do not be angry with yourselves that you sold me here, for it was to be a provider that God sent me before you…And God sent me ahead of you to insure your survival in the land and to keep you alive for a great deliverance* (*Bereishis* 45: 5, 7).

Thus, one of the crucial lessons that is emphasized in the last fourteen chapters of the Book of *Bereishis* is that events that at first glance seemed terrible, such as the sale of Yosef by his brothers and Yaakov's temporary loss of his favorite son, Yosef, were orchestrated by God and were ultimately beneficial. The *Midrash* discusses this lesson in a few locations. According to the *Midrash Bereishis Rabbah* 91:10, with the limited insight that human beings have, even our forefather Yaakov erred when he told his children, "Why did you do such harm to me?" (*Bereishis* 43:6). This *Midrash* teaches that God rebuked Yaakov for this comment by saying, "I am busy arranging for Yosef to be the Viceroy of Egypt, [so why does Yaakov complain] and say 'Why did you do such harm to me?'" Earlier in the Book of *Bereishis*, the *Midrash Bereishis Rabbah* 86:2 teaches:

> Yaakov should have gone down to Egypt in chains [since this was the beginning of Israel's slavery in Egypt], but God declares, "He is My firstborn son; shall I then bring him down in disgrace!…Therefore, I will bring down his son before him and Yaakov will follow…" (also see *Midrash Tanchuma, Parshas Vayeshev* 4).

Based on the text (*Bereishis* 45:5, 7 and 50:20) and these Midrashic teachings, one of the major themes of chapters 37–50 is that God manipulated everything that happened so that Yosef would become the Viceroy of Egypt, in order for Yaakov and his family to descend to Egypt in an honorable fashion to begin the enslavement of the Jewish people. The slavery of the Jewish people ultimately leads to their miraculous exodus from Egypt, the formation of the Jewish nation, and God's giving of the Torah at Mount Sinai.

Our Sages also point out that events that seem favorable can sometimes turn out not to be truly beneficial. Rabbi Zelig Pliskin, a contemporary scholar, writes in *Growth Through Torah* (page 110), based on an insight from Rabbi Leib Lopian, the *Rosh Yeshiva* of Gateshead:

> Later on when Yaakov, Yosef's father, went down to Egypt, anyone viewing the scene would have considered it a very positive one. Yaakov was going to be reunited with his favorite son after many years of separation. His son was a powerful leader and he would be treated with all the honors of royalty. But what was the total picture? This was the first stage in the exile of the Children of Israel. Their enslavement in Egypt was beginning at this very moment…

Only God knows definitively whether an event will be beneficial or harmful.

This theme that Yosef emphasizes at the end of *Parshas Vayechi* when he tells his brothers, וְאַתֶּם חֲשַׁבְתֶּם עָלַי רָעָה אֱלֹהִים חֲשָׁבָהּ לְטֹבָה, *And you intended to hurt me, but God meant it for good*, can also be appreciated in an entirely different context at the beginning of *Parshas Vayechi*! Towards the beginning of *Parshas Vayechi* (*Bereishis* 47:29), Yaakov asked Yosef to swear, וְעָשִׂיתָ עִמָּדִי חֶסֶד וֶאֱמֶת אַל נָא תִקְבְּרֵנִי בְּמִצְרָיִם, *And do kindness and truth with me – please do not bury me in Egypt*. Rashi explains, based on *Midrash Bereishis Rabbah*, that only acts of kindness done for the dead are considered חֶסֶד שֶׁל אֱמֶת, true kindness. The plain explanation of this is that although acts of kindness done for the living often have an ulterior motive to be repaid, this motive does not apply when acts of kindness are done for the dead.

There is a magnificent collection of Torah insights entitled *Likutei Yehoshua* (*Collections of Yehoshua*) published around 1958 by Rabbi Yehoshua Scheinfeld. Rabbi Scheinfeld suggests another reason that only acts of kindness done for the dead are considered חֶסֶד שֶׁל אֱמֶת. Rabbi Scheinfeld quotes *Ohel Yaakov*, which states that when a person tries to do an act of kindness for a living person, because of the imperfection of human reasoning, the act of kindness may not actually turn out to be beneficial. Only when acts of kindness are done for the dead do they always turn out to be beneficial, or חֶסֶד שֶׁל אֱמֶת.

According to *Ohel Yaakov*, as quoted in *Likutei Yehoshua*, our forefather Yaakov teaches at the beginning of *Parshas Veyechi* a similar lesson to that which is emphasized by Yosef at the end of *Parshas Vayechi* – that only God knows definitively whether an event or action is beneficial or detrimental. Sometimes an event that seems terrible, such as the sale of Yosef by his brothers, is ultimately beneficial, and sometimes well-intentioned actions are detrimental, except when they are חֶסֶד שֶׁל אֱמֶת, acts of kindness, done for the dead.

Likutei Yehoshua adds that this concept enables us to understand a phrase in the prayer that is recited prior to the beginning of each new month. Based on the *Gemara Berachos* 16b, we pray יְהִי רָצוֹן מִלְּפָנֶיךָ י־וה אֱלֹקֵינוּ... וְתִתֵּן לָנוּ... חַיִּים שֶׁיְמַלֵּא י־וה מִשְׁאֲלוֹת לִבֵּנוּ לְטוֹבָה, "May it be Your will, Hashem, our God, …that You give us …a life in which our heartfelt requests will be fulfilled for the good." The *Likutei Yehoshua* wonders why it is not sufficient just to request that God fulfill our requests. Why is it necessary to add that God fulfill our requests *"for the good"*?

Rabbi Scheinfeld, in *Likutei Yehoshua*, explains that, as described above, since human reasoning is imperfect, people don't truly know whether or not their wishes and requests will ultimately be beneficial or detrimental. Therefore, Rabbi Scheinfeld explains, it is necessary to ask, "May it be Your will, *Hashem*, our God…that You give us…a life in which our heartfelt requests will be fulfilled *for the good*," because only God knows which of our requests will really turn out to be benefical.

The *Mishnah* in the ninth chapter of *Berachos* teaches, "One is obliged to bless [God] for the evil, just as one blesses [God] for the good." The Rambam codifies this *Mishnah* as *Halachah* (law) in *Mishneh Torah*, Laws of Blessings 10:3. Rav Yosef Karo (1488–1575) also codifies this *Mishnah* as *Halachah* in the classic Code of Jewish Law, the *Shulchan Aruch, Orach Chayim* 222:3. Based on the *Gemara* in *Berachos* 60b, Rav Yosef Karo in the *Shulchan Aruch, Orach Chayim* 230:5, also codifies as *Halachah* the teaching of Rabbi Akiva, "A person should always be accustomed to say, 'Whatever the Merciful One does, He does for the best.'"

For me this law has always been somewhat difficult to understand, because at first glance, it is difficult to comprehend why a person should be obliged to bless God for bad things that happen to him. Probably the most common explanation for this law is that attributed to Rabbeinu Yonah of Gerona (c.1180–1263), that a person is obliged to bless God for the bad, because the bad things that happen to people serve as atonement for their sins.

The Rambam offers a different, magnificent explanation for this in his commentary on this *Mishnah*. (It is remarkable that at the conclusion of his commentary on all of the *Mishnah*, the Rambam writes that he wrote this entire commentary between the ages of 23-30.) The Rambam explains the rationale for the *Mishnah*'s teaching that "One is obliged to bless [God] for the evil" as follows:

> Our Sages taught, "Everything Heaven does is for the good"... Although many matters may originally look unfavorable, ultimately they will bring great good. Conversely, there are many things which, at the onset, appear good, and ultimately are very bad. Therefore, an understanding person should not be upset when beset with terrible difficulties because he does not know the ultimate outcome...but the writings of the Prophets are very clear that a person is warned not to be in a state of anxiety or worry. (Adapted from the translation by Rabbi Eliyahu Touger.)

Thus, according to the Rambam, one is obliged to bless God for the bad, because our Sages taught, "Everything Heaven does is for the good" and "Although many matters may originally look unfavorable, ultimately they will bring great good."

The Rambam's explanation is similar to Yosef's comment to his brothers near the end of *Parshas Vayechi*, וְאַתֶּם חֲשַׁבְתֶּם עָלַי רָעָה אֱלֹהִים חֲשָׁבָהּ לְטֹבָה, *And you intended to hurt me, but God meant it for good*, and to the *Midrash Bereishis Rabbah* quoted above, that God rebuked Yaakov and said, "I am busy arranging for Yosef to be the Viceroy of Egypt, [so why does Yaakov complain] and say 'Why did You do such harm to me?'" Both Yosef in his conversation with his brothers, and the *Midrash* regarding Yaakov's complaint, emphasize that the ultimate outcome of a seemingly terrible event such as the sale of Yosef was orchestrated by God to be beneficial.

In his commentary on *Parshas Metzora* in *Living Each Week*,

Rabbi Abraham J. Twerski, M.D. explains that it is comforting to note that since the concept that "One is obliged to bless [God] for the evil" is a difficult one, the *Gemara* in *Bava Basra* 16b teaches that "a person is not held accountable [for harsh words] uttered while in pain." The law is merciful and well-balanced, and teaches that since it is difficult, one is not punished if one is unable, at the time of a bad occurrence, to bless God.

In *Parshas Vayigash*, the Torah portion immediately preceding *Parshas Vayechi*, Yosef reveals his true identity to his brothers and tells them, "And now, don't be sad, and do not be angry with yourselves that you sold me here, for it was to be a provider that God sent me before you…And God sent me ahead of you to insure your survival in the land and to keep you alive for a great deliverance" (*Bereishis* 45:5 and 7). Unlike the English alphabet, each letter of the Hebrew alphabet has a numerical value. Our Sages noted that there are 106 sentences in *Parshas Vayigash* and that 106 is also the numerical value of יְהַלֵּל אֵל, which means "he shall praise God" (10+5+30+30+1+30=106=יְהַלֵּל אֵל). As quoted in the *ArtScroll Stone Chumash*, Rabbi David Feinstein, the current *Rosh Yeshiva* of Mesivta Tiferes Yerushalayim and son of Rav Moshe Feinstein, teaches that יְהַלֵּל אֵל, "he shall praise God," may allude "to the praise due to God for orchestrating the events that led to the Egyptian bondage. For just as the Jew is obliged to praise God for the goodness that He bestows, so must we praise Him for that which appears evil." Thus, the number of sentences in *Parshas Vayigash* reflects one of the major lessons of the last 14 chapters of the Book of *Bereishis*, that God is the master conductor who orchestrates world events and that even if events seem terrible, the ultimate outcome for the Jews, as it was for Yosef, is often beneficial.

As the Ramban quoted above emphasizes:

> *I will tell you a principle by which you will understand all the upcoming portions of the Torah…*"Whatever has happened to the Patriarchs is a sign to the children." It is for this reason

that the verses *narrate at great length* the account of the journeys of the Patriarchs…and other events. Now someone may consider them unnecessary and of no useful purpose, but in truth they all serve as *a lesson for the future*…

It seems that one of the reasons that the Torah "*narrates at great length*" the story of the sale of Yosef is that this is "*a lesson for the future.*" Events that appear terrible, such as the sale of Yosef by his brothers, are orchestrated by God and often beneficial. As the Rambam writes in his commentary on the *Mishnah* in *Berachos* quoted above, "an understanding person should not be upset when beset with terrible difficulties because he does not know the ultimate outcome." According to the Rambam, this concept is the basis for the *Mishnah* that teaches in the ninth chapter of *Berachos*, "One is obliged to bless [God] for the evil, just as one blesses [God] for the good," because, as the Rambam explains, "Our Sages taught, 'Everything Heaven does is for the good.'"

Sefer Shemos

פרשת שמות

Parshas Shemos

› **THE EARLIEST AND MOST RESPECTED BIBLICAL COMMENTARY**

The *Gemara* in *Megillah* 32a teaches that the Torah should be read with נְעִימָה, a pleasant tone. Most of the words in the Torah are associated with a written symbol that explains how they are to be sung. These musical accents are sometimes described as notes of cantillation, and are referred to in the *Gemara* as פִּיסְקֵי טְעָמִים (*Megillah* 3a, *Nedarim* 37b) or as טַעֲמֵי תּוֹרָה (*Berachos* 62a). In his commentary on *Berachos* 62a, Rashi refers to them as נְגִינוֹת טַעֲמֵי מִקְרָא. These written symbols can be found in most printed editions of the *Chumash* (the Five Books of the Torah), but not in Torah scrolls. A Torah scroll with written musical accents is invalid (ArtScroll commentary on *Gemara Berachos* 62a, based on various *halachic* sources). There is an argument quoted in the *Gemara Nedarim* 37a-b between Rav and Rabbi Yochanan as to whether the musical accents are of biblical origin or a rabbinic innovation. Either way, it seems clear that the musical accents are of tremendous importance and were well known in the Talmudic era (approximately 200–500 C.E.), and probably also in the era of the *Mishnah* (compiled and edited by Rabbi Yehuda HaNasi around 200 C.E.).

The ArtScroll commentary on *Nedarim* 37a explains that, according to the Rosh (acronym for Rabbi Asher ben Yechiel, who lived from approximately 1250 to 1327, and wrote a classic *halachic* commentary on the *Gemara*), the musical accents establish the correct sentence structure of a verse joining words into phrases, and marking pauses between discrete phrases or clauses.

Judah David Eisenstein is the editor of a magnificent ten-volume Jewish encyclopedia written in Hebrew, entitled *Otzar Yisrael*. He was born in Poland in 1854, immigrated to the United States in 1872, and died in 1956. Mr. Eisenstein authored many of the entries in the encyclopedia himself. It is amazing how much information he gathered without the aid of computers. He was also a successful coat manufacturer. Yet he succeeded in publishing numerous other books, including *Otzar Dinim U'minhagim*, which is a well-known anthology of laws and customs, and *Otzar Musar U'midoth*, which is an anthology of morals and ethics.

Mr. Eisenstein writes that the טַעֲמֵי מִקְרָא, the musical accents, are כְּנְשָׁמָה לְגוּף, like a soul to its body, and that they are the first and most respected of all the commentaries. He quotes Avraham Ibn Ezra (1089–c.1164, great biblical commentator, poet, and grammarian), that there are 21 different musical accents, and that you should not accept any explanation of the Torah that doesn't agree with the explanation suggested by the musical accents. Because all explanations of the Torah must agree with the pauses suggested by the musical accents, *the musical accents are clearly the only commentary with which everyone must agree*. Occasionally, commentators argue even with the explanations of Rashi or the Ramban, but according to the Ibn Ezra quoted above, everyone must agree with the pauses and phrases that are defined by the musical accents. **Therefore, the musical accents are clearly the most respected commentary.**

The Vilna Gaon, Rabbi Eliyahu ben Shlomo Zalman (1720–1797), had amazing insight and often revealed wonderful explanations that were previously not apparent. In his commentary on the musical accents of the words וַיְמָרֲרוּ אֶת חַיֵּיהֶם, [*The Egyptians*] *embittered the lives of the Jewish people with hard work* (*Shemos* 1:14), the Vilna Gaon teaches a fascinating idea. God told Avraham that his descendants would be slaves for four hundred years in a land that was not theirs (*Bereishis* 15:13). Later in *Bereishis* 42:2, Yaakov told his children רְדוּ שָׁמָּה, *Go down there* to Egypt to purchase food. Rashi, quoting the *Midrash Bereishis Rabbah*, explains that the word רְדוּ alludes to the 210 years that the Jews were actually slaves in Egypt. Unlike the English alphabet, each letter of the Hebrew alphabet has a unique numerical value. The *gematria* (numerical value) of רְדוּ equals 210 (ו=6, ד=4, ר=200). God, in His mercy, reduced His original promise to Avraham of 400 years of slavery to 210 years. God did this by calculating the 400 years from the birth of Yitzchak until the Jews left Egypt (commentary of Rashi on *Bereishis* 15:13).

According to the Vilna Gaon, another reason that God was able to reduce the time of actual slavery is because of the sentence וַיְמָרֲרוּ אֶת חַיֵּיהֶם, [*The Egyptians*] *embittered the lives of the Jewish people with hard work* (*Shemos* 1:14). God calculated that because of the extraordinary severity of the slavery, 400 years of servitude were accomplished in just 210 years. The same idea appears in the *Midrash Hagadol* and perhaps the *Gemara Yerushalmi* (see *Torah Sheleimah* on *Shemos* 2:23, letter קפב). The Vilna Gaon points out that the טַעֲמֵי מִקְרָא (musical accents) on וַיְמָרֲרוּ אֶת חַיֵּיהֶם are קַדְמָא וְאַזְלָא. These words mean 'came early and left' and allude to the reduction *of slavery from 400 to 210 years because of* וַיְמָרֲרוּ אֶת חַיֵּיהֶם. The musical accents on וַיְמָרֲרוּ אֶת חַיֵּיהֶם are קַדְמָא וְאַזְלָא, because the bitterness of the slavery caused the promise of 400 years of slavery to come early and leave.

Itturei Torah is a magnificent collection of Torah insights by Rabbi Aharon Yaakov Greenberg, which was published posthumously in 1965. *Itturei Torah* quotes Rabbi Zvi Hirsch Ashkenazi (1660–1718, scholar and communal leader who was also known as the Chacham Zvi), that the *gematria* (numerical value) of קַדְמָא וְאַזְלָא is **190** (30=ל, 7=ז, 1=א, 6=ו, 1=א, 40=מ, 4=ד, 100=ק, 1=א,). This is exactly equal to the number of years that God subtracted from His original promise to Avraham of 400 years of slavery. 400 minus 190 equals 210, which, as noted above, is the number of years that the Jews were actually slaves in Egypt. 190 is the exact number of years that קַדְמָא וְאַזְלָא *came early and left* because of וַיְמָרֲרוּ אֶת חַיֵּיהֶם.

Rabbi Yitzchak Zev Soloveichik, (1886–1960, great Talmudic scholar, Rabbi in Brisk and Jerusalem) taught that this same idea is expressed in the *Haggadah* that is read at the Passover *Seder*. The *Haggadah* praises God because He חִשַּׁב אֶת הַקֵּץ ("calculated the end of the slavery"). According to Rabbi Soloveichik, the *Haggadah* is praising God for being able to calculate exactly that because of the extraordinary bitterness of the slavery, the original decree of 400 years of slavery was accomplished 190 years early. Only God could calculate the extent of their suffering and expedite their redemption accordingly (from *The Pesach Haggadah* by Rabbi Moshe Lieber). Therefore, the *Haggadah* praises God because He calculated the end (קֵץ). קֵץ means end and has a numerical value of 190 (90=צ, 100=ק), *similar to* קַדְמָא וְאַזְלָא. *God calculated that because of the extraordinary bitterness of the slavery, the original decree of 400 years should be reduced by 190 years.* The *Haggadah* is praising God for subtracting קֵץ (equals 190) from the original decree, so that the Jews were able to leave Egypt 190 years early. The *Haggadah* is praising God for making this exact calculation, that the work that was supposed to be done in 400 years was actually accomplished in 210 years. This is something that only God could figure out exactly.

The musical accents (טַעֲמֵי מִקְרָא) *are the first and most respected of all the commentaries.* The Vilna Gaon had amazing vision and revealed the beauty of the musical accents on וַיְמָרֲרוּ אֶת חַיֵּיהֶם, *They embittered their lives.* This idea and many others of the Vilna Gaon's magnificent insights are collected in a book entitled *Kol Eliyahu*, including a wonderful explanation on the very beginning of the Torah portion *Vayigash*, also relating to musical accents.

Parshas Shemos · 131

▸ KINDNESS EQUALS TORAH

The Torah says that the daughter of Pharaoh went to bathe by the river and saw Moshe's basket among the reeds. When she saw Moshe, who was then approximately three months old, crying, וַתַּחְמֹל עָלָיו וַתֹּאמֶר מִיַּלְדֵי הָעִבְרִים זֶה, *she took pity on him and said*, "This is one of the Hebrew boys" (*Shemos* 2:6). The Torah points out that the daughter of Pharaoh *first had pity* on Moshe, and then realized that he was one of the Hebrew babies. The Torah tells us over the next several sentences that, despite this realization, she rescued the baby, named him Moshe, and raised him as a son.

Rabbi Yissocher Frand is a well-known contemporary author of many magnificent Torah thoughts and a teacher in Yeshivas Ner Israel in Baltimore. Rabbi Frand quotes Rav Nissan Alpert (who passed away in 1986, and was a scholar, communal leader, teacher, and a student of Rabbi Moshe Feinstein):

> It is no coincidence that the word חֶסֶד (kindness) always precedes the word אֱמֶת (truth) wherever the two terms are used together in the Torah (for example: *Bereishis* 24:49, *Shemos* 34:6, *Yehoshua* 2:14). If אֱמֶת (truth) would precede חֶסֶד (kindness), we would never reach חֶסֶד....A person's natural reaction must be חֶסֶד first. It may subsequently be tempered with אֱמֶת, but the initial response must be חֶסֶד.

Similarly, if Pharaoh's daughter, whom God named Basya (בַּתְיָה), had thought about the situation logically, before feeling pity for Moshe, she probably would never have adopted him. She would have reasoned that he was a Hebrew baby, and her father had decreed that newborn Hebrew boys should be killed. However, the Torah points out that *she had pity* on him, and only afterwards took into account that he was a Hebrew baby. *Basya adopted Moshe because* חֶסֶד (*kindness*) *came before* אֱמֶת (*truth*).

The *Midrash* in *Vayikra Rabbah* 1:3 states that God named Pharaoh's daughter Basya, which means daughter of God, because of the kindness she showed to Moshe. This *Midrash* teaches, "He

[Moshe] was not your son and you called him your son, so too you are not my daughter, and I will call you my daughter, as it says וְאֵלֶּה בְּנֵי בִּתְיָה בַת פַּרְעֹה, 'and these are the sons of Bisya, the daughter of Pharaoh'" (Divrei Hayamim I 4:18).

The above insight, that חֶסֶד (kindness) should always precede אֱמֶת (truth), is found in Rabbi Alpert's book, *Limudei Nissan*, which was published posthumously. Rabbi Frand mentions that Rabbi Alpert quoted this insight when he delivered a eulogy for his teacher, Rav Moshe Feinstein. Rav Moshe Feinstein (1895–1986) was the *Rosh Yeshiva* (Dean) of Mesivta Tifereth Yerushalayim in New York City, and was one of the foremost leaders and *halachic* authorities of his time. Rabbi Alpert said that Rabbi Feinstein always viewed a situation from a חֶסֶד perspective, before examining the situation from the angle of אֱמֶת. For this reason, Rav Alpert pointed out, many Rabbis found that it was easy to obtain letters of recommendation for their publications from Rabbi Feinstein. In addition, needy people who were looking for reference letters found that it was easy to get help from Rabbi Feinstein.

Rabbi Moshe Feinstein personified Basya's example and the teaching of our Torah that חֶסֶד should always precede אֱמֶת. According to Rabbi Frand, "That was Basya's spirit, and that was the spirit she imbued into Moshe Rabbeinu (our teacher). For that is the spirit that a Jewish leader must have, the spirit of חֶסֶד and then אֱמֶת. If we allow אֱמֶת to come first, we will never reach חֶסֶד."

Rabbi Alpert, in his book *Limudei Nissan*, points out that the lesson to be learned from Basya is that if you see a person in danger, pity should be the overriding factor so that you will do whatever is possible to save the person, even if it is very difficult. Moshe learned this lesson well, as the Torah tells us in the next few sentences that Moshe saved a Jew who was being attacked by an Egyptian (*Shemos* 2:12). A few sentences later, Moshe saved Yisro's daughters from the shepherds (*Shemos* 2:17). These two examples are found in the Torah only a few sentences after Basya "...*took pity* on him and said, 'This is one of the Hebrew boys'" (*Shemos* 2:6). Perhaps this is because Moshe learned from Basya the importance of placing חֶסֶד before אֱמֶת, and to do whatever is possible to save a person in danger.

The *Midrash* in *Shemos Rabbah* 1:26, which was probably edited between 400–500 C.E., states, "From here you can infer how great is the reward of those who perform kind acts (גּוֹמְלֵי חֲסָדִים); for although Moshe had many names, the name by which he is known throughout the Torah is the one which Basya, the daughter of Pharaoh, called him, and even God called him by no other name." The *Gemara*, in *Megillah* 13a, records that Moshe had six other meaningful names, and the *Midrash* in *Vayikra Rabbah* 1:3 says that Moshe had ten names in total. Basya had mercy and showed great kindness by raising Moshe. The only name that the Torah and God used was Moshe, the name given to him by Basya, to repay her for this kindness.

Rabbi Moshe Yechiel Epstein (1890–1971), who was known as the Rebbe from Ozhorov, writes in *Ba'ar Moshe* that Moshe's name should always remind us how great is the reward of those who perform kind acts (גּוֹמְלֵי חֲסָדִים). As the *Midrash* quoted above teaches, despite the fact that Moshe had many meaningful names, the Torah and God use only the name Moshe, to repay Basya for the חֶסֶד that she showed to Moshe. Thus, whenever one sees or hears Moshe's name, it should remind one of the greatness of חֶסֶד.

The Rebbe from Ozhorov quotes the *Gemara* in *Sotah 14a*, תּוֹרָה תְּחִלָּתָהּ גְּמִילוּת חֲסָדִים וְסוֹפָהּ גְּמִילוּת חֲסָדִים, "The Torah – its beginning is the performance of kindness and its end is the performance of kindness." The *Gemara* explains that towards the beginning of the Torah, in *Bereishis* 3:21, God made garments and put them on Adam and Chava, and towards the end of the Torah, in *Devarim* 34:6, God personally buried Moshe. This *Gemara* emphasizes, according to the Maharsha (acronym for Rabbi Shmuel Eliezer Adels, 1555–1631, one of the foremost *Gemara* commentators), that the Torah is essentially a book of חֶסֶד. The second *Mishnah* in *Pirkei Avos* lists the performance of acts of kindness as one of the three things on which the world stands. The *Gemara* in *Avodah Zarah* 17b teaches that if one occupies himself with the study of Torah, without the performance of acts of kindness, it is as if he has no God. The Maharsha explains that it is as if he has no God to save him, because God performs acts of kindness and he should emulate God to also perform acts of kindness. Perhaps what the Maharsha means is that if one doesn't perform acts of kindness, he will not be deserving, when he is in trouble, to have God perform acts of kindness to save him.

Perhaps our doing acts of kindness is our way to pay back God for all the kindness that He does for us. Indeed, Rabbi Moshe Lieber, in his commentary on *Pirkei Avos*, quotes another contemporary scholar, Rabbi Avrohom Chaim Feuer, that the term גְּמִילוּת חֲסָדִים literally means the *repaying* of acts of kindness. Performing acts of kindness is the best way to repay God for the acts of kindness that God does. The *Gemara*, also in *Sotah* 14a, teaches that people are responsible to emulate God's attributes, which consist of the performance of acts of kindness such as supplying clothes for those in need, visiting the sick, comforting mourners, and burying the dead. The *Gemara* in *Shabbos* 133b states similarly, "Just as [God] is gracious and compassionate, you also should be gracious and compassionate." This is consistent with the *Gemara* in *Sotah* 14a and the explanation of the Maharsha quoted above that the Torah is essentially a book of חֶסֶד. The Rebbe from Ozhorov writes in *Ba'ar Moshe* that the idea that the Torah is essentially a book of חֶסֶד teaches that one shouldn't perform acts of kindness because they are logical or because one hopes to be paid back in some fashion, but only because the Torah commands us to do them.

The Rebbe from Ozhorov points out beautifully that the numerical value of the word תּוֹרָה (Torah) is equivalent to the numerical value of the words גְּמִילוּת חֲסָדִים (performing acts of kindness)! The letters of the Hebrew alphabet, unlike English, are each assigned a specific numerical value. The word תּוֹרָה adds up to 611 as follows: 611=400+6+200+5; 5=ה, 200=ר, 6=ו, 400=ת. This is exactly equivalent to the numerical value of גְּמִילוּת חֲסָדִים which is also 611 (3+40+10+30+6+400+8+60+4+10+40=611). *These numerical values are exactly equivalent because, as noted above, the Torah is essentially a book of* חֶסֶד!

In addition, the Rebbe from Ozhorov points out, וְרֶמֶז נִפְלָא 'בְּדָבָר כִּי 'מֹשֶׁה רַבֵּינוּ' עוֹלֶה' בְּגִימַטְרִיָּא 'בִּגְמִילוּת חֲסָדִים', "And there is a wonderful hint, because 'מֹשֶׁה רַבֵּינוּ' (Moshe, our teacher) has the same numerical value as 'בִּגְמִילוּת חֲסָדִים' (with acts of kindness)." The numerical value of מֹשֶׁה רַבֵּינוּ (Moshe, our teacher) is 613, which is exactly equal to the number of commandments in the Torah, and also the numerical value of בִּגְמִילוּת חֲסָדִים (with acts of kindness). This is reminiscent of the ideas emphasized above, that the Torah's utilization of the name Moshe is a repayment for Basya's חֶסֶד and an important reminder of the greatness of חֶסֶד. Thus, מֹשֶׁה רַבֵּינוּ, the 613 commandments, תּוֹרָה, and גְּמִילוּת חֲסָדִים (performing acts of kindness) are intertwined conceptually and numerically.

(If desired, see related essays on גְּמִילוּת חֲסָדִים – performing acts of kindness, that I have written, with God's help, on *Parshios Eikev, Ki Seitzei, and Vezos HaBerachah*.)

פרשת וארא

Parshas Vaeira

> FREEDOM

In the Torah portion *Vaeira* (וָאֵרָא), the process of the Jewish exodus from Egyptian slavery toward freedom moves forward quickly. Rabbi Moshe Green, in his book entitled *Impressions on the Heart*, which was culled from the thoughts of Rabbi Shlomo Freifeld, (1923–1988, beloved teacher and founder of Yeshiva Sh'or Yoshuv), discusses the concept of freedom as it exists in American society, and compares it to the Torah's understanding of freedom.

Freedom in American society can be described as "the free rein to do as one pleases…as long as one doesn't hurt anybody." The history of American society has shown that this can lead to all sorts of problems. For instance, as Rabbi Freifeld and Rabbi Green ask: "Is a drug addict who has open access to heroin a free man? Is a child allowed to run wild better off than the child who has parents that do not allow such behavior? License to do whatever one wants, whenever one wants, makes one a slave to his base desires, rather than securing liberty."

Rabbi Freifeld and Rabbi Green explain:

> Freedom requires form. One must have definitions of what is positive, decent, and moral…Only with principles…to channel behavior…can the benefits of freedom be reaped… The Torah is the "owner's manual" for life. The Sages are teaching us that *freedom starts with humbling oneself to the awesome clarity and depth of the Torah*. Only within its four walls can the human spirit soar…Without real and concrete guidelines…freedom becomes meaningless…As it states in *Pirkei Avos* 6:2, "One cannot be a free man unless he immerses himself in the Torah."

To be truly free, one needs the framework provided by the Torah. "License to do whatever one wants, whenever one wants, makes one a slave to his base desires." Without the guidance of the Torah, one is not free at all.

▸ BROTHERLY LOVE

In his commentary on *Shemos* 6:26, Rashi explains that sometimes the Torah writes Moshe's name before his brother Aaron's, and sometimes Aaron's before Moshe's, because "they were equal." This seems difficult to understand because the Torah tells us that Moshe was the greatest prophet who ever lived (*Devarim* 34:10), and that God spoke to him פֶּה אֶל פֶּה, *mouth to mouth* (*Bamidbar* 12:8). Also, the Torah was given through Moshe. What does Rashi mean by stating that Moshe and Aaron were equal?

Rav Moshe Feinstein, explains that they were still considered equal because they were both needed for the redemption of the Jews. To give an analogy, even though one partner in a business has a greater role than the other, if the business could not function without both of them, they are equals in that sense. For example, there may be to two partners in a business – one who makes sure that everything inside the business runs well, and one who focuses outside the business, dealing with customers, other retailers, and wholesalers. Even though one may appear to be more important than the other, they can be considered equal because they are both essential for the business. So too, Rav Moshe Feinstein explains, Moshe and Aaron were considered equal because they were both essential for the redemption of the Jewish people.

Perhaps one can offer another explanation of this Rashi: they were equal because they looked at each other as equals and were not jealous of each other. After all, Aaron, who was older than Moshe, could easily have been jealous of Moshe and his greater role. *However this was the greatness of Moshe and Aaron, in that they looked at each other as equals and one was not jealous of the other.* As the Torah says regarding Aaron, הֲלֹא אַהֲרֹן אָחִיךָ הַלֵּוִי...וְרָאֲךָ וְשָׂמַח בְּלִבּוֹ, *Is there not Aaron your brother, the Levite?...and when he sees you he will rejoice in his heart* (*Shemos* 4:14).

This is one example of the personality trait that characterized Aaron. The *Mishnah* in *Pirkei Avos* 1:12 tells us that Aaron loved peace (שָׁלוֹם) and chased after peace. Since this was the essence of Aaron's personality, he was not jealous of the leading role that his younger brother, Moshe, was given.

Aaron and Moshe's excellent relationship compares favorably to the sibling rivalries described in סֵפֶר בְּרֵאשִׁית (the Book of *Bereishis*). The relationships between the brothers Kayin and Hevel, Yitzchak and Yishmael, Yaakov and Eisav, and Yosef and his brothers were characterized by major sibling rivalries. Yehuda was one of the first to correct this, when he was willing to give his life so that his brother Binyamin would be returned to Yaakov (*Bereishis* 44:32). Our Rabbis have emphasized מַעֲשֵׂי אָבוֹת סִימָן לְבָנִים, "The actions of the forefathers are a sign for their children" (commentary of the Ramban on *Bereishis* 12:6, based on the *Midrash*). Yehuda's repentance led to the reversal of the tendency toward sibling rivalry that was very prominent throughout the Book of *Bereishis*. Perhaps, since the actions of the forefathers are a sign for their children, this led to the good relationship that existed between Yosef's sons, Ephraim and Menasheh. They were not jealous of each other, even though Yaakov, during his blessing, placed his right hand on the younger brother, Ephraim (*Bereishis* 48:14). Similarly, the wonderful brotherly relationship between Ephraim and Menasheh lay the foundation for the excellent relationship that existed between Moshe and Aaron. It is possible that this is one of the reasons that Ephraim and Menasheh have the same initials as Aaron and Moshe (in Hebrew, both of their names begin with א and מ).

Itturei Torah is a magnificent collection of Torah insights by Rabbi Aharon Yaakov Greenberg, which was published posthumously in 1965. At the beginning of the Torah portion entitled *Bechukosai*, *Itturei Torah* points out that many of the redeemers of the Jews have these initials א and מ; אַהֲרֹן and מֹשֶׁה (Aaron and Moshe), אֶסְתֵּר and מָרְדְּכַי (Esther and Mordechai), and אֵלִיָּהוּ מָשִׁיחַ (Eliyahu Messiah). Perhaps the absence of jealousy between אֶפְרַיִם and מְנַשֶּׁה (Ephraim and Menasheh) was the impetus that led to these other examples that have the same initials.

Our Rabbis have emphasized that exile is sometimes caused by the sin of שִׂנְאַת חִנָּם (groundless and unwarranted hatred) (see related *Gemara* in *Yuma* 9b). Therefore, a good interpersonal relationship, as in the example of Ephraim and Menasheh, which is the opposite of שִׂנְאַת חִנָּם, is the essential element that is necessary for the redemptions symbolized by the other three examples listed above that begin with the same initials, א and מ. **Perhaps Rashi writes that Aaron and Moshe were equal because they represent the ideal sibling relationship in that they looked at each other as equals, and were not jealous of each other.**

Our Sages place great emphasis on not being jealous. The *Mishnah* in *Pirkei Avos* 4:21 teaches that jealousy can cause a person to exit this world. At a neighbor's house I was fortunate, with God's help, to notice a small thin book entitled פְּנִינֵי נֶפֶשׁ (*Pearls of the Soul*) which I had never seen before. I found that it contained some magnificent insights. It is written by someone whom I had never heard of. The author's name is Rabbi Yuval Yosef Ordentlich from B'nei Brak, Israel. In his comments on the Torah portion entitled *Vayechi*, Rabbi Ordentlich wrote a magnificent essay that discusses jealousy. Rabbi Ordentlich points out that because God decides what each person has, if one is jealous and desires what

God gave someone else, in that sense he is doubting God's judgment. God wants us to accept His judgment and not be jealous.

The *Mishnah* in *Pirkei Avos* 4:1 teaches, אֵיזֶהוּ עָשִׁיר הַשָּׂמֵחַ בְּחֶלְקוֹ, "Who is it that is rich? It is he who is happy with *his* portion." Rabbi Ordentlich points out that the word *his* could refer to his friend's portion. Therefore, the *Mishnah* can be read, אֵיזֶהוּ עָשִׁיר? הַשָּׂמֵחַ בְּחֶלְקוֹ [שֶׁל חֲבֵרוֹ], "Who is it that is rich? It is he who is happy with *his* [friend's] portion." The *Mishnah* is instructing us to be happy not only with what we have, but also with what our friend has. If we accept God's judgment, and are happy with what our friend has, it should be easy to avoid jealousy and be happy with our own share.

The word for *rich* in Hebrew is עָשִׁיר. Rabbi Ordentlich teaches that the letters of the word עָשִׁיר stand for עֵינַיִם, שִׁנַּיִם, יָדַיִם, רַגְלַיִם – eyes, teeth, hands, legs. Therefore, the *Mishnah* may be suggesting that if one has all his limbs, that should be enough to make one עָשִׁיר (rich) and שָׂמֵחַ בְּחֶלְקוֹ (happy with his portion).

Rabbi Ordentlich discusses *Bamidbar* 24:5, מַה טֹּבוּ אֹהָלֶיךָ יַעֲקֹב, *How goodly are your tents, O Jacob*. Rashi quotes the *Gemara Bava Basra* 60a that teaches that the tents were goodly because the opening of each tent did not face the opening of any other tents. Usually, this is taken to mean that the tents were purposely arranged to protect personal modesty, so that each person was unable to see inside any other tent. Rabbi Ordentlich offers an insightful, additional explanation for this sentence. Each person did not look into his neighbor's tent because each person respected God's judgment, and didn't desire what his neighbor had, and was satisfied with his own portion. The tents didn't face each other because each person focused only on his own tent. According to this explanation, when the Torah writes, מַה טֹּבוּ אֹהָלֶיךָ יַעֲקֹב, *How goodly are your tents, O Jacob*, it was because each person was satisfied with what he had in his own tent, and was not jealous of anything in his friend's tent.

Perhaps Rashi points out that Aaron and Moshe "were equal" because they viewed each other as equals and were not jealous of each other. Our Sages want us to be happy and satisfied with what each of us has, and this lack of jealousy, according to the *Mishnah* in *Pirkei Avos* quoted above, makes us rich. Rabbi Ordentlich offers magnificent insights into the concept of jealousy, into the *Mishnah* אֵיזֶהוּ עָשִׁיר הַשָּׂמֵחַ בְּחֶלְקוֹ, "Who is it that is rich? It is he who is happy with his portion," and into the sentence מַה טֹּבוּ אֹהָלֶיךָ יַעֲקֹב..., *How goodly are your tents, O Jacob...*

פרשת בא

Parshas Bo

> REFLECTIONS

The first commandment given specifically to the Jewish nation is in the Torah portion entitled *Bo*, near the beginning of the twelfth chapter of the Book of *Shemos*. The *Sefer HaChinuch*, which was written by an anonymous thirteenth-century Spanish Rabbi, describes this as the commandment to sanctify the months. According to the *Sefer HaChinuch*, "This is the substance of this commandment: Two reputable Israelites come before the court and testify that they saw the new moon. They [the judges] set the beginning of the month according to their word by saying 'the day is holy'..." This commandment establishes that the Jews will have a lunar calendar. The *Gemara* in *Sukkah* 29a recognizes that "the Jews calculate according to the moon, and the gentiles calculate according to the sun."

The *Gemara* in *Sanhedrin* 42a ermphasizes the great significance of this commandment. The *Gemara* teaches, "Anyone who blesses the new month in its proper time, it is as if he greets the Divine Presence (מְקַבֵּל פְּנֵי שְׁכִינָה). For it is written here [regarding the commandment to sanctify the months] הַחֹדֶשׁ הַזֶּה לָכֶם, *This month shall be for you* (*Shemos* 12:2), and it is written elsewhere

144 · SEFER SHEMOS

זֶה אֵלִי וְאַנְוֵהוּ, *This is my God and I will glorify Him* (*Shemos* 15:2). The ArtScroll commentary on this *Gemara* explains, "This second verse refers to the Divine Presence, which was experienced during the Splitting of the Sea. Since the term 'זֶה,' '*this*,' is used in both verses, we may deduce through [the principle of] *gezeirah shavah* that the first verse, which refers to the new moon, also alludes to experiencing the Divine Presence." The *Gemara* goes on to emphasize the importance of this commandment and says that if the Jews were not privileged to perform any other commandments except for sanctifying the new moon, it would be sufficient.

Rashi, at the very beginning of his commentary on the Torah, suggests that this commandment is so important that one would have thought that the Torah should have started with it. Why did God choose the sanctification of the months as the first commandment given to the Jewish nation, and not something seemingly more fundamental such as faith in God, or *Shabbos*, or the obligation to respect one's parents? Why does the *Gemara* in *Sanhedrin* quoted above say that if the commandment to sanctify the months were our only commandment, it would suffice? Why does the *Gemara* quoted above compare the commandment to sanctify the months to the declaration of the Jews at the Splitting of the Sea, זֶה אֵלִי וְאַנְוֵהוּ, *This is my God and I will glorify Him* (*Shemos* 15:2)? Is there any rational connection between the commandment to sanctify the months and the statement, "This is my God and I will glorify Him"? The lunar calendar requires the addition of a thirteenth month (*Adar* 2) seven times every nineteen years, in order for Passover to occur in the spring and for *Sukkos* to occur in the fall. Why does the Torah emphasize the need for a lunar calendar, which seems less practical than the solar calendar?

Many explanations have been suggested to answer these questions. Rabbi Chaim Wakslak, in *Words of Torah*, suggests that the Torah emphasizes the sanctification of the new moon because of the nature of the moon's light. The moon has no light of its own, and only radiates the reflected light of the sun. Similarly, the Jews are obligated to reflect the principles of the Torah and God's attributes. When we sanctify the new moon, we should concentrate our thoughts on the nature of the moon's light and subsequently on our responsibility to reflect the principles of the Torah and God's attributes. This is such a crucial concept that it is the first commandment given specifically to the Jewish nation and is equivalent, according to the *Gemara* in *Sanhedrin* quoted above, to greeting the Divine Presence (מְקַבֵּל פְּנֵי שְׁכִינָה). This commandment is so fundamental that the *Gemara* in *Sanhedrin* also says that if the Jews would not be privileged to perform any other commandments except for sanctifying the new moon, it would be sufficient. Perhaps this most important lesson derived from the moon, that the Jews should reflect the principles of the Torah and God's attributes, is one of the reasons that all of our holidays are based on the somewhat impractical lunar calendar, and not on the solar calendar.

The Rambam lists the *mitzvah* (commandment) "to imitate [God's] good deeds and lofty attributes" in his סֵפֶר הַמִּצְוֹת (*Book of the Commandments*) as the eighth positive commandment. The Rambam also codifies this principle as law in *Mishneh Torah*, Laws of *De'os* 1:6 by stating, "…A person is obligated to accustom himself to these paths and to resemble Him to the best of his ability."

The *Gemara* in *Shabbos* 133b also discusses the sentence זֶה אֵלִי וְאַנְוֵהוּ, *This is my God and I will glorify Him*, and derives from the word וְאַנְוֵהוּ that the Jews are responsible to be like Him. Just as He is gracious and compassionate, you also should be gracious and compassionate. This is also emphasized in *Gemara Sotah* 14a, where we are told that it is our responsibility to reflect God's attributes. Just as God provides clothes for the needy, visits the sick, comforts mourners, and buries the dead, the *Gemara* in *Sotah* 14a teaches that we are commanded to reflect these attributes of God.

Based on these ideas, one can offer a logical explanation for the *Gemara* in *Sanhedrin* quoted above, which compares the commandment to sanctify the months, הַחֹדֶשׁ הַזֶּה לָכֶם, *This month shall be for you* (*Shemos* 12:2), to the statement of the Jews at the

Splitting of the Sea, זֶה אֵלִי וְאַנְוֵהוּ, *This is my God and I will glorify Him* (*Shemos* 15:2). Perhaps there is a logical connection besides the fact that the word זֶה, *this*, is used both at the Splitting of the Sea and at the sanctification of the new moon.

The sanctification of the new moon, according to the idea proposed by Rabbi Wakslak quoted above, teaches that just as one of the major characteristics of the moon is that it radiates only reflected light, so too one of the major characteristics of the Jews should be that they reflect the principles of the Torah and God's attributes. Therefore, both the sanctification of the new moon and זֶה אֵלִי וְאַנְוֵהוּ teach that the Jews should reflect God's attributes, as the *Gemara* in *Shabbos* 133b derives from the word וְאַנְוֵהוּ, "Just as He is gracious and compassionate, you also should be gracious and compassionate."

Based on this, it seems that there is also a logical reason that the *Gemara* in *Sanhedrin* 42a compares these two sentences, besides the fact that the word זֶה, *this*, is used both at the Splitting of the Sea and at the sanctification of the new moon. *Both the sanctification of the new moon and* זֶה אֵלִי וְאַנְוֵהוּ *teach that it is our responsibility to always try to reflect the principles of the Torah and God's attributes.*

(If desired, see related essay on *Parshas Vezos HaBerachah* entitled "Man of God," where the *mitzvah* to imitate God's attributes is discussed in more detail.)

▸ TIME AND RENEWAL

In the Torah portion entitled *Bo*, in *Shemos* 12:2, the Torah describes the first commandment given specifically to the Jewish nation. The *Sefer HaChinuch* describes this as the commandment to sanctify the months, according to the lunar calendar. The *Gemara* in *Sanhedrin* 42a emphasizes the great significance of this commandment by teaching that if the Jews were not privileged to perform any other commandments except for sanctifying the new moon, it would be sufficient. Why is this commandment so important that it is the first commandment given to the Jewish nation? Why does the *Gemara* say that if it were our only commandment it would suffice?

The previous essay presents an explanation by Rabbi Chaim Wakslak, that the significance of the lunar calendar is related to one of the major characteristics of the moon. Just as the moon radiates only reflected light, so too the major characteristic of the Jews should be that they reflect the principles of the Torah and God's attributes. The *Midrash* in *Bamidbar Rabbah* 13:15–16 teaches, שִׁבְעִים פָּנִים בַּתּוֹרָה, "There are seventy different ways of interpreting the Torah." This essay will offer some other ideas related to the commandment to sanctify the months according to the lunar calendar, yet will still not approach the seventy interpretations that are possible.

Rabbi Moshe Green, in *Impressions on the Heart*, a collection of essays based on the thoughts of Rabbi Shlomo Freifeld, (1923–1988, beloved teacher and founder of Yeshiva Sh'or Yoshuv), writes that "Just as the moon renews itself month after month, so too we, as a people, have the power to revitalize ourselves." Just as the moon seems to disappear, and is able to return to its original size, each Jew should have a "deep appreciation of the power of rejuvenation. The emerging sliver of light in the evening sky is a symbol of hope…It inspires us to reach out for something better," and to focus on the future.

Rabbi Moshe Green and Rabbi Nosson Weisz (*Internet Parshah Sheet on Bo* – 5760) both point out that the Hebrew word for month, חֹדֶשׁ (*Shemos* 12:2), has the identical letters as the Hebrew word for new. King Solomon taught, וְאֵין כָּל חָדָשׁ תַּחַת הַשָּׁמֶשׁ, *and there is nothing new under the sun* (*Koheles* 1:9). Rabbi Weisz explains, "For the sun rises and sets each day without change, whereas the moon waxes and wanes, renewing itself each month. There is never a new sun, but there is a new moon each month."

Sanctification of the new moon is the first commandment given to the Jewish nation, because the moon symbolizes the potential to always make a fresh start, to focus on the future, and to reach out for something better. This is reminiscent of the ability that the Torah has given us to do *teshuvah* (Repentance). If a person commits a sin, that person has the ability to start anew, like the moon does each month, by doing *teshuvah*. The *Gemara* in *Pesachim* 54a teaches that *teshuvah* preceded the creation of the physical world, perhaps because repentance allows one to start anew, and to erase the past. In this way, *teshuvah* supercedes our usual concept of time, and thereby precedes the creation of the physical world. Also, our Sages emphasize repeatedly that the words of the Torah should always seem new, as if you heard them from God on that same day (commentary of Rashi on *Devarim* 6:6, 11:13, and 26:16, based on the *Gemara Berachos* 63b and the *Midrash*).

The commandment to sanctify the new moon is the ultimate symbol of the importance of having a positive outlook and the potential to make a fresh start. This was the first law given to the Jews who were leaving Egypt, because the ability to make a fresh start was crucial to their redemption. Our Rabbis teach that the Jewish nation, as it was being rescued from the servitude of the Egyptians, was just above the lowest depth of spiritual contamination, and if they had not been redeemed then, it would have been too late (ArtScroll commentary on *Shemos* 12:11, in the Stone edition of the *Chumash*, probably based on a saying by Rabbi Shimon bar Yochai, in the *Zohar Chadash* on *Shemos* 20:2, that most Jews in Egypt were at the 49th level of impurity, prior to their redemption). **The commandment to sanctify the new moon, which emphasizes the potential to make a fresh start, thereby enabled the redemption of the Jews from Egypt and was therefore the first commandment given to the Jewish nation.**

Rabbi Ovadiah Sforno (c.1470–1550), who wrote one of the most important commentaries on the *Chumash*, emphasizes a different facet of the commandment to sanctify the months. The Torah writes, הַחֹדֶשׁ הַזֶּה לָכֶם רֹאשׁ חֳדָשִׁים רִאשׁוֹן הוּא לָכֶם לְחָדְשֵׁי הַשָּׁנָה, *This month shall be for you the beginning of the months, it shall be for you the first of the months of the year* (*Shemos* 12:2). It seems that this sentence would have made just as much sense without the word לָכֶם, *for you*. The word לָכֶם seems superfluous. Why is it written twice in this sentence?

Rashi, in his commentary on *Bereishis* 12:1, teaches that the words *for you* indicate that God is doing something "for your benefit and for your good." Therefore, the Sforno explains, the commandment to sanctify the months that is taught in this sentence (*Shemos* 12:2) is for our benefit and good. Concerning this sentence, the Sforno writes: "Henceforth, months of the year shall be yours, to do with them as you will. During the period of the bondage, your time did not belong to you; it was used to work for others and to fulfill their will. Therefore, '…it shall be *for you* the first of the months of the year' for in this month your existence as a people of free choice began" (based on the translation by Rabbi Steven Finkelstein in *Kol Torah* 2/3/2001). The Sforno is teaching that the first commandment given to the Jewish nation, to sanctify the months, is לָכֶם, for the good and benefit of the Jewish nation, because their redemption from Egypt meant that they were now masters of their time. With the first commandment given to the Jewish nation, the Torah is pointing out that we are responsible for using time properly, and we must establish each month in its proper time.

The *Gemara* in *Shabbos* 31a teaches that after death, at the time of final judgment, a person is asked several questions relating to his use of time. One of those questions is קָבַעְתָּ עִתִּים לַתּוֹרָה? This is usually translated as, "Did you establish fixed times [during your routine schedule] for Torah study?"

Rabbi Samson Raphael Hirsch, (1808–1888, leader of German Orthodox Jewry and brilliant biblical commentator), as quoted by Rabbi Yehoshua Kaufman in *Words of Torah*, offers a magnificent alternative translation for קָבַעְתָּ עִתִּים לַתּוֹרָה? Rabbi Hirsch translates, "Have you established your times according to the Torah and not, God forbid, adjusted the Torah according to the spirit of the times?" Rabbi Hirsch is teaching that the Jew must utilize and arrange time according to the principles of the Torah, and that the Torah must not be adjusted according to the spirit of the times.

Rabbi Kaufman similarly points out that there is a commonly-held sociological view that "man is a product of his environment, reacting to circumstances over which he has little or no control. The Torah tradition repudiates this environmental... interpretation of man's conduct. The individual, the Torah teaches, is not the puppet of his environment, but rather the architect of his society, the master builder of his house." Just as Rabbi Samson Raphael Hirsch teaches that the times should be adjusted based on the principles of the Torah, so too, according to Rabbi Kaufman, Judaism teaches us to mold the environment according to the moral teachings of the Torah. The Jew is not solely a product of his environment. Every Jew, for his own personal benefit and for society's benefit, should mold the environment according to the principles of the Torah.

Rabbi Abraham J. Twerski, M.D., explains in his magnificent commentary on the Torah, *Living Each Week*, that the type A personality is a slave to time. The type A personality is always rushing and feels pressured to accomplish a certain amount per unit time. In this day and age, we clearly have so many more time-saving devices than our ancestors had even twenty-five or fifty years ago. Yet we still don't seem to have more time, and in many ways many people are slaves to time now more than they were twenty-five to fifty years ago, despite the great increase in time-saving devices. Many people expect to accomplish much more, and more quickly. Therefore, the Torah tells us הַחֹדֶשׁ הַזֶּה לָכֶם, *This month shall be for you* (*Shemos* 12:2). As Rashi teaches in his commentary on *Bereishis* 12:1 quoted above, the word לָכֶם, *for you* often implies for your benefit. **The Torah, in its first commandment to the Jewish nation, is teaching that we use time for our benefit** and not feel pressured by time itself.

According to Rabbi Twerski, similar to the Sforno's explanation, "the very first *mitzvah* given to the Israelites...was to be masters over time." Their freedom from the Egyptians is crucial, but it is incomplete unless "one is also free from the unrelenting domination by time…Hence, the *mitzvah* of establishing a calendar or regulating your time should be לָכֶם, for your own true interest." **Our ancient, yet most modern Torah, is warning us about the dangers of the type A personality, and that even though we are free from slavery, we must not be slaves to time.** These ideas are so important that they are included in the first commandment given to the Jewish nation.

פרשת בשלח
Parshas Beshalach

› HAPPINESS AND TORAH

The Torah tells us, וְלֹא יָכְלוּ לִשְׁתֹּת מַיִם מִמָּרָה כִּי מָרִים הֵם, *And they were not able to drink the waters of Marah because they were bitter.* (*Shemos* 15:23). Rabbi Zelig Pliskin quotes an explanation of this sentence by Rabbi Menachem Mendel of Kotzk (1787–1859, known as the Kotzker Rebbe). Rabbi Abraham J. Twerski, M.D., quotes an explanation by Rabbi Yisrael ben Eliezer (1700–1760, the founder of Chasidism who is known as the Ba'al Shem Tov). Both the Kotzker Rebbe and the Ba'al Shem Tov interpret this verse in exactly the same way. These rabbis both explain the words *because they were bitter* as referring not only to the waters of Marah, but also to the Jews themselves who were bitter. Rabbi Pliskin and Rabbi Twerski, quoting the Kotzker Rebbe and the Ba'al Shem Tov, point out that the reason the waters tasted bitter was because the Jews themselves had a bitter attitude. According to Rabbi Pliskin: "Anyone looking for flaws and defects will always be able to find them. A bitter person makes himself miserable…the source of the problem is not out there but within himself. **By sweetening one's own outlook one will live in a much sweeter world**." According to Rabbi Twerski: "There are many times when we judge things to be bitter when they are not so in reality, and it is only because of a distorted perception that we consider them bitter."

The Torah is compared to an עֵץ חַיִּים, a tree of life (*Mishlei* 3:18). When God takes a tree, which represents the Torah, and throws it into the bitter waters, they become sweet (*Shemos* 15:25). The tree of life, the Torah, has the ability to sweeten a bitter attitude, as the Torah's perspective on life leads to sweetness and to a positive outlook.

Rabbi Pliskin quotes Rabbi Yechezkel Abramsky (1886–1976, a Talmudic scholar and leader of Jewish communities in Europe and Israel), speaking at a *siyum*, a celebration in honor of the conclusion of Tractate *Yevamos* in the Slobodka Yeshiva. Rabbi Abramsky said:

> A person becomes angry easily when he is not satisfied with his life. He is bitter and does not have satisfaction…Any true Torah scholar is full of happiness, satisfaction, pleasure, and joy…Because he is so full of pleasure and satisfaction from his studies, he does not become frustrated over mundane matters. Only Torah and good deeds are important to him and this increases peace in the world.

Likewise, the *Gemara* in *Berachos* 64a teaches, "Rabbi Elazar said in the name of Rabbi Chanina, 'תַּלְמִידֵי חֲכָמִים מַרְבִּים שָׁלוֹם בָּעוֹלָם' 'Torah scholars increase peace in the world.'" That is because they have the proper outlook on life, and are happy and satisfied, and not bitter.

Rabbi Twerski writes: "With the guidance of Torah, much bitterness can be averted. God showed Moses the tree, the עֵץ חַיִּים (tree of life) of Torah, through whose perspective the bitter waters can be sweetened." The Torah teaches each person to be satisfied with his lot (*Pirkei Avos* 4:1), and emphasizes that one should not be jealous of what another person has (*Shemos* 20:14 and *Devarim* 5:18). It is attitudes such as these that lead to happiness and satisfaction, as opposed to bitterness.

The Jews in the desert had a problem כִּי מָרִים הֵם, *because they were bitter*. This bitter attitude led to much complaining. God taught them that with the עֵץ חַיִּים, with the Torah perspective on life, their bitter attitude would become sweet. Rabbi Pliskin quotes the Kotzker Rebbe and Rabbi Twerski quotes the Ba'al Shem Tov, who both explain this section of the Torah in this fashion. Perhaps the reason the Torah teaches us the lesson of the bitter waters even before the Ten Commandments is to emphasize the importance of this concept – that **a Torah perspective on life makes bitter waters sweet and leads to happiness and satisfaction.** As King David writes in *Tehillim* (*Psalms* 19:9), פִּקּוּדֵי יְהוָה יְשָׁרִים מְשַׂמְּחֵי לֵב, *The commandments of God are upright, gladdening the heart.*

▸ RABBI DEUTCH'S PRECIOUS JEWEL

The Torah tells us that as the Jews were leaving Egypt, וַיִּקַּח מֹשֶׁה אֶת עַצְמוֹת יוֹסֵף עִמּוֹ, *And Moshe took Yosef's bones with him* (*Shemos* 13:19). The *Gemara* in *Sotah* 13a teaches that this shows "how beloved the *mitzvos* (commandments or good deeds) were to Moshe our teacher, for the whole Jewish people in their entirety were busy gathering the booty [of Egypt], and he [Moshe] was involved with *mitzvos*, as it says חֲכַם לֵב יִקַּח מִצְוֹת, *The wise of heart will seize mitzvos*" (*Proverbs* 10:8).

Why is Moshe's decision to take out Yosef's bones instead of pursuing Egyptian booty specifically called an act of *wisdom* rather than an act of piety or an act of leadership? Rabbi Frand (contemporary author of many magnificent Torah insights and teacher at Yeshivas Ner Israel in Baltimore) explains that the *Gemara* in *Sotah* quoted above emphasizes that Moshe is a חָכָם, a wise man, because of a statement in the *Gemara* in *Tamid* 32a, "Who is a wise man? A wise man is he who sees the future [based on his understanding of the world around him]." Moshe was wise because he understood that it was better to do the great *mitzvah* of taking Yosef's bones out of Egypt than to spend time gathering money and jewels from the Egyptians. Moshe understood that gathering money and becoming rich can lead to all sorts of trouble, as it clearly did when the Egyptian spoils were used to help make the Golden Calf. So instead, he chose to pursue the *mitzvah* of taking Yosef's bones out of Egypt.

The Torah, in *Shemos* 13:19 quoted above, emphasizes that Moshe took Yosef's bones out עִמּוֹ, with him. The Torah could have just written that Moshe took out Yosef's bones. What other message is the Torah trying to teach us by emphasizing that Moshe took the bones עִמּוֹ, with him?

Rabbi Baruch HaLevi Epstein, (1860–1940), in his classic commentary on the Torah entitled *Torah Temimah*, quotes two portions of the *Gemara* that offer two different reasons why the Torah tells us that Moshe took Yosef's bones with him. Consistent with the *Midrash* in *Bamidbar Rabbah* 13:15–16 that teaches שִׁבְעִים פָּנִים בַּתּוֹרָה, "There are seventy different ways of interpreting the Torah," another interpretation is given by Rabbi Yehoshua Scheinfeld, in his magnificent collection of Torah insights entitled *Likutei Yehoshua* (*A Collection by Yehoshua*), which was published around 1958. Rabbi Scheinfeld and others point out, based on the teaching in *Pirkei Avos* (*Ethics of the Fathers* 6:9) quoted below, that the only things that a person really takes with him after death are the *mitzvos* that he performs. That is why the Torah says that Moshe took Yosef's bones out עִמּוֹ, with him.

According to Rabbi Scheinfeld, the Torah is alluding to the teaching in *Pirkei Avos* 6:9 that says, "Furthermore, when a man departs from this world, neither silver, nor gold, nor precious stones, nor pearls escort him, but only Torah study and good deeds..." Rav Moshe Yitzchak Deutch, was the *Mashgiach* (מַשְׁגִּיחַ – chief teacher of ethics and spiritual matters) of the *Kollel Chazon Ish* (כּוֹלֵל חֲזוֹן אִישׁ) in B'nei Brak, Israel. Rabbi Deutch used to quote this portion of *Pirkei Avos* frequently. I had the privilege of visiting with Rabbi Deutch on several occasions. He was a great scholar who wrote commentaries on various sections of the *Gemara* and whose life was totally dedicated to studying the Torah and performing its *mitzvos*. Rabbi Deutch lived in a small apartment in the *Kollel* building one or two floors beneath the main study hall

(בֵּית מִדְרָשׁ), where he spent almost all of his time engrossed in Torah study. His kindly appearance and personality were radiant with the beauty of Torah. During the last few years of Rabbi Deutch's life, I was fortunate to receive several letters from him. Rabbi Deutch quoted this portion of *Pirkei Avos* in almost every letter. I believe that Rabbi Deutch also mentioned this portion of *Pirkei Avos* to me on several occasions.

The *Gemara* says in several places (*Berachos* 17a, *Sanhedrin* 50b, and *Zevachim* 36b) that there were several rabbis who had favorite sayings or teachings. The *Gemara* uses the term מַרְגְּלָא בְּפוּמֵיהּ to describe this. Rashi explains that the word מַרְגְּלָא is derived from the word רָגִיל, which means usual, habitual, or customary. Therefore, according to Rashi, מַרְגְּלָא בְּפוּמֵיהּ is translated as "a usual and customary [lesson] in his mouth." Rabbi Meir HaLevi Abulafia (c.1180 to c.1244) wrote an important commentary on *Gemara Sanhedrin* entitled *Yad Ramah*. In *Yad Ramah*, Rabbi Abulafia explains that מַרְגְּלָא is derived from מַרְגָּלִית, which means jewel or pearl (according to the dictionary by Professor Marcus Jastrow). The concept is identical to Rashi's explanation, but מַרְגְּלָא בְּפוּמֵיהּ would be translated as a jewel (or pearl) in his mouth. According to both Rashi and the *Yad Ramah*, מַרְגְּלָא בְּפוּמֵיהּ refers to a rabbi's favorite teaching.

This teaching of *Pirkei Avos* (*Ethics of the Fathers*) 6:9 quoted above was Rabbi Deutch's מַרְגְּלָא בְּפוּמֵיהּ, favorite teaching. Rabbi Deutch reminded me, whenever he had a chance, that when a person leaves this world, he takes with him only his Torah study and good deeds. The other related teaching that Rabbi Deutch frequently emphasized to me is the importance of setting aside scheduled time for Torah study, קוֹבֵעַ עִתִּים לַתּוֹרָה, as discussed in *Gemara Shabbos* 31a.

Rabbi Scheinfeld and others explain that this is why the Torah says that Moshe took Yosef's bones עִמּוֹ, with him; because the only thing that a person takes with him when he leaves this world is his Torah study and the good deeds that he performs. While the rest of the Jews were busy gathering the spoils of Egypt, Moshe was wiser and gathered the true riches, the *mitzvos* that are a person's only permanent possessions. Moshe's good deed became his personal possession for eternity. By writing the word עִמּוֹ, with him, the Torah reminds us of the teaching in *Pirkei Avos* (*Ethics of the Fathers*) 6:9 that was Rabbi Deutch's precious jewel – that Torah study and good deeds are a person's only eternal possessions.

פרשת יתרו

Parshas Yisro

> **WHAT DID YISRO HEAR?**

The first sentence of the Torah portion entitled *Yisro* tells us that Yisro heard "everything that God did to Moshe and to Israel, His people, that God had taken Israel out of Egypt." Yisro was Moshe's father-in-law and a minister of the Midianite people. Rashi quotes two of the three ideas given in the *Gemara Zevachim* 116a regarding exactly what Yisro heard that convinced him to travel to be with the Jewish people. Rashi writes that Yisro heard about the splitting of the Red Sea and the war with Amalek. Why does Rashi omit the third idea of the *Gemara Zevachim* 116a that Yisro came because he heard about the giving of the Torah? In addition, what was so special about the war with Amalek that made Yisro come to join the Jews? Actually, the fact that God allowed the Jews to be attacked by another nation immediately after leaving Egypt would seem to be a reason not to join them.

Rav Moshe Feinstein explains in *Darash Moshe*, volume two, that "Yisro saw in the war with Amalek that people who live without *Hashem*'s Torah are capable of sinking to depths beyond our imagination."

Amalek was our forefather Yitzchak's great-grandson. His

father was Elifaz, who was the son of Eisav and the grandson of Yitzchak. Rashi, in his commentary on *Bereishis* 29:11, quotes the *Midrash* that teaches that Elifaz was raised on Yitzchak's lap. Amalek's mother was Timna. She was a Horite princess who married Elifaz only because she held our forefather, Avraham, in high esteem and wanted to marry a descendant of Avraham (commentary of Rashi on *Bereishis* 36:12, based on the *Gemara Sanhedrin* 99b and the *Midrash Bereishis Rabbah* 82:14). According to the *Gemara* in *Sanhedrin* 99b, Timna said, "It is better to be a maidservant to this [Avraham's] nation, than to be a princess to another nation."

Despite the fact that Amalek's father was raised on Yitzchak's lap, and that his mother had remarkable respect for Avraham, Amalek had the audacity to attack the Jews, even after knowing about the incredible miracles that God did for the Jews when they left Egypt! **This taught Yisro that a nation that does not fear God can become incredibly evil.** Even though God was clearly performing amazing miracles for the Jewish nation, Amalek attacked them. Amalek had tremendous hatred for the Jews. This was shocking, especially since Amalek was a great-grandson of Yitzchak. Indeed, even though there was something special about both of Amalek's parents, he became so evil that he attacked the Jews despite the great miracles that God performed for the Jews.

In this respect, Amalek's hatred for the Jews was somewhat similar to the hatred of the Egyptians. The Egyptians hated the Jews so much that they continued to chase after them even though they had already been stricken by ten miraculous plagues. The Egyptians were finally destroyed at the splitting of the Red Sea.

Rashi, quoted above, teaches that Yisro left his homeland and traveled to be with the Jewish people because he heard about the splitting of the Red Sea and the war with Amalek. Perhaps Rashi quotes only two of the three ideas offered by the *Gemara Zevachim* 116a for Yisro's joining the Jews, because these two ideas both suggest that Yisro joined the Jews when he saw that nations can become incredibly evil when they don't fear God. The Torah emphasizes in *Devarim* 25:18 that one of the major characteristics of Amalek is וְלֹא יָרֵא אֱלֹהִים, *and he did not fear God*. When Yisro saw the extreme evil that can evolve without fear of God, he left his homeland and traveled to be with the Jewish people.

Rav Moshe Feinstein adds: "This concept is not a new one. Centuries earlier, when Avraham traveled with his wife to the land of Gerar, he told Avimelech, the king, that he felt it necessary to hide the fact that Sarah was his wife because 'there is but no fear of God in this place, and they will slay me because of my wife' (*Bereishis* 20:21)…Avraham knew that because there was no fear of *Hashem* among the people, they were capable of perpetrating as base an act as killing him to take his wife." Similarly, Rashi (quoted above) suggests that when Yisro understood how evil people can become when they do not fear God, based on Amalek's attack and the attack of the Egyptians prior to the splitting of the Red Sea, he decided to travel to be with the Jewish people.

Rabbi Zelig Pliskin, in *Growth Through Torah*, found this same idea in the writings of Rabbi Eliyahu Lopian (1876–1970), who taught Torah in Kelm, London, and later in Israel. Rabbi Pliskin wrote that Rabbi Lopian taught: "Amalek also heard about the crossing of the Red Sea. They themselves were in no danger from the Israelites, nevertheless they cruelly tried to wipe them out. Hearing this, Yisro was moved. He realized how one needs the Almighty in his life for basic values."

Unfortunately, we have seen a powerful example of this in our times. Before World War II, Germany was considered to be among the most advanced nations in the world, from every perspective. The Germans were leaders philosophically, scientifically, and culturally. Some of the world's best universities were in prewar Germany. Yet, without fear of God, the Germans committed the most barbaric acts in the history of the world.

Yisro learned from Amalek's attack, and the attack of the Egyptians prior to the splitting of the Red Sea, a most important lesson regarding fear of God. As Rav Moshe Feinstein wrote, "Yisro saw in the war with Amalek that people who live without *Hashem*'s Torah are capable of sinking to depths beyond our imagination." As Rabbi Pliskin wrote, quoting Rav Eliyahu Lopian, "Hearing this, Yisro was moved. He realized how one needs the Almighty in his life for basic values." As King Solomon wrote, סוֹף דָּבָר הַכֹּל נִשְׁמָע אֶת הָאֱלֹהִים יְרָא וְאֶת מִצְוֹתָיו שְׁמוֹר כִּי זֶה כָּל הָאָדָם, *The sum of the matter when all has been considered: Fear God and keep His commandments, for that is man's whole duty* (Koheles 12:13).

(If desired, see related essay that I have written, with God's help, on *Parshas Yayeira* entitled "An Essential Lesson.")

▶ LEFT AND RIGHT

The Ten Commandments are divided into two groups. The first five, on the left side of the tablets, are those that guide the relationship that a person has with God, whereas the other five commandments, on the right side of the tablets, emphasize the laws that are necessary for a proper relationship between man and his fellow man. Why is the commandment to honor your parents placed on the left side of the tablets with those commandments that guide the relationship that a person has with God? Wouldn't the commandment to honor your parents have fit better on the right side of the tablets with the other commandments that guide interpersonal relationships?

Perhaps the commandment to honor your parents is placed with those that guide the relationship that a person has with God, because honoring one's parents is often a prerequisite for honoring God. This is because it is the primary responsibility of parents to hand over the principles of the Torah to their children, as the Torah writes וְשִׁנַּנְתָּם לְבָנֶיךָ, *And you shall teach them thoroughly to your children* (Devarim 6:7, translation by *ArtScroll Stone Chumash*). Our Sages in *Gemara Sotah* 10b, *Gemara Chullin* 63b, and *Pirkei Avos* 3:13 refer to the Oral Tradition as the *Masoret* (מָסוֹרֶת), which is derived from the verb מָסַר to hand over. Children need to honor their parents in order to make it easier for their parents to teach the *Masoret* (מָסוֹרֶת) to them. If children honor their parents, they will be more willing to absorb the *Masoret* that their parents are trying to hand over to them. By honoring their parents

Parshas Yisro · 163

and learning the *Masoret* from them, children will be able to live according to the principles of the Torah, and have a proper relationship with God. Therefore, the commandment to honor your parents is placed with the other commandments that guide one's relationship with God.

This may help us to better understand the *Gemara* in *Kiddushin* 30b that teaches, "There are three partners in a human being: The Holy One, Blessed is He, his father, and his mother." Perhaps they are partners because God, the father, and the mother are involved in teaching the principles of the Torah to the children. All three are partners in this endeavor.

God said that one of the main reasons that He loved our forefather Avraham is because Avraham was careful to transmit the principles of the Torah to his children. As the Torah says, כִּי יְדַעְתִּיו לְמַעַן אֲשֶׁר יְצַוֶּה אֶת בָּנָיו, *For I have loved him, because he commands his children* (*Bereishis* 18:19).

Rav Moshe Feinstein wondered why the Torah doesn't tell us anything about most of the students who studied in the Yeshiva of Shem and Ever. Shem is the son of Noach, and Ever is the great-great-grandson of Noach (*Bereishis* 10:21). One of the only well-known students of their Yeshiva is our forefather Yaakov. Rashi tells us that Yaakov studied in the Yeshiva of Shem and Ever for fourteen years, between the time he left his parents' house and the time that he arrived at Lavan's house (commentary of Rashi on *Bereishis* 28:9, 11 based on the *Gemara Megillah* 17a and the *Midrash Bereishis Rabbah* 68:11). According to the Aramaic translation of the Torah ascribed to Yonasan ben Uziel on *Bereishis* 22:19, our forefather Yitzchak studied in the Yeshiva of Shem for three years. Our forefathers Yitzchak and Yaakov seem to be the only well-known students of the Yeshiva of Shem and Ever.

Rav Feinstein wondered what happened to all the other students who studied in the Yeshiva of Shem and Ever. Why doesn't the Torah tell us anything about them? Rav Feinstein suggests that perhaps the Torah and our Oral Tradition don't mention anything about the other students because they weren't careful to hand over their traditions to their children, and consequently there wasn't any permanence to their studies. The Yeshiva of Shem and Ever has no legacy because, unlike our forefathers, the other students of the Yeshiva didn't transmit their studies to their children (*Darash Moshe*, vol. 1, *Bereishis* 11:32).

Honoring one's parents is crucial, because it makes it easier for parents to transmit the principles of the Torah to their children. This may be one reason that the commandment to honor parents is on the left side of the Tablets with laws that are concerned with the relationship that a person has with God. In addition, the *Sefer HaChinuch* (written by an anonymous thirteenth-century Spanish Rabbi) explains that by honoring one's parents, children learn to appreciate and express gratitude to their parents for everything that they do for them, and in this way, children learn הַכָּרַת הַטּוֹב, to appreciate and thank God for all that God does for them.

It is fascinating that the *Halachah* (legal ruling according to Jewish law) requires that the period of mourning, which a child must observe for a parent, lasts a full year. In contrast, the *Halacha*h is that a parent only mourns one month for a child. One of our Sages explained that children must observe a full year of mourning for their parents, because children learn the *Masoret* from their parents. Even though a parent may love a child very much, possibly more than a child loves a parent, the mourning period that a parent has for a child is only one month, because children are not obligated to teach their parents the *Masoret*. **Since children learn the Masoret from their parents, children must observe a full year of mourning for a parent.**

This essay suggests two possible reasons why the Torah commands that children are required to honor their parents. Firstly, honoring one's parents makes it possible for the parents to teach the principles of the Torah to their children. Secondly, by honoring and expressing gratitude to their parents, children learn to express gratitude to God for everything that He has done for them (הַכָּרַת הַטּוֹב). Since these are essential ideas associated with one's relationship with God, the commandment to honor parents is listed on the left side of the tablets with the other commandments that guide the relationship that a person has with God.

Therefore, honoring one's parents indirectly teaches the children to honor God. Perhaps this is one of the reasons that the *Gemara* in *Kiddushin* 30b teaches, "When a person honors one's father and mother, the Holy One, Blessed is He, says, 'I consider it as if I had lived among them and they had honored me.'" May everyone be privileged to be part of a family in which the parents are honored, so that God can say, "I consider it as if I had lived among them and they had honored Me."

(Some of these ideas are based on an essay by Rabbi A. Leib Scheinbaum in the *Internet Parshah Sheet on Yisro* – 5760, who quotes Rabbi Matisyahu Salomon, the *Mashgiach* of the Lakewood Yeshiva, who quotes Rabbi Ovadiah Sforno [1470–1550].)

פרשת משפטים

Parshas Mishpatim

> EVERYTHING IS HINTED AT IN THE TORAH

The first sentence in the Torah portion entitled *Mishpatim* is וְאֵלֶּה הַמִּשְׁפָּטִים אֲשֶׁר תָּשִׂים לִפְנֵיהֶם, *And these are the laws that you shall place before them.* This sentence introduces *Parshas Mishpatim*, which begins to describe in detail the legal framework of the Torah.

The Rambam writes in *Mishneh Torah*, Laws of the *Sanhedrin* 22:4, based on *Gemara Sanhedrin* 6b, that "It is a *mitzvah* to tell the litigants at the beginning 'would you prefer a legal judgment, or to try to reach a compromise?' If they want a compromise, the court works out a compromise. And every court that continuously negotiates a compromise is praiseworthy..." The Rambam began his *Commentary on the Mishnah* at the age of 23 and completed it when he was 30. In his introduction to his *Commentary on the Mishnah* (section 6), the Rambam also writes that a judge is praiseworthy even if every case ends with a compromise, without ever rendering a nonnegotiated legal judgment.

Why isn't this crucial law, that compromise is preferred over legal judgment, written in *Parshas Mishpatim*, since it is the portion that introduces in detail the legal framework of the Torah?

Rabbi Yaakov ben Asher (c.1269–c.1343) wrote the אַרְבָּעָה הַטּוּרִים (*Four Rows*), a monumental codification of all the laws upon which Rabbi Yosef Karo (1488–1575) later based the *Shulchan Aruch*, which is the foundation for *Halachah* (Jewish law) until today. Because of the importance of the אַרְבָּעָה הַטּוּרִים (*Four Rows*), Rabbi Yaakov ben Asher became known as the בַּעַל הַטּוּרִים (Ba'al HaTurim). The Ba'al HaTurim also wrote a commentary on the Torah in two parts: a short one containing "…appetizers, numerical calculations, and interpretations of masoretic notes to attract [the reader's] heart," and a comprehensive and much longer commentary. Despite the fact that the Ba'al HaTurim had a magnificent grasp of the entire Talmud and its commentaries and wrote a monumental codification of all the laws, the Ba'al HaTurim seems also to have enjoyed explanations that revolve around the numerical value of words (גִימַטְרִיָא), ideas that come from the letters that make up a particular word (רָאשֵׁי תֵבוֹת), and other similar explanations. This shorter commentary that the Ba'al HaTurim wrote to "attract [the reader's] heart" has been very popular and has recently been translated into English.

The Ba'al HaTurim suggests that compromise is such an important concept that it is hinted to in the very first sentence of *Parshas Mishpatim*. The word הַמִשְׁפָּטִים (*HaMishpatim*) stands for הַדַיָן מְצֻוֶה שֶׁיַעֲשֶׂה פְּשָׁרָה טֶרֶם יַעֲשֶׂה מִשְׁפָּט, "A judge is commanded to negotiate a compromise prior to judging a case." The very next word following הַמִשְׁפָּטִים, in the first sentence of *Parshas Mishpatim*, is אֲשֶׁר. The Ba'al HaTurim points out that this stands for אִם שְׁנֵיהֶם רוֹצִים, "if both [litigants] want." Thus, the very first sentence of *Parshas Mishpatim* hints that, as the Rambam rules based on *Gemara Sanhedrin* 6b, compromise is only legally binding if both litigants accept it.

According to the Ba'al HaTurim, the next word in the same sentence, תָּשִׂים stands for, תִּשְׁמַע שְׁנֵיהֶם יַחַד מְדַבְּרִים, "listen to both of them speaking together," which refers to a law discussed in *Gemara Sanhedrin* 7b that both litigants should appear before the judge prior to hearing the case from either one of them.

Thus, the Ba'al HaTurim explains how several important legal concepts that seem to be totally left out of *Parshas Mishpatim* are magnificently hinted to in the very first sentence. As our Sages have taught, לֵיכָּא מִידֵי דְּלֹא רְמִיזֵי בְּאוֹרַיְתָא, "There is nothing that is not hinted at in the Torah."

The source for this teaching is not entirely clear, as this exact phrase does not appear in the *Gemara* or *Midrash*. A similar, but more limited idea appears in *Gemara Ta'anis* 9a, where the *Gemara* teaches that everything written in the נְבִיאִים (*Prophets*) and כְּתוּבִים (*Writings*) is hinted to in the Torah. Rabbi Yehuda Aszod (1794–1866, one of the major authorities on Jewish law in Hungary during his era) writes in a responsa that the teaching of the *Gemara* in *Ta'anis* 9a should certainly be extended to all of the Oral Laws given to Moshe at Sinai, which are also hinted to in the Torah (*Yehuda Ya'aleh*, vol. 1, *Orach Chayim*: 198).

Perhaps, לֵיכָּא מִידֵי דְּלֹא רְמִיזֵי בְּאוֹרַיְתָא, "There is nothing that is not hinted at in the Torah" is also based on the last *Mishnah* in the fifth chapter of *Pirkei Avos* (*Ethics of the Fathers*) that teaches, בֶּן בַּג בַּג אוֹמֵר הֲפֹךְ בָּהּ וַהֲפֹךְ בָּהּ דְּכֹלָּא בָהּ..., "Ben Bag Bag said, 'Search in it and continue to search in it, for everything is in it...'" The ideas of the Ba'al HaTurim quoted above, on the first sentence of *Parshas Mishpatim*, are a wonderful example of לֵיכָּא מִידֵי דְּלֹא רְמִיזֵי בְּאוֹרַיְתָא, "There is nothing that is not hinted at in the Torah."

(If desired, see other essays that I have written, with God's help, on *Parshios Bereishis, Vayeitzei, Tetzaveh, Shimini, Beha'aloscha, Re'eh, Ki Savo,* and *Vezos HaBerachah* that also discuss this principle.)

▸ STARTING A SENTENCE WITH THE WORD *AND*

The *Midrash Mechilta* was written by Rabbi Yishmael, who lived in the 1st–2nd century of the Common Era, and his students. Rashi tells us, based on the *Midrash Mechilta*, that the Torah portion entitled *Mishpatim* begins with the word *and* to connect it with the עֲשֶׂרֶת הַדִּבְּרוֹת (Ten Commandments) that were read in last week's Torah portion. The purpose of this connection is to teach that just as the Ten Commandments were given by God on Mount Sinai, so too all the laws that govern man's relationship with his fellow man taught in *Mishpatim* were given by God on Mount Sinai.

This is reminiscent of an idea offered by Rabbi Joseph B. Soloveitchik (1903–1993, great Talmudic scholar, teacher, and one of the foremost leaders of his era) to explain another *Midrash Mechilta* that Rashi quotes in his commentary on *Shemos* 20:1 that teaches that God mentioned all of the Ten Commandments in one utterance. Rabbi Soloveitchik explains that God vocalized all of the Ten Commandments together in one utterance even though they could not be understood with this sort of vocalization, to emphasize that the first five commandments that deal with man's relationship with God and the second five commandments that deal with man's relationship with his fellow man, are of equal importance and emanate directly from God. Similarly, Rashi explains at the beginning of the Torah portion entitled *Mishpatim*, that *Mishpatim* begins with the word *and* to emphasize that all of the laws in this Torah portion that deal with man's relationship with his fellow man are like the preceding Ten Commandments, because all of these laws were given by God at Sinai.

A similar point is taught by Rabbi Ovadiah of Bartenura (c.1440–1516) in his commentary on the first *Mishnah* in *Pirkei Avos* (*Ethics of the Fathers*). Rabbi Ovadiah of Bartenura writes that the first words of *Pirkei Avos* are "Moshe accepted the Torah from Sinai…," to emphasize that all of the *ethics* taught in *Pirkei Avos* emanate directly from Sinai, just as all 613 commandments emanate directly from Sinai. Rabbi Ovadiah of Bartenura points out that many nations have a code of ethics. What makes the Jewish code of ethics (*Pirkei Avos*) different from any other code of ethics, is that it comes from God Who gave it to us at Sinai.

In this way, it becomes clear that even the *mitzvos* (commandments) between man and man are really *mitzvos* between man and God. There really is no separation, since all commandments and ethics come from Sinai. This thought was written by

Rabbi Steven Finkelstein in an essay published by the Frisch Yeshiva High School. Rabbi Finkelstein also points out that this may provide a fascinating insight into the concept quoted in the *Gemara* in several places (*Kiddushin* 31a, *Bava Kama* 38a and 87a, and *Avodah Zarah* 3a) that Rabbi Chanina teaches: גָּדוֹל הַמְצֻוֶּה וְעוֹשֶׂה יוֹתֵר מִמִּי שֶׁאֵינוֹ מְצֻוֶּה וְעוֹשֶׂה, "One who is commanded to perform the commandments is greater than one who volunteers to perform the *mitzvos*." Why is someone who is commanded greater than someone who volunteers to do good deeds from his own free will?

The traditional explanation, quoted by *Tosefos*, a group of twelfth and thirteenth-century commentators, in their commentary on the *Gemara* in *Avodah Zarah* 3a, is that the commanded person is greater because a commanded individual needs to overcome a greater evil inclination, or יֵצֶר הָרַע, which tries to persuade him not to observe the *mitzvos*. A person who is commanded has a greater evil inclination to combat than one who volunteers to do a *mitzvah*, and for this reason a person who is commanded to do a *mitzvah* is more praiseworthy.

Rabbi Steven Finkelstein quotes an unnamed commentator who offers another wonderful explanation into Rabbi Chanina's teaching that a person who is commanded to perform the commandments is greater than one who volunteers. **The commanded individual is greater than the volunteer, because the commanded individual accepts that all mitzvos and ethics were commanded by God at Sinai.** This is preferable to the volunteer who does *mitzvos* just because they make sense and not because God commanded them. Someone who performs *mitzvos* because they were commanded at Sinai, is greater than someone who performs commandments because he feels that they are just the right thing to do.

Someone who volunteers to do the commandments, based on common sense, can possibly make a mistake, because human judgment is far from perfect and can be influenced by one's desires. Relying on human judgment is dangerous since even the most brilliant human mind can be misled because of one's desires. The desires of Pharaoh and Amalek clearly ruined their ability to utilize reasonable judgment. Even though they witnessed great miracles, they still tried to attack the Jews. We have seen a powerful example of this closer to our own times. Before World War II, the Germans were considered to be among the most advanced nations in the world, from every perspective. The Germans were leaders philosophically, scientifically, and culturally. Some of the world's best universities were in pre-war Germany. Despite this, the desires of the Nazi regime clearly ruined their ability to utilize reasonable judgment and they committed the most barbaric acts in the history of the world.

Therefore, the *Gemara* instructs us not to rely on common sense to voluntarily perform *mitzvos*, but to observe the commandments because they are a framework and guide for life that God commanded at Mount Sinai. God does not want us to rely on our own logic to decide proper behavior. Amalek, Pharaoh, and the Nazis have shown us that human logic is too often corrupted by human desires. As the *Gemara* teaches, "One who is commanded is greater, [or better off,] than someone who volunteers to do *mitzvos*." Rabbi Chaim Shmulevitz (1902–1978, *Rosh Yeshiva* of the Mirrer Yeshiva) offers an explanation similar to this in *Sichos Mussar*, Essay 16, 5732.

These concepts may help us to better understand the last *Mishnah* in *Makkos*. This *Mishnah* is traditionally recited after studying each chapter of *Pirkei Avos* (*Ethics of the Fathers*). The *Mishnah* teaches רָצָה הַקָּדוֹשׁ בָּרוּךְ הוּא לְזַכּוֹת אֶת יִשְׂרָאֵל, לְפִיכָךְ הִרְבָּה לָהֶם תּוֹרָה וּמִצְווֹת..., "The Holy One, Blessed is He, wanted to grant merit to the Jewish people; therefore He gave them Torah and *mitzvos* in abundance..." Isn't it possible that an abundance of *mitzvos* can also bring punishment to the Jews if they find it difficult to keep all of them? What is so special about having so many *mitzvos*? Having 613 commandments may make it difficult to observe all of them. Would it not have been better to have a smaller number of *mitzvos* that the people could observe carefully?

Perhaps this *Mishnah* is teaching, similar to the idea discussed above, that God generously gave us so many *mitzvos* at Sinai because it is better for us to be commanded in the *mitzvos* rather than trying to rely on imperfect human reasoning. Therefore, God gave us an abundance of commandments that provide a framework and guide for every step of our lives.

The word לְזַכּוֹת in the phrase, רָצָה הַקָּדוֹשׁ בָּרוּךְ הוּא לְזַכּוֹת אֶת יִשְׂרָאֵל, is usually translated as being related to the word זְכוּת, that God wished to grant merit or reward, and therefore gave the Jews an abundance of commandments. One of the commentators suggests that the word לְזַכּוֹת is related to the word זַךְ, which means pure, as in, שֶׁמֶן זַיִת זַךְ, which means pure olive oil. According to this approach, the *Mishnah* is teaching that God wanted, לְזַכּוֹת to purify the Jews, and therefore gave the Jews an abundance of *mitzvos*.

God has given us so many *mitzvos*, because they provide a framework and guide for every step of our lives. In addition, as the *Sefer HaChinuch*, which was written by an anonymous thirteenth-century Rabbi, teaches in his commentary on *Parshas Bo*, the actions of performing so many commandments help to mold and improve one's character. Therefore, the Rambam rules in his Commentary on the *Mishnah* (*Pirkei Avos* 3:15) that it is preferable to give one dollar to one hundred poor people, than one hundred dollars to one poor person. This is because the action of performing each *mitzvah* molds and improves one's character.

Rabbi Akiva, the great sage who lived from approximately 40–135 of the Common Era, summarized this idea and taught (*Midrash Tanchuma, Tazria* 5) that God gave the commandments to the Jews *only* in order to purify their character, as King David wrote in *Tehillim* 18:31, אִמְרַת יְהֹוָה צְרוּפָה, *The words of God purify*.

Rashi, as described above, explains that *Parshas Mishpatim* begins with the word *and* to connect it to the preceding Ten

Commandments. This connection teaches that all of the laws in *Mishpatim* that govern man's relationship with his fellow man are similar to the preceding Ten Commandments, since all of these laws were given by God at Sinai. Similarly, Rabbi Soloveitchik explains the *Midrash* that God vocalized the Ten Commandments together in one utterance, even though they could not be understood with this sort of vocalization, to emphasize that the first five commandments that deal with man's relationship with God and the second five commandments that deal with man's relationship with his fellow man, are of equal importance and emanate directly from God. Similarly, Rabbi Ovadiah of Bartenura writes that the first words of *Pirkei Avos* are "Moshe accepted the Torah from Sinai…" to emphasize that the ethics taught in *Pirkei Avos* emanate directly from Sinai, just like all the other commandments. God gave us so many *mitzvos* at Sinai, because God does not want us to rely on human rationality to decide proper behavior. Amalek, Pharaoh, and the Nazis have shown us that human reasoning is too often twisted by human desires. As the *Gemara* quoted above also teaches, "One who is commanded is greater, [or better off,] than someone who volunteers to do *mitzvos*."

(If desired, see related essay that I have written, with God's help, on *Parshas Kedoshim*.)

פרשת תרומה

Parshas Terumah

> INSIDE OUT

The last fifteen chapters of the Book of *Shemos* (*Exodus*), from the Torah portion entitled *Terumah*, until the end of the Torah portion entitled *Pekudei*, are mostly related to the construction of the *Mishkan*. The *Mishkan*, which is usually translated as Tabernacle, is the Temple that was built by the Jews in the desert after they received the Ten Commandments at Mount Sinai.

One of the most important structures within the *Mishkan* was the *Aron* (Ark), which housed the Ten Commandments. Regarding the *Aron*, the Torah writes וְצִפִּיתָ אֹתוֹ זָהָב טָהוֹר מִבַּיִת וּמִחוּץ, *You shall cover it with pure gold, from within and without* (*Shemos* 25:11). The *Gemara* in *Yuma* 72b quotes in the name of Rava, who passed away in 352 C.E., that the Ark was the same on the outside as the inside, to teach, כָּל תַּלְמִיד חָכָם שֶׁאֵין תּוֹכוֹ כְּבָרוֹ אֵינוֹ תַּלְמִיד חָכָם, "Any Torah scholar whose inside is not as his outside, is not a [true] Torah scholar." Rava emphasizes that it is crucial to be completely honest. A person's actions, speech, and attire should match their innermost thoughts.

Complete honesty is also emphasized in last week's Torah portion entitled *Mishpatim*, in which it is written מִדְּבַר שֶׁקֶר תִּרְחָק,

Distance yourself from a false word (*Shemos* 23:7). Both Rabbi Simcha Bunam of Pshischa (1762–1827, a prominent Polish Chasidic Rebbe), as quoted in the commentary in the *ArtScroll Stone Chumash*, and his student, the first Gerrer Rebbe, Rabbi Yitzchak Meir Alter (1799–1866), taught that this is the only instance in which the Torah commands us to distance ourselves from a sin. God dislikes falsehood (שֶׁקֶר) so much that God commands us to distance ourselves from it. There is no biblical command to distance ourselves from any sin, except for falsehood (שֶׁקֶר). The Torah emphasizes in both *Mishpatim* and *Terumah* the great importance of honesty, the need to distance yourself from falsehood, and that a person's outward appearance should be consistent with his thoughts.

In English, the words *face* and *facade* emphasize the exterior and exclude the interior. It is amazing that the Hebrew word for face, פָּנִים, is very similar to the word בִּפְנִים, which means inside. In Hebrew, the words for face and inside are almost identical, perhaps to emphasize the teaching of Rava quoted above, that the outside should be the same as the inside (תּוֹכוֹ כְּבָרוֹ), and that one should be completely honest. (The similarity between פָּנִים, face, and בִּפְנִים, inside, is pointed out by Dr. Joel M. Berman in *Kol Torah* 2/5/2000).

The importance of complete honesty is also stressed by the *Gemara* in *Sanhedrin* 64a and the *Gemara* in *Shabbos* 55a. Both quote Rabbi Chanina who teaches that God's seal is אֱמֶת (truth). Rabbi Lipman Podolsky, was born in Bangor, Maine, and became a beloved teacher at Yeshivat HaKotel in Jerusalem. I never met him, yet he made a long-lasting impression upon me with his excellent essays on the weekly Torah portions. Rabbi Podolsky wrote, based entirely on *Gemara Shabbos* 104a:

> The letters that comprise אֱמֶת (truth) come from the beginning, middle, and the end of the *Alef-Beis* (Hebrew alphabet), respectively. This provides symbolic stability – an alphabetical tripod. The three letters comprising שֶׁקֶר (falsehood), though, are sequential. It cannot stand. Moreover, *each of*

the letters spelling the word אֱמֶת *has two legs. It stands strong. With* שֶׁקֶר*, each letter has only one leg, with the central* ק *longer than the others.* שֶׁקֶר *falters.*

שֶׁקֶר is clearly unstable as each letter has only one leg, and the central ק that extends below the other letters adds instability (*Internet Parshah Sheet on Mishpatim*, 5760).

There are individuals who don't observe the laws of *Kashruth*, except for the law that teaches not to eat the meat of a pig (*Vayikra* 11:7; *Devarim* 14:8). Perhaps the pig has become a model of a non-kosher animal because its outside is very different from its inside. The two major requirements for an animal to be kosher are that it chews its cud and has split hooves (*Vayikra* 11:3; *Devarim* 14:6). The *Gemara* in *Chullin* 59a teaches that the pig is the only animal that externally appears kosher because it has split hooves, but upon closer inspection internally is not kosher because it does not chew its cud. Perhaps the pig has become a model of a non-kosher animal because it reminds us of dishonesty – it looks kosher but really isn't.

Each of our forefathers was known for excellence in a particular character trait, which he passed on to his descendants. Avraham specialized in חֶסֶד – showing kindness to others and Yitzchak specialized in יִרְאַת שָׁמַיִם – fear of Heaven, as was exemplified by Yitzchak's behavior when Avraham took Yitzchak to be sacrificed. Our forefather Yaakov specialized in אֱמֶת, as is written, תִּתֵּן אֱמֶת לְיַעֲקֹב, *Give truth to Yaakov* (*Michah* 7:20). Rabbi Eliyahu Eliezer Dessler, (1892–1953, director of the *Kollel* in Gateshead, England and later the *Mashgiach* – spiritual guide of the Ponevezh Yeshiva in Israel) provides a magnificent explanation based on the idea that Yaakov's אֱמֶת – truth – is derived from a combination of Avraham's חֶסֶד – kindness – and Yitzchak's יִרְאַת שָׁמַיִם – fear of Heaven.

(If desired, please see the first essay on *Parshas Vayishlach* where this is described in detail.)

Another approach to Yaakov's specialization in אֱמֶת might

relate to Yaakov's complete honesty. The Torah in *Bereishis* 25:27 describes Yaakov as an אִישׁ תָּם (a wholesome man). Rashi defines אִישׁ תָּם as כְּלִבּוֹ כֵּן פִּיו (as his heart is, so is his mouth). Rashi emphasizes that Yaakov was completely honest – his outside was the same as his inside (תּוֹכוֹ כְּבָרוֹ).

Rashi, in his commentary on *Bereishis* 37:4, quotes the *Midrash Bereishis Rabbah* that teaches that all of Yosef's brothers were unable to speak kindly to Yosef because שֶׁלֹּא דִבְּרוּ אַחַת בַּפֶּה וְאַחַת בַּלֵּב..., "...they did not speak one thing with their mouth and another in their heart." Melissa Raymon, who is an accomplished educator and the original typist of almost all of these essays, pointed out that Yosef's brothers were taught this trait by their father, Yaakov, who as described above was also completely honest, כְּלִבּוֹ כֵּן פִּיו ("as his heart is, so is his mouth").

Eisav, on the other hand, pretended that he was righteous and attempted to deceive his father, Yitzchak, by asking such insincere questions as "How are salt and straw tithed?" even though Eisav knew that tithes are not taken from salt and straw (Rashi on *Bereishis* 25:27, based on the *Midrash*). Eisav, similar to the pig, exemplifies a model of dishonesty – the outside is different from the inside.

Since מַעֲשֵׂי אָבוֹת סִימָן לְבָנִים, "The happenings of the forefathers are a sign for the children," (as discussed in the first essay on *Parshas Lech Lecha*), let us hope that Yaakov's trait, אֱמֶת – truth, will be passed on to all of his descendants. Subsequently, Yaakov's descendants will find it easier to fulfill מִדְּבַר שֶׁקֶר תִּרְחָק (*Distance yourself from a false word*) (*Shemos* 23:7), and the great lesson of the *Aron* (Ark), that one's actions, speech, and attire should be consistent with his innermost thoughts (תּוֹכוֹ כְּבָרוֹ).

> **JEWISH JOY**

The Torah portion entitled *Terumah* is often read during *Adar*, the twelfth month of the Jewish year. The *Gemara* in *Ta'anis* 29a teaches, מִשֶּׁנִּכְנַס אֲדָר מַרְבִּים בְּשִׂמְחָה..., "...when *Adar* begins we increase happiness." This law is not mentioned at all in most of the major books of Jewish law, including *Mishneh Torah* by Rambam and *Shulchan Aruch* by Rabbi Yosef Karo (1488–1575), but is codified by Rabbi Shlomo Ganzfried (1804–1880) in the *Kitzur (Abridged) Shulchan Aruch*. The *Gemara* and the *Kitzur Shulchan Aruch* do not explain the details of the obligation to increase happiness during *Adar*. None of these great books explain what we are supposed to do to increase happiness during *Adar*. Does this mean that we should attend parties, or movies, or play more sports during *Adar*? Also, since happiness is an emotion and emotions are not always within human control, why is it fair for the *Gemara* to instruct that happiness should be increased during *Adar*?

The *Gemara* quoted above teaches that a person should increase happiness(שִׂמְחָה) during *Adar*. שִׂמְחָה is best defined as happiness or joy, but not as fun. Happiness seems to be an important concept in Judaism since the Torah commands us on numerous occasions to be happy (for example, *Devarim* 26:11 and 27:7) and reemphasizes this concept in *Psalms* 100:2 עִבְדוּ אֶת יְהֹוָה בְּשִׂמְחָה, *Serve God with happiness*. We are commanded to be happy, but not to have fun. It is fascinating that the concept of fun is so foreign to Judaism, that there isn't any word identical to the English word fun in the Hebrew language. In the English-Hebrew dictionary, all of the Hebrew words listed for fun are not really synonymous.

Rabbi Shmuel Goldin, a communal leader and Torah scholar, wrote in an essay published in *The Jewish Standard* (3/2/01):

> Fun is superficial, while happiness is deep…Fun is usually a short-lived, temporary experience and happiness can be longer lasting…Fun is a self-centered attempt to acheive immediate gratification, to satisfy a particular desire or need. Happiness, according to the Torah…can be found only when one moves out of the center.

The self-centered process of seeking fun is often doomed to failure because, as Rabbi Goldin explains, "the moment you satisfy one need, another will develop, and you are never happy, you are never satisfied." Perhaps this helps explain some of the unhappiness that is common in our society even in the face of wealth and luxury. Achieving wealth doesn't necessarily lead to happiness because the moment one need is satisfied, another will develop. Our Sages warned us against self-centered attempts to satisfy desires and needs, when Rabbi Yudan said in the name of Rabbi Aibu, "Nobody departs from this world with half of his desires satisfied, because a person who has one hundred wants two hundred, and a person who has two hunded wants four hundred" (*Midrash Koheles Rabbah* 1:13).

Rabbi Shmuel Goldin writes that "Happiness (שִׂמְחָה), according to the Torah…can be found only when one moves out of the center." This is very different from fun, which is a self-centered attempt to satisfy desires and needs. The Torah tells us on three occasions, וְשָׂמַחְתָּ לִפְנֵי יְהוָה אֱלֹהֶיךָ, *And you shall be happy before Hashem, your God* (*Devarim* 12:18, 16:11, 27:7). The Torah emphasizes that happiness should be related to one's relationship with God, and not on the self-centered immediate gratification of one's desires.

Rabbi Avrohom Chaim Feuer, a contemporary scholar, explains that the word שִׂמְחָה contains the word מָחָה, which means erase. Rabbi Feuer writes on page 40 of his commentary on the *Ramban's Letter to His Son*, "If one truly wishes to rejoice, he must first abandon the conscious desire to place his own needs first." In a sense, he must erase himself. Thus, Rabbi Feuer and Rabbi Goldin independently come to the same conclusion – that happiness begins with erasing one's own desires and is one hundred percent different from fun, which is entirely self-centered. Perhaps the word fun doesn't exist in the Hebrew language because a *self-centered* attempt to satisfy one's desires is not as beneficial as happiness (שִׂמְחָה), which is derived from attempting to move closer to God, the Jewish people, and Jewish ideals.

Rabbi Goldin explains that true happiness only comes by focusing outside of ourselves, by connecting to something greater than ourselves, "to Jewish history, to Jewish experience, to Jewish thought, to God's will, to God's commandments. Life becomes valuable and breaks the constraints of its own mortality when we become part of that higher good, when we attach ourselves to something greater than ourselves, and when we realize our role and our place within the context of that whole." Happiness comes from "belonging and playing a part and not always taking center stage."

Rabbi Goldin suggests that we should teach our children that the happiness (שִׂמְחָה) of becoming a bar or bat mitzvah is not a self-centered extravaganza seeking to fulfill the desires of a 12- or 13-year-old child, and not only an event celebrating who they are, but an event "celebrating who they can become." The happiness of becoming a bar or bat mitzvah marks their entry into the world of responsibility and belonging. In this way, our children will learn that true happiness can be found only by moving ourselves out of the center, and determining the role that each of us is meant to play in the world.

The Torah writes on two other occasions, וּשְׂמַחְתֶּם לִפְנֵי יְהֹוָה אֱלֹהֵיכֶם, *And you shall be happy before Hashem, your God* (*Vayikra* 23:40 and *Devarim* 12:12). Happiness is acheived by seeking a proper relationship with God and by attaching oneself to Jewish faith and ideals. This leads to happiness (שִׂמְחָה) because it gives a person true purpose, and helps one not to focus on one's own desires. Just as a blind person suddenly given the abilty to see would be incredibly happy, each person should be incredibly happy for even commonplace things like vision, which are often taken for granted (as is also discussed in an essay on the Torah portion *Ki Savo*, entitled *Happiness*).

The *Gemara* in *Ta'anis* 29a quoted above teaches that happiness should be increased during *Adar*. This is obviously related to Purim, the monumental event celebrated in the middle of the month of *Adar*, when the Jews were saved from Haman's evil decree calling for their annihilation. Mordechai and Esther were clearly willing to give their lives to save the Jewish nation (*Megillas Esther* 4:16), and this led to the great happiness that is celebrated on Purim (*Megillas Esther* 9:22). Rabbi Goldin explains that Mordechai and Esther demonstrated by their actions that happiness is not achieved by a self-centered effort to satisfy one's desires, but by pursuing a proper relationship with God and by attaching oneself to Jewish faith and ideals. This adds purpose and direction to one's life.

The nation of Amalek is infamous for attacking the Jews immediately after God performed great miracles and rescued the Jews from Egypt (*Shemos* 17:8–16 and *Devarim* 25:17–19). Rashi points out in his commentary on *Devarim* 25:18, that Amalek believed that everything happens by chance and that is why they weren't afraid of God and attacked the Jews. Haman was a descendant of Amalek (*Megillas Esther* 3:1), and also believed that everything happens by chance, and therefore felt that he would succeed in his plan to destroy the Jews. The name Esther (אֶסְתֵּר) is derived from the word סֵתֶר, which means *hidden*. God's name is not written in *Megillas Esther*! Perhaps this teaches us that even though one might suggest that the Jews were saved from Haman because the king, by chance, fell in love with Queen Esther, the Jewish perspective is that it was God's *hidden* control of the events that led the king to love a Jewish queen. Thus, in a *hidden*, natural fashion, God orchestrated the events that saved the Jews. Because the Jews were saved in a hidden fashion, God's name doesn't appear in the *Megillah*.

Purim teaches us that Amalek and Haman were wrong; nothing happens by chance, and God often operates without obvious miracles, in a hidden, natural fashion. The realization that even though God's control is sometimes hidden, that God still cares, looks after this world, and wants all of humanity to live up to the morals and commandments of the Torah, should be the basis of a person's relationship with God. This realization, and each person's efforts to come closer to Jewish faith and ideals, gives purpose to one's life and leads to happiness. The Jews in the era of the *Megillah* understood this and thereby achieved great happiness (*Megillas Esther* 9:22). To commemorate and celebrate the happiness of the Jews in the era of the *Megillah*, we are told by the *Gemara* in *Ta'anis* 29a that happiness should be increased during *Adar*.

As noted at the beginning of this essay, the Torah portion entitled *Terumah* is often read during *Adar*. *Parshas Terumah* describes every Jew's contribution to the building of the *Mishkan* (מִשְׁכָּן), the Tabernacle that accompanied the Jews in the desert. The connection between the events and lessons of *Adar*, and *Parshas Terumah* is sweet. Both the events of *Adar* and *Parshas Terumah* demonstrate that happiness is not achieved by a self-centered effort to satisfy one's desires, but by contributing to the well-being of the Jewish people and by attaching oneself to Jewish faith and ideals.

(If desired, see related essays that discuss happiness, which I have written, with God's help, on *Parshas Beshalach*, *Parshas Devarim*, and *Parshas Ki Savo*.)

פרשת תצוה

Parshas Tetzaveh

➤ GOD'S KEYS

The *Gemara*, on the first page of Tractate *Ta'anis*, tells us that God retains three keys (מַפְתְּחוֹת) for Himself, and that these keys are not given to an angel. These are the keys of childbirth (חַיָּה), resurrection of the dead (תְּחִיַּת הַמֵּתִים), and rain (מָטָר). God looks after these things Himself, rather than delegating these jobs to angels to perform.

Rabbi Eliyahu ben Shlomo Zalman (1720–1797) is commonly referred to as the Vilna Gaon, or as the גְּרָ"א (initials of גָּאוֹן רַבִּי אֵלִיָּהוּ – Gaon Rabbi Eliyahu) and is one of the greatest Torah scholars of the last few centuries. The Vilna Gaon possessed amazing vision and revealed many fascinating insights that are hinted to beneath the plain meaning of the words of the Torah.

The Vilna Gaon explained that the *Gemara* in *Ta'anis* that teaches that God retains three keys (מַפְתְּחוֹת) for Himself, is hinted to in the Torah portion entitled *Tetzaveh*. The Torah tells us in *Parshas Tetzaveh* regarding the Head-plate (צִיץ) of the High Priest, וּפִתַּחְתָּ עָלָיו פִּתּוּחֵי חֹתָם קֹדֶשׁ לַיהוָה, *And you should engrave upon it, engraved like a signet ring, 'Holy to God'* (*Shemos* 28:36). The Vilna Gaon teaches that the word חֹתָם in this sentence stands for חַיָּה (childbirth), תְּחִיַּת הַמֵּתִים (resurrection of the dead), and מָטָר (rain). According to the Vilna Gaon, the words פְּתוּחֵי חֹתָם קֹדֶשׁ לַיהוָה are a hint that the keys (פְּתוּחֵי is similar to the word מַפְתֵּחַ, which means key) of חַיָּה (childbirth), תְּחִיַּת הַמֵּתִים (resurrection of the dead), and מָטָר (rain), are קֹדֶשׁ לַיהוָה, *Holy to God*, and are not given to an angel.

Our Sages have often taught, לֵיכָּא מִידֵי דְּלֹא רְמִיזֵי בְּאוֹרַיְתָא, "There is nothing that is not hinted at in the Torah." This is a magnificent hint for the *Gemara* in *Ta'anis*, quoted above, that teaches that God retains three keys (מַפְתְּחוֹת) for Himself: the keys of childbirth (חַיָּה), resurrection of the dead (תְּחִיַּת הַמֵּתִים), and rain (מָטָר).

My *rebbe*, Rabbi Shmuel Scheinberg, taught this thought in the name of the Vilna Gaon, to my class over thirty years ago. Because of its beauty, this thought still remains in my memory.

(If desired, see other essays that I have written, with God's help, on *Parshios Bereishis, Vayeitzei, Mishpatim, Shimini, Beha'aloscha, Re'eh, Ki Savo,* and *Vezos HaBerachah* that offer other examples of the principle, לֵיכָּא מִידֵי דְּלֹא רְמִיזֵי בְּאוֹרַיְתָא, *There is nothing that is not hinted at in the Torah.*)

▶ IS MOSHE'S NAME REALLY MISSING?

Rabbi Yaakov ben Asher (c.1269–c.1343) wrote the אַרְבָּעָה הַטּוּרִים (*Four Rows*) which is a monumental codification of all the laws upon which Rabbi Yosef Karo (1488–1575) later based the *Shulchan Aruch*, which is the foundation for *Halachah* (Jewish law) until today. Because of the importance of the אַרְבָּעָה הַטּוּרִים, Rabbi Yaakov ben Asher became known as the בַּעַל הַטּוּרִים (Ba'al HaTurim). The Ba'al HaTurim points out that the Torah portion entitled *Tetzaveh* is unusual because Moshe's name is conspicuously absent. This is the only Torah portion between Moshe's birth and the Book of *Devarim*, in which Moshe's name is not mentioned. This is the reason that *Parshas Tetzaveh* begins with the phrase וְאַתָּה תְּצַוֶּה אֶת בְּנֵי יִשְׂרָאֵל, *And you shall command the children of Israel* rather than וַיְדַבֵּר יְהוָה אֶל מֹשֶׁה לֵּאמֹר. צַו אֶת בְּנֵי יִשְׂרָאֵל,

And God spoke to Moshe saying. Command the children of Israel… (*Vayikra* 24:1-2).

Even though God left Moshe's name out of *Parshas Tetzaveh*, the hidden numerical value (גִּימַטְרִיָּא נִסְתָּר, מִסְפָּר נֶעֱלָם) of Moshe's name appears in *Parshas Tetzaveh*. Unlike English, each letter in Hebrew is assigned a numerical value. Moshe's name consists of three Hebrew letters: מ, ש, and ה. The *numerical value of the addition of the unwritten portion of these three letters* adds up to one hundred and one. The letter 'מ' is pronounced as מֵם. The ם is pronounced, but not written. Its numerical equivalent is the hidden value of the letter 'מ' and equals 40. The letter 'ש' is pronounced as שִׁין. The ין is pronounced, but not written. Its numerical equivalent is the hidden value of the letter 'ש' and equals 60 (10+50=נ + י). The letter 'ה' is spelled הֵא. The hidden value of the letter 'ה' is the numerical equivalent of א, which is 1. The sum of the unwritten portion of the letters of Moshe's name is its hidden value (גִּימַטְרִיָּא נִסְתָּר, מִסְפָּר נֶעֱלָם) and is 40+60+1=101, which is equivalent to the number of sentences in *Parshas Tetzaveh*. Therefore, even though Moshe's name is not clearly written in *Parshas Tetzaveh*, the hidden value (גִּימַטְרִיָּא נִסְתָּר, מִסְפָּר נֶעֱלָם) of Moshe's name (101) equals the number of sentences in the *parshah* (101). In this way, Moshe's name, although not explicitly written, is present in *Parshas Tetzaveh*. This suggests that even when Moshe is not clearly seen, he is present.

This idea regarding the hidden numerical value of Moshe's name is usually attributed to Rabbi Eliyahu ben Shlomo Zalman (1720-1797), who is commonly referred to as the Vilna Gaon. *Talelei Oros, Itturei Torah*, and *Divrei Eliyahu* attribute this thought to the Vilna Gaon.

Rabbi Yaakov Koppel Reinitz, a contemporary scholar, points out in his commentary on the *Ba'al HaTurim*, that this exact idea is found in the commentary of Rabbi Saul Katzenellenbogen of Vilna on *Gemara Berachos* 32a. This brief commentary is printed in the Vilna edition of the *Gemara* soon after the commentary of the *Maharsha*. According to the *Encyclopedia Judaica* (Vol. 8, page 269), the Yeshiva of Rabbi Saul Katzenellenbogen existed in the late 1600s, which is prior to the birth of the Vilna Gaon, and Rabbi Abraham Katzenellenbogen was involved in the education of the Vilna Gaon, when the Vilna Gaon was a child (Vol. 6, page 651). Therefore it is clear that the above thought regarding the hidden numerical value of Moshe's name predated the Vilna Gaon. However, it may have been known in Vilna since it had been written by Rabbi Saul Katzenellenbogen of Vilna and may have been taught to the young Vilna Gaon by his teacher, Rabbi Abraham Katzenellenbogen.

Even though Moshe's name doesn't appear in *Parshas Tetzaveh*, the great angel מִיכָאֵל (Michael) is present. As discussed above, there are 101 sentences in *Parshas Tetzaveh*. The masoretic notes at the end of *Parshas Tetzaveh* teach that these 101 sentences correspond to the numerical value of the great angel מִיכָאֵל, which is also 101 (30=ל, 1=א, 20=כ, 10=י, 40=מ). Therefore, despite the fact that Moshe's name is not written in this *parshah*, מִיכָאֵל is present, because the number of sentences in *Parshas Tetzaveh* is equivalent to the numerical value of מִיכָאֵל. מִיכָאֵל (Michael) is described as הַשַּׂר הַגָּדוֹל, "the great prince," (*Daniel* 12:1 and *Gemara Chagiga* 12b). The *Midrash Shemos Rabbah* 2:5 writes that whenever מִיכָאֵל appears, the glory of God [the *Shechinah*] is present.

Torah LaDaas, by the contemporary scholar Rabbi Matis Blum, quotes a related thought by *Chanukas HaTorah* on the first sentence of *Parshas Tetzaveh*. *Chanukas HaTorah* points out that because of the sin of the Golden Calf, God threatened Moshe, הִנֵּה מַלְאָכִי יֵלֵךְ לְפָנֶיךָ, *Behold, my angel* מַלְאָכִי *shall go before you* (*Shemos* 32:34). God threatened Moshe that His angel would lead the Jewish people instead of Him. The Ba'al HaTurim writes that the word מַלְאָכִי (my angel) is the same letters as מִיכָאֵל, because God was threatening that the angel מִיכָאֵל (Michael) would lead the Jews instead of Him. Indeed, our Rabbis tell us that after Moshe responded to God's threat by praying, אִם אֵין פָּנֶיךָ הֹלְכִים אַל תַּעֲלֵנוּ מִזֶּה, *If Your Presence does not go along, do not bring us forward from here* (*Shemos* 33:15), the decree regarding the angel מִיכָאֵל was postponed until Yehoshua became the leader of the Jews. The *Midrash Bereishis Rabbah* 97:3 and *Shemos Rabbah* 32:3 both teach that while Moshe was their guide, God Himself led the Jews in the desert, but that Yehoshua was led by an angel. Rashi explains that מִיכָאֵל is the angel that appeared to Yehoshua prior to his attack on Jericho (*Yehoshua* 5:15).

Chanukas HaTorah points out, based on the above, that as long as Moshe was present, the angel מִיכָאֵל did not lead the Jews. Since Moshe's name is absent from *Parshas Tetzaveh*, the number of sentences (101) in *Parshas Tetzaveh* has the same numerical value as מִיכָאֵל (101), since the angel מִיכָאֵל is present when Moshe is absent. Even though God didn't write Moshe's name explicitly in Parshas Tetzaveh, the hidden numerical value of Moshe's name and the angel מִיכָאֵל are present.

› **LET THE SPOTLIGHT SHINE ON YOUR BROTHER**

Rabbi Yaakov ben Asher (c.1269–c.1343) is known as the Ba'al HaTurim, because of the importance and popularity of his codification of Jewish law, which is entitled אַרְבָּעָה הַטּוּרִים (*Four Rows*). The Ba'al HaTurim points out that the Torah portion entitled *Tetzaveh* is unusual because Moshe's name is conspicuously absent. This is the only Torah portion between Moshe's birth and the Book of *Devarim*, in which Moshe's name is not mentioned.

The Ba'al HaTurim explains that Moshe's name is absent because Moshe told God, in the next Torah portion, *Ki Sisa*, that if God did not forgive the Jews for the sin of the Golden Calf, מְחֵנִי נָא מִסִּפְרְךָ אֲשֶׁר כָּתָבְתָּ, *erase me now from Your book that You have written* (*Shemos* 32:32). The Ba'al HaTurim quotes *Gemara Makkos* 11a that says that a curse of a wise person will come true, even if the curse depends on a condition that never occurs. Therefore, even though God forgave the Jews, Moshe's name is erased from *Parshas Tetzaveh*.

Many of our Sages have wondered why God chose to erase Moshe's name specifically from *Parshas Tetzaveh*. Even if Moshe's name needed to be erased from some Torah portion, why did God choose *Parshas Tetzaveh*?

Many answers have been suggested to explain this dilemma. Moshe said, וְאִם אַיִן מְחֵנִי נָא מִסִּפְרְךָ אֲשֶׁר כָּתָבְתָּ, *And if not, erase me now from Your book that You have written* (*Shemos* 32:32). Unlike English, each letter in Hebrew is assigned a numerical value. Our Rabbis point out that the numerical value of the word אֲשֶׁר is five hundred and one (1+300+200), and that the numerical value of the word תְּצַוֶּה (*Tetzaveh*) is also five hundred and one (400+90+6+5). Perhaps this is one reason that Moshe's name is left out of *Parshas Tetzaveh*.

Torah LaDaas, by the contemporary scholar Rabbi Matis Blum, offers another reason. Moshe said in the next Torah portion, *Ki Sisa*, *And if not, erase me now from Your book that You have written* (*Shemos* 32:32). Moshe said this in the past tense; so God erased his name from the Torah portion that immediately precedes *Ki Sisa*, which is *Parshas Tetzaveh*. Rabbi Mordechai Kamenetzky (*Internet Parshah Sheet on Tetzaveh*, 5760) explains that Moshe asked מְחֵנִי נָא מִסִּפְרְךָ (*Shemos* 32:32). The word מִסִּפְרְךָ is spelled with the letter 'כ' at the end of it (the numerical value of 'כ' is 20). This hints that Moshe asked to have his name erased from the twentieth סֵפֶר (book) in the Torah (ספר כ' = מספרך), and the twentieth Torah portion in the Torah is *Parshas Tetzaveh*.

These are magnificent hints as to how the sentence, וְאִם אַיִן מְחֵנִי נָא מִסִּפְרְךָ אֲשֶׁר כָּתָבְתָּ alludes to *Parshas Tetzaveh*. However, is there is any logical reason that Moshe's name is not mentioned specifically in *Parshas Tetzaveh*?

The Vilna Gaon points out that Moshe passed away on the seventh day of *Adar*, and this day always occurs in very close proximity to the reading of *Parshas Tetzaveh*. Therefore, to commemorate Moshe's passing, God omitted Moshe's name from *Parshas Tetzaveh*. But, once again one should wonder, what is the rational reason that Moshe's name is specifically left out of *Parshas Tetzaveh*?

Rabbi Mordechai Kamenetzky (*Internet Parshah Sheet on*

Tetzaveh, 5760) offers a logical explanation why Moshe's name is specifically omitted from *Parshas Tetzaveh*. Sibling rivalries are a prominent, recurrent theme in the Book of *Bereishis* (Kayin and Hevel, Yitzchak and Yishmael, Yaakov and Eisav, and Yosef and his brothers). Yehuda corrected this situation when he offered his life for his brother, Binyamin (*Bereishis* 44:32). Yehuda's actions marked the absence of jealousy in brotherly relationships and this characteristic became ingrained in his descendants. As our Sages teach, מַעֲשֵׂי אָבוֹת סִימָן לְבָנִים, "The happenings of the forefathers are a sign for their children" (as discussed in the first essay on *Parshas Lech Lecha*). Yehuda's repentance led to the reversal of the tendency toward sibling rivalry that was very prominent throughout the Book of *Bereishis*. Perhaps, since the happenings of the forefathers are a sign for their children, this led to the good relationship that existed between Yosef's sons, Ephraim and Menasheh. They were not jealous of each other, even though Yaakov, during his blessing, placed his right hand on the younger brother, Ephraim (*Bereishis* 48:14). Similarly, the wonderful brotherly relationship between Ephraim and Menasheh laid the foundation for the excellent relationship that existed between Moshe and Aaron. It is possible that this is one of the reasons that Ephraim and Menasheh have the same initials as Aaron and Moshe (in Hebrew, both of their names begin with א and מ).

Moshe and Aaron had the ideal brotherly relationship. God chose Moshe to lead the Jews, even though Aaron was older. Our Sages tell us that one of the reasons that Moshe initially did not want to lead the Jews out of Egypt was because he was afraid of hurting Aaron's feelings (commentary of Rashi on *Shemos* 4:10, based on *Midrash Shemos Rabbah* 3:16). Therefore, God told Moshe, "Is there not Aaron your brother, the Levite? ...When he sees you, he will rejoice in his heart" (*Shemos* 4:14). God told Moshe not to worry, because Aaron would be very happy about God's choosing Moshe to lead the Jews out of Egypt.

Rashi, commenting on this same sentence, quotes the *Gemara Zevachim* 102a that teaches that because of Moshe's initial reluctance to accept God's suggestion that he lead the Jews out of Egypt, the כְּהֻנָּה (priesthood) was taken away from Moshe and his children, and given to Aaron and his descendants. Therefore, all of the priestly responsibilities that Moshe taught Aaron to perform in *Parshas Tetzaveh* were originally meant for Moshe and his descendants. God punished Moshe and gave these duties to Aaron. Despite this, Moshe taught Aaron as well as he possibly could. Just as Aaron was happy about Moshe's elevation to be the leader of the Jews, so too Moshe accepted God's decision that Aaron should be the priest instead of him. In *Parshas Tetzaveh*, Moshe wholeheartedly taught Aaron everything that he needed to know to be the כֹּהֵן גָּדוֹל (High Priest).

In order to emphasize that he was not upset over Aaron's elevation to the priesthood, Moshe's name is left out of *Parshas Tetzaveh*. According to Rabbi Mordechai Kamenetzky:

> Moshe did not want to diminish Aaron's glory in any way. He wanted the entire spotlight to shine on Aaron…Therefore, in the portion in which Moshe charges, guides, and directs the entire process of the priesthood, his name is conspicuously omitted. One of the greatest attributes of true humility is to let others shine in their own achievement without interfering or announcing your role in their success.

The absence of Moshe's name in the *parshah* that describes Aaron's priesthood serves to emphasize Moshe's greatest attribute, which was humility (*Bamidbar* 12:3), and the ideal brotherly relationship that Aaron and Moshe shared.

Conflicts between brothers caused many problems in the Book of *Bereishis*. The Book of *Shemos* emphasizes how brotherly love enabled Moshe and Aaron to lead the Jewish people. One can almost say that the Book of *Bereishis* is about sibling rivalries and their unfortunate consequences, and that the Book of *Shemos* is about the exceptional accomplishments of an ideal brotherly relationship – the relationship between Moshe and

Aaron. Since *Parshas Tetzaveh* describes Aaron's elevation to the priesthood, Moshe's name is omitted so that Aaron could be in the spotlight.

It must also be noted that *Megillas Esther* is usually read in very close proximity to the reading of *Parshas Tetzaveh*. There probably is a very significant connection between the absence of Moshe's name in *Parshas Tetzaveh*, and the absence of God's name in *Megillas Esther*. Without addressing this in detail, perhaps one can suggest that just as Moshe guides the events in *Parshas Tetzaveh* even though his name isn't present, so too God guides all the events in *Megillas Esther*, even though God's name isn't written in the *Megillah*.

(If desired, see related essays that I have written, with God's help, on *Parshas Vaeira* regarding sibling rivalry, and on *Parshas Terumah* that discusses *Megillas Esther*.)

פרשת כי תשא

Parshas Ki Sisa

> A LIFE SAVING MEASURE

The Torah teaches, at the beginning of the Torah portion entitled *Ki Sisa*, that the proper method for counting the Jews is for each person to donate a מַחֲצִית הַשֶּׁקֶל, half-shekel (*Shemos* 30:13). According to the Ramban, the shekel is a silver coin that was instituted by Moshe. In his commentary on *Shemos* 30:15, Rashi explains, based on the *Gemara Megillah* 29b and the *Gemara Shekalim* 2b, that the funds were to be used for communal offerings and for the sockets (אֲדָנִים) upon which the walls of the *Mishkan* (Tabernacle) rested. The Torah says that exactly a half-shekel should be collected from each person and that "the wealthy shall not increase and the poor shall not decrease from half a shekel" (*Shemos* 30:15). To commemorate this important law, it is customary, on the holiday of Purim, for each person to donate *half* of their country's standard coin.

It seems worthwhile to try to understand why the Torah says that exactly *half* of a shekel should be donated. What would have been wrong with donating a full shekel? Rabbi Yissachar Dov Rubin is a contemporary Torah scholar, and author of *Talelei Oros*, which is a wonderful collection of insights on each Torah portion that has been translated into English. Rabbi Rubin quotes Rabbi Shlomo Alkabetz (c.1505–1576, Kabbalist and author of the Shabbos prayer *Lecha Dodi*) who explains that the half-shekel "is meant to highlight the solidarity of the Jewish people; that no one is an island unto himself able to live totally independently. No, every Jew is only a 'half,' who cannot reach his full potential without connecting to his fellow Jews." Thus, the half-shekel suggests the concept that a Jew is incomplete without being connected to the Jewish community.

Rabbi Abraham J. Twerski, M.D., explains in *Living Each Week* that the great Chasidic Rebbe, Rabbi Aaron of Karlin (1736–1772) taught that the letter צ in the middle of the word מַחֲצִית stands for צְדָקָה, which means charity. The letters next to the letter צ, in the word מַחֲצִית are ח and י, which spells חַי (life); and the letters removed from the צ, are מ and ת, which spells מֵת (death). This teaches that one who gives צְדָקָה (charity) comes close to חַי (life), and one who distances himself from צְדָקָה, comes close to מֵת (death).

King Solomon probably felt that this is a very important lesson because he wrote the identical sentence twice in *Mishlei* (10:2 and 11:4) וּצְדָקָה תַּצִּיל מִמָּוֶת, *And charity saves from death*. Perhaps one of the reasons that the Torah says that exactly מַחֲצִית (half) of a shekel should be donated is to remind us of this lesson that King Solomon also emphasized. The צ in מַחֲצִית (half) stands for צְדָקָה (charity), and as taught by Rabbi Aaron of Karlin, the word מַחֲצִית reminds us that צְדָקָה (charity) has the ability to keep each Jew close to חַי (life) and away from מֵת (death).

This identical idea regarding מַחֲצִית is also found in *Divrei Eliyahu*, a collection of Torah thoughts attributed to Rabbi Eliyahu ben Shlomo Zalman, commonly referred to as the Vilna Gaon, one of the greatest Torah scholars of the last few centuries. The Vilna Gaon was a contemporary of Rabbi Aaron of Karlin and lived from 1720–1797. Perhaps this idea regarding מַחֲצִית, can be found in both of their writings because it was well known to the scholarly rabbis of that era.

(If desired, see related essay that I have written, with God's help, on *Parshas Pinchas* entitled *A Matter of Life and Death*.)

▸ DON'T CONFUSE THE BIG LETTERS

After the sin of the Golden Calf, God told Moshe לֶךְ רֵד כִּי שִׁחֵת עַמְּךָ, *Go down, for your people have become corrupt* (*Shemos* 32:7). In his commentary on this sentence, Rashi quotes the *Gemara* in *Berachos* 32a that Moshe was told, רֵד מִגְּדֻלָּתְךָ, "Go down from your [position of] greatness."

There is a beautiful thought regarding this *Gemara* quoted in *Likutei Yehoshua*, *Itturei Torah*, and *Torah LaDaas*. At the end of the sentence, שְׁמַע יִשְׂרָאֵל יְהֹוָה אֱלֹהֵינוּ יְהֹוָה אֶחָד, *Hear, O Israel: Hashem is our God, Hashem is one* (*Devarim* 6:4), the last letter, ד, is enlarged. The last word in this sentence is אֶחָד, which means "one," and the ד, as it is written in the Torah scroll, is enlarged. Later in this Torah portion, it is written, כִּי לֹא תִשְׁתַּחֲוֶה לְאֵל אַחֵר, *For you shall not bow down to another god* (*Shemos* 34:14). The last word in this sentence is אַחֵר, which means "another," and the last letter in this word, the ר, as it is written in the Torah scroll, is enlarged. It's possible that the reason for the large ד in the word אֶחָד and the large ר in the word אַחֵר, is to help prevent these words from being mixed up with each other. ר and ד have a similar appearance and in the two sentences quoted above, perhaps these letters are enlarged so that these words won't be interchanged. In the sentence "Hear, O Israel...", there is a large ד in the word אֶחָד, so that we **don't** say אַחֵר, which would translate, God forbid, as, "Hear, O Israel: *Hashem is our God, Hashem is another*." To avoid this, the word אֶחָד is written with a large ד. Similarly, in the sentence כִּי לֹא תִשְׁתַּחֲוֶה לְאֵל אַחֵר, *For you shall not bow down to another god* (*Shemos* 34:14), the word אַחֵר is written with a big ר, so that we **don't** read, God forbid, כִּי לֹא תִשְׁתַּחֲוֶה לְאֵל אֶחָד, "*For you shall not bow down to one God*."

With this in mind, *Likutei Yehoshua*, *Itturei Torah*, and *Torah LaDaas*, offer a beautiful explanation of the *Gemara* in *Berachos* 32a quoted above. Moshe was told that since the Jews made a

Golden Calf, they were clearly mixing up the word אֶחָד (one) and the word אַחֵר (another), even though the ר and ד are enlarged in the Torah scroll. Therefore, the Gemara in Berachos 32a quoted above writes, רֵד מִגְּדֻלָּתְךָ, the letters ר and ד which make up the word רֵד, *may go down from your greatness.* The letters ר and ד no longer need to be enlarged, since the Jews are mixing them up anyway.

Rabbi Matis Blum, a contemporary Torah scholar and author of *Torah LaDaas*, expands on this and quotes a related idea from *Yalkut HaUrim*. The *Midrash Yalkut Shimoni* (a Midrashic anthology which was probably compiled in the 13th century) on *Song of Songs* (תתקצ) writes that if one mixes up any of these letters ה,ד,ר,כ,ב – the end result could be very negative. For instance, according to this *Midrash*, if someone, God forbid, confuses the ד with a ר in שְׁמַע יִשְׂרָאֵל יְהוָה אֱלֹהֵינוּ יְהוָה אֶחָד, *Hear, O Israel: Hashem is our God, Hashem is one* (Devarim 6:4), it is as if one destroys the world. Similarly, the *Midrash* continues, if one mixes up the letter ר in, כִּי לֹא תִשְׁתַּחֲוֶה לְאֵל אַחֵר, *For you shall not bow down to another god* (Shemos 34:14) with a ד, it is as if one destroys the world. Similarly, the Torah says, וְלֹא יְחַלְּלוּ אֶת שֵׁם קָדְשִׁי, *And they should not desecrate My holy Name* (Vayikra 22:2). If one confuses the ח in יְחַלְּלוּ with a ה, because ח and ה have a similar appearance (desecrate would then mean praise), it is as if one destroys the world. The *Midrash* continues and discusses the last sentence in the book of *Psalms*, כֹּל הַנְּשָׁמָה תְּהַלֵּל יָהּ, *All souls will praise God.* If one confuses the ה in תְּהַלֵּל with a ח (praise would then mean desecrate), it is as if one destroys the world. Hannah said, אֵין קָדוֹשׁ כַּיהוָה, *There is none as holy as Hashem* (Samuel I 2:2). כ and ב have a similar appearance. The *Midrash* adds that if someone confuses the כ with a ב, the sentence would read, God forbid, אֵין קָדוֹשׁ בַּיהוָה, "There is nothing holy about God," and it is as if one destroys the world.

In *Torah LaDaas*, Rabbi Matis Blum quotes *Yalkut HaUrim* that the Jews were mixing up all these letters when they served the Golden Calf, and that the entire *Midrash Yalkut Shimoni* quoted above is hinted to in one sentence in this *parshah*. When God told Moshe that the Jews had sinned, God said, סָרוּ מַהֵר מִן הַדֶּרֶךְ, *They have turned* (סָרוּ) *quickly from the way* (הַדֶּרֶךְ). (*Shemos* 32:8). *Yalkut HaUrim* explains that this hints that the Jews that served the Golden Calf *turned* around, or confused, the letters of the word הַדֶּרֶךְ. They mixed up the letters – ה,ד,ר,כ – as described in the *Midrash Yalkut Shimoni* quoted above. Because they mixed up these letters, God told Moshe to go down from the mountain to try to straighten things out. Moshe was told in the prior sentence לֶךְ רֵד כִּי שִׁחֵת עַמְּךָ, *Go down, for your people have become corrupt* (*Shemos* 32:7). Similarly, the Jews that served the Golden Calf corrupted the letters of the word רֵד. They were mixing up the, ד and ר, as described above.

Rabbi Yaakov Neuburger, the rabbi of the shul in which I pray and *rebbe* at Yeshiva University, added that a similar hint is present toward the beginning of the Torah. One of the ways that God punished Adam when he ate from the tree by telling him, וְקוֹץ וְדַרְדַּר תַּצְמִיחַ לָךְ, *And thorns and thistles shall it sprout for you* (*Bereishis* 3:18). Rabbi Neuburger suggested that the unusual word דַרְדַּר might hint that Adam is being punished for confusing the ד and ר, as described above.

Unlike English, each letter in the Hebrew alphabet has a numerical value. When some of the Jews sinned by serving a Golden Calf, God told Moshe, לֶךְ רֵד, *Go down*. The numerical value of the word רֵד is 204 (200=ר and 4=ד). This is equivalent to the numerical value of the word צַדִּיק, which means righteous (100=ק, 10=י, 4=ד, 90=צ). Therefore, it is as if God told Moshe when some of the Jews sinned by serving a Golden Calf, לֶךְ רֵד, *Go down*, and you are still righteous. Even though some of the Jews (Moshe's students) sinned, Moshe is still considered righteous and should go down to help his nation and pray for them. Shortly thereafter, Moshe prayed for the Jews, as the Torah says, וַיְחַל מֹשֶׁה אֶת פְּנֵי יְהֹוָה אֱלֹהָיו, *And Moshe pleaded before Hashem, his God* (*Shemos* 32:11).

The numerical value of the word רֵד, and the letters of רֵד and הַדֶּרֶךְ provide fascinating insights into the Torah reading.

(If desired, see *Itturei Torah* on *Bereishis* 3:18 regarding the numerical value of דַרְדַּר, and *Gemara Berachos* 32a regarding Moshe's prayers for the Jews.)

פרשיות ויקהל־פקודי
Parshios Vayakhel and Pekudei

❯ THE TORAH OF LIFE – HOW FORTUNATE ARE WE!

The Torah tells us, וַיַּעַשׂ אֵת הַכִּיּוֹר נְחֹשֶׁת וְאֵת כַּנּוֹ נְחֹשֶׁת בְּמַרְאֹת, *He made the wash-basin out of copper and its base out of copper, from the mirrors* (*Shemos* 38:8). Doesn't it seem strange that the wash-basin in the *Mishkan* (Tabernacle) was made out of mirrors? Rashi teaches us why these mirrors were special. Rashi, based on the *Midrash Tanchuma*, explains:

> The daughters of Israel possessed mirrors into which they would look when adorning themselves. Even those [mirrors] they did not withhold from bringing as a contribution to the *Mishkan*. However, Moshe found them repulsive, since their purpose was to incite the evil inclination. God said to him, "Accept [them] for *they are dearer to Me than everything else*, because through them the women raised huge multitudes in Egypt." When their husbands were exhausted from their crushing labor, they [the women] would go and bring them food and drink, and feed them. They would then take the mirrors and each one would look at herself and her husband in the mirror, and entice him with words, saying, "See, I am

more beautiful than you," thereby awakening their husbands' desire and they would cohabit with them. They conceived and gave birth...

What a fascinating *Midrash*! Let us try to understand why God says that these mirrors *are dearer to Me than everything else*.

The sanctification of the physical is one of the major doctrines of Judaism. Our Sages teach that all the physical aspects of this world should be used according to the guidelines of the Torah, and that God's commandments enable us to transform the physical into the spiritual. For instance, when one makes a blessing and thanks God for his food, eating is raised to a higher spiritual level. Similarly, when one rests in order to have strength to study Torah, sleeping is raised to a higher spiritual level. The Jewish women in Egypt used the mirrors to channel their sexual desire towards the service of God and perpetuate Jewish existence, despite the miserable conditions that the Jews endured as slaves in Egypt. These mirrors represent an example of utilizing the physical according to the ideals of the Torah; even mirrors can be used to enhance our spiritual well-being. God said that these mirrors *are dearer to Me than everything else*, because they are symbolic of one of the major doctrines of Judaism, that all the physical aspects of this world should be used according to the guidelines of the Torah.

In his discussion of the significance of these mirrors, Rabbi Abraham J. Twerski, M.D., echoes this doctrine: "The highest degree of *kedushah* [holiness] is achieved when the mundane and physical are elevated and are transformed into the spiritual and sacred." Perhaps Rabbi Twerski based this doctrine on the writings of Rabbi Eliyahu Eliezer Dessler, one of the most profound Jewish thinkers of the last century. Rabbi Dessler (1892–1953) was the director of the *Kollel* in Gateshead, England and later spiritual guide of the Ponevezh Yeshiva in Israel. Rabbi Dessler's writings were published posthumously in a multivolume edition entitled *Michtav MiEliyahu*. Rabbi Dessler writes:

Parshios Vayakhel and Pekudei · 203

All of the [physical] things of this world are there to serve the ends of holiness… This is the deep and wonderful significance of the *Gemara* in *Berachos* 55a that teaches that the table of the Torah scholar is like an altar and his eating resembles a *korban* (sacrifice). Eating for such a person is a sanctified act, since it enables him to reinforce his powers for the fulfillment of the Torah (adapted from the translation of *Michtav MiEliyahu*, Vol. 1, pages 38–39, by Rabbi Aryeh Carmell).

Rabbi Twerski points out how wonderfully different Judaism is in this regard, when compared to other religions. It seems that they have difficulty dealing with the physical pleasures of this world. Often their response to physical pleasure is that it is best to abstain from it. For instance, Roman Catholic priests are not allowed to marry. Judaism is quite different in this respect. According to the *Sefer HaChinuch*, which was written by an anonymous thirteenth-century Torah scholar, the first commandment in the Torah is to *Be fruitful and multiply* (*Bereishis* 1:28). The *Sefer HaChinuch* writes, "This is an important commandment, by virtue of which all the commandments in the world are fulfilled: For to human beings were they given, not to the ministering angels." The Roman Catholic position is that celibacy is preferred and that it is best to avoid sexual relations. The Jewish position is that the Torah was given for human beings, and that procreation, when performed according to the precepts of the Torah, is such an important commandment, that it is the first of the 613 commandments. The *Halachah* (Jewish law) emphasizes the importance of this commandment. The *Halachah* is that "Every man must marry a wife in order to beget children and he who fails in this duty… diminishes the image of God and causes the Divine Presence to depart from Israel" (*Shulchan Aruch, Even HaEzer*, 1:1; translation by Rabbi Dr. Charles B.Chavel).

In Hebrew, the inital act of marriage is often termed קִדּוּשִׁין

(*kiddushin*). The entire tractate of the *Gemara* that deals with the laws of marriage is also called קִדּוּשִׁין. The term קִדּוּשִׁין (*kiddushin*) is clearly derived from the word, קֹדֶשׁ (holy). Perhaps one of the reasons for this is that marriage transforms the physical act of sexual relations into one of the most important holy commandments.

Both Christianity and Buddhism consider a monk who secludes himself in a monastery to abstain from the normal activities and pleasures of this world to be praiseworthy. The Torah tells us, וּבָחַרְתָּ בַּחַיִּים, *And you shall choose life* (*Devarim* 30:19), and King Solomon wrote, עֵץ חַיִּים הִיא לַמַּחֲזִיקִים בָּהּ, *It is a tree of life to those who grasp it* (*Mishlei* 3:18). In the *Shemoneh Esrei*, which is the most important of our prayers, the Torah is described as תּוֹרַת חַיִּים, the Torah of *life*, possibly because the Torah is a manual for daily living that encourages participation in the activities and pleasures of this world, according to its principles. As Rabbi Twerski writes in his discussion of the mirrors that the Jewish women used in Egypt to arouse their husbands, "The highest degree of *kedushah* [holiness] is achieved when the mundane and physical are elevated and are transformed into the spiritual and sacred."

Every day in the daily morning service (*Shacharis*), we declare: אַשְׁרֵינוּ מַה טּוֹב חֶלְקֵנוּ וּמַה נָּעִים גּוֹרָלֵנוּ וּמַה יָּפָה יְרֻשָּׁתֵנוּ, "We are fortunate – how good is our portion, how pleasant our lot, and how beautiful our heritage!" How fortunate are we that our Torah is a Torah of *life* that teaches us how to properly partake in the activities and pleasures of this world, elevating our entire lives into the realm of the spiritual and sacred.

(I am indebted to Rabbi Shlomo Riskin, who is the rabbi of Efrat and the chancellor of the Ohr Torah Stone Institutions of Israel, for an inspiring essay he wrote on this topic.)

› **JUST TRY!**

The Torah portions, *Vayakhel* and *Pekudei*, review the details of the construction of the *Mishkan*. The *Mishkan* is the Tabernacle that

God instructed the Jews to build to accompany them during their travels in the desert. God promised that He would dwell among the Jews in the *Mishkan* that they would build (*Shemos* 25:8).

The fifth sentence in the Torah portion entitled *Vayakhel* says, קְחוּ מֵאִתְּכֶם תְּרוּמָה לַיהֹוָה כֹּל נְדִיב לִבּוֹ, *Take from yourselves a portion for God, everyone whose heart motivates him.* The twenty-first sentence in *Parshas Vayakhel* says, וַיָּבֹאוּ כָּל אִישׁ אֲשֶׁר נְשָׂאוֹ לִבּוֹ, *Every man whose heart inspired him came.* The Torah clearly emphasizes that the hearts of the Jewish people should motivate them to donate to and construct the *Mishkan*.

Why regarding the construction of the *Mishkan* does the Torah place so much emphasis on the inspired hearts of the Jews? The Ramban points out that the Jewish people had recently left Egypt, where they were slaves, and primarily worked with mortar and bricks (*Shemos* 1:14). They were not artisans and lacked the training and skills required to build the *Mishkan* and its utensils. They did not have significant experience with most of the skills required to construct the *Mishkan*, such as embroidery, weaving, stone-cutting, wood-carving, and working with gold, silver, and copper (*Shemos* 35:32–35). The Torah emphasizes, "Every man *whose heart inspired him* came," because it took great courage and faith for the Jews, who had very little education in the skills that were needed, to attempt to build the *Mishkan* and its utensils. The Ramban explains in his commentary on *Shemos* 31:2 and 35:21 that even though the Jewish people did not have the skills required, since they had the courage and faith to attempt to build the *Mishkan* and its utensils, God helped them to complete the task.

In four locations (*Yuma* 38b, *Shabbos* 104a, *Menachos* 29b, and *Avodah Zarah* 55a) the *Gemara* teaches this concept as a general principle: בָּא לְטַהֵר מְסַיְּיעִים אוֹתוֹ, "If someone comes to purify himself, he is given assistance [from God]." God wants us to make an effort, and, if necessary, He will help complete the task.

In all four locations this concept is attributed to the great Torah sage Reish Lakish, who lived in the third century C.E., and was an important contributor to the *Gemara*. This is especially interesting and relevant, because Reish Lakish states in the *Gemara Bava Metzia* 84a that he was the leader of a group of thieves before he repented and devoted his life to Torah study. Reish Lakish enjoyed incredible success in his Torah study, as he was able to become one of the great Torah sages of his era, despite his beginnings as a thief. Clearly, Reish Lakish was speaking from his own personal experience when he taught, בָּא לְטַהֵר מְסַיְּיעִים אוֹתוֹ, "If someone comes to purify himself, he is given assistance [from God]."

This idea is reemphasized just a few chapters later in the Torah portion entitled *Pekudei*. In his commentary on *Shemos* 39:33, Rashi quotes the explanation of the *Midrash Tanchuma*. The *Midrash Tanchuma*, which has been ascribed to the fourth-century *Amora* Tanchuma bar Abba, teaches that the Jews brought the unassembled *Mishkan* to Moshe because they were unable to erect it because of the weight of the planks. Moshe asked God, "How is it possible for man to erect it [because it is too heavy]?" God answered Moshe, עֲסוֹק אַתָּה בְּיָדֶךָ, "You busy yourself [in erecting the *Mishkan*] with your hand." God wanted Moshe to make an effort to erect the *Mishkan*, even though Moshe couldn't possibly do so without assistance. Once Moshe tried to lift up the heavy planks, God helped him finish the job. This is another example of the principle quoted above: בָּא לְטַהֵר מְסַיְּיעִים אוֹתוֹ, "If someone comes to purify himself, he is given assistance [from God]."

Rabbi Benjamin Yudin (contemporary scholar, teacher, and communal leader) points out that this idea is also taught later in the Torah in the Book of *Bamidbar*. The Torah says: וַיִּפְקֹד אֹתָם מֹשֶׁה עַל פִּי יְהֹוָה, *And Moshe counted them [the Levites] according to the word of God* (*Bamidbar* 3:16). Rabbi Yudin writes:

> Rashi [based on the *Midrash Tanchuma*] teaches that Moshe was troubled as to how he would succeed in counting the *Leviim* from the age of thirty days. Could he possibly enter each tent and count the number of suckling infants? Thereupon *Hashem* said to him, 'עֲשֵׂה אַתָּה שֶׁלְּךָ, וַאֲנִי אֶעֱשֶׂה שֶׁלִּי,' 'You

do yours and I will do Mine.' Moshe stood outside the entrance of each tent and a בַּת קוֹל, a heavenly voice, proclaimed the number of male children in each tent. One could ask: If the census was coming from the בַּת קוֹל (the heavenly voice), why did Moshe have to go from tent to tent? The answer is: he had to do his part, and only then did *Hashem* finish (*Internet Parshah Sheet on Vayakhel-Pekudei*, 5761).

Another example of בָּא לְטַהֵר מְסַיְּיעִים אוֹתוֹ, "If someone comes to purify himself, he is given assistance [from God]" is found earlier in the Book of *Shemos*. Rashi, in his commentary on *Shemos* 2:5, quotes a *Gemara* and a *Midrash* that Basya, the daughter of Pharoah, reached for Moshe's basket that had been placed among the reeds near the river, but it was beyond her reach. According to the *Gemara* and *Midrash*, her arm miraculously extended to reach the basket. Rabbi Menachem Mendel of Kotzk (1787–1859, a great Chasidic Rebbe) explains, as quoted in the commentary in the *ArtScroll Stone Chumash*, that her example teaches us that one should never assume that a task is impossible. She was far from the basket, yet she reached out for it – and God enabled her to attain her goal.

These are some examples of the general principle that the *Gemara*, as quoted above, teaches in four separate locations, that Reish Lakish said, בָּא לְטַהֵר מְסַיְּיעִים אוֹתוֹ, "If someone comes to purify himself, he is given assistance [from God]." our Sages have also expressed this idea in other words: "God tells the Jews, 'My children, open for Me an opening as large as the eye of a needle, and I will enlarge it as wide as the opening of a large reception room'" (similar to *Midrash Shir HaShirim Rabbah* 5:2). Similarly, the *Gemara Makkos* 10b teaches, בְּדֶרֶךְ שֶׁאָדָם רוֹצֶה לֵילֵךְ, בָּהּ מוֹלִיכִין אוֹתוֹ, "A person is led in the way that he wants to go."

The examples quoted above teach us that God says, "עֲשֵׂה אַתָּה שֶׁלְּךָ, וַאֲנִי אֶעֱשֶׂה שֶׁלִּי, You do yours and I will do Mine" and "עֲסוֹק אַתָּה בְּיָדְךָ, You busy yourself with your hand." God wants us to try to complete worthwhile tasks with desire, courage, and enthusiasm and not to be lazy or afraid of failure. Even if a task seems impossible, God wants us to try so that He might help finish the task.

Many self-help books have been published in the last decade that emphasize these fundamental principles: that you can't succeed if you don't try and if you are afraid to fail. I recently purchased one such book entitled *Yes, You Can!* As God told Moshe, "עֲשֵׂה אַתָּה שֶׁלְּךָ, וַאֲנִי אֶעֱשֶׂה שֶׁלִּי."

The examples quoted above illustrate that God wants each of us not to be lazy and to have the enthusiasm and courage to try, because as the *Gemara* teaches, בָּא לְטַהֵר מְסַיְּיעִים אוֹתוֹ, "If someone comes to purify himself, he is given assistance [from God]." As Rabbi Zelig Pliskin writes, "Have the courage to accept upon yourself to do what is needed. A person who has a strong drive to accomplish something will find that he has many [hidden] talents and abilities that will enable him to be successful and complete the task."